One Family, Two Worlds

Buenos Aires, 31 Dicembre 1922

Carissimo cugino,

Che dire? Il nostro dolore è troppo grande, troppo intimo per poterlo comunicare. Impossibile ogni conforto. I nostri migliori desideri si sono infranti! Troppo anelammo l'agognato momento del più puro e sublime amplesso per persuaderci che non ci sarà più dato abbracciare e baciare il Caro Babbo nostro! Proprio nel momento stesso che stavamo per stringerselo al cuore. Non possiamo che ringraziare sinceramente per tutto quanto avete fatto per Lui e per noi. Speriamo rivederci presto. Un caro abbraccio e baci al caro Aldo, Angiolino ed a te.

Vostri addolorati affⁿ cugini
Abele, Oreste e Corinna

ONE FAMILY, TWO WORLDS

An Italian Family's Correspondence

across the Atlantic, 1901–1922

Edited, with an Introduction by

Samuel L. Baily and Franco Ramella

Translated by John Lenaghan

Rutgers University Press

New Brunswick and London

Library of Congress Cataloging-in-Publication Data

One family, two worlds.

Bibliography: p.
Includes index.
1. Italians—Argentina—Buenos Aires—Correspondence.
2. Sola family—Correspondence. 3. Buenos Aires
(Argentina)—Biography. 4. Biella (Italy)—Biography.
5. Immigrants—Argentina—Correspondence. I. Baily, Samuel L.
II. Ramella, F. (Franco) III. Title: 1 family, 2 worlds.
F3001.9.I8054 1988 982'.11 88-11487
ISBN 0-8135-1331-6
ISBN 0-8135-1354-5 (pbk.)

British Cataloging-in-Publication information available

DEDICATED TO THE MEMORY OF

Luigi Sola (1851–1922)

Contents

List of Illustrations

Photographs

Maps and Charts

Tables

Preface

One of us, Franco Ramella, first came across an extensive set of emigrant letters in 1984 while pursuing an investigation of the Biellesi abroad for the Sella Foundation. In the personal archive of Dr. Aldo Sola—who was born in Buenos Aires, Argentina, but for most of his life resided in Valdengo near Biella in Italy—were hundreds of letters sent between Biella/Valdengo and Buenos Aires during the first two decades of the twentieth century. Ramella discussed the letters with his wife Luciana and she began the work of systematically examining them. He also mentioned this discovery and described the Sola family correspondence to the other of us, Samuel Baily. We both were enormously excited since we had for some time shared the belief that personal letters were essential documents for understanding the subjective reality and the social organization of migration, and the Sola correspondence was by far the most extensive collection of letters between members of one family that either of us had seen. Not only did the collection of 351 letters span a period of more than twenty-one years, it also contained contributions from the parents in Italy as well as from the children in Argentina. The children sent their letters to the family homes in Biella and Valdengo, where they were kept and preserved. Equally important, the father, Luigi, wrote first drafts of his letters in a notebook before he wrote the final drafts to send to Argentina. These notebooks of first drafts were also preserved in Valdengo. Thus the collection uniquely provides both sides of the correspondence. We agreed that the letters were of such importance that they had to be published. Marlie Wasserman, editor-in-chief of the Rutgers University Press, showed much interest in the letters, and thus it was agreed that for the English-language edition we would translate them and publish them with Rutgers.

The project has truly been a collaborative one involving four people and spanning three continents—Europe, North America, and South America. Although each person did the initial work on some parts of the project alone, all reviewed, improved, and approved the first, intermediate, and final drafts of everything. After consultation with Baily and Franco Ramella on the content and organization of the book, Luciana Ramella did the initial selection and editing of the letters, proposed the division into chapters, and transcribed the letters for translation and editing in the United States. Later, when it became apparent that the manuscript was still too long, additional cuts were mutually agreed upon. The difficult translation into English was artfully done by John Lenaghan of the Rutgers Department of History with the help of Lisa Di Santi, Lynn Berrettoni, and Roy Dominico. The initial editing of the manuscript and the chapter introductions were done by Baily with major input from Lenaghan. We both—Baily and Ramella—wrote the Introduction. We have found it a stimulating and delightful experience to work together so closely on this project.

We have incurred a number of debts in the preparation of the book and wish to acknowledge them here. Luciana Ramella spent many, many hours transcribing the letters, checking errors and inconsistencies, and collecting needed additional information. It is difficult to find the words in either language to thank her for what she had done. John Lenaghan devoted time well beyond the call of duty to produce an outstanding translation of an extraordinarily difficult text. Without his commitment to perfection and consistency this would not be nearly so precise and readable a manuscript. Joan Baily took time out of her busy schedule to read the Introduction and the body of the book and to give us the benefit of her comments. Marlie Wasserman recognized the extraordinary significance of the letters and encouraged us to translate, edit, and publish them. Her suggestions have greatly improved the final product, and we thank her for her support.

Our greatest debt, however, is to Dr. Aldo Sola, who now lives in Vigliano near Valdengo. As a child in Buenos Aires, he knew Oreste and Abele, his cousins once removed. Most importantly he preserved the letters of the Sola family when others less sensitive to their historical value might have discarded them. Without his good judgment and his willingness to give us permission to translate and publish the letters the project obviously would have been impossible. We wish to thank him especially for all that he has done to bring this book to light.

The letters will appeal to both the general reader and to the specialist in migration history. On the one hand, they tell a compelling story of the day-to-day life of an immigrant family—a story that can be enjoyed in its own right. On the other hand, the letters illustrate and document many aspects of the migration process that will be of interest to some general readers and particularly to immigration scholars. Those who wish to learn more about letters as evidence, the migration process, the Sola family, and Italian migration to Argentina will find the Introduction especially useful. All who come from immigrant families, even into the third and fourth generations, will be touched by the many similarities in the history of their own families and that of the Solas.

Samuel L. Baily, New Brunswick, N.J., U.S.A.
Franco Ramella, Turin, Italy
Fall 1987

Translator's Note

A translation of private letters written in the recent past should not present extraordinary problems. It is easy enough to set forth aims and intentions. One wishes above all to be accurate, to get the meaning in its exact sense. Next in importance is presenting the letter writers' words in clear, readable, colloquial English. These goals in the translation of ordinary prose are almost universal. However, some aspects of these letters present problems that need to be mentioned. They are not peculiar to these letters, nor do I imagine that I have completely solved them.

The letters come from five people and vary widely in style, composition, and accuracy of syntax and spelling. The letters of Margherita, the mother, and especially those of Corinna, the wife of one of the brothers who emigrated, are interesting for the rough Italian. Those of Corinna are badly spelled, and the words are incorrectly divided. Doubled consonants especially are neglected. For the most part these mistakes reflect a lack of education and polish, not a lack of clarity or vigor. The mistakes in fact reflect her pronunciation; Corinna simply did not transliterate spoken Italian into normal written Italian. She, and Oreste and Abele (the brothers) as well, spell words with the Spanish "cu . . ." instead of the Italian "qu . . .". There is no point in disfiguring the translation with an attempt to bring these mistakes over into English. Corinna, however, does make real grammatical errors; in letter #119 she uses the correct and incorrect form of "we went" in the same sentence (*abiamo* [sic] and *siamo andati*). It would be nice to capture this change in English, but the result tends to be clumsy and obtrusive, so I have not attempted to produce a deliberately ungrammatical English. The brothers, whose original letters were saved, were both educated young men. Accordingly, their Italian presents no special problems to the translator. The same applies to their father's letters.

The letters are intimate and often effusive; for the most part they are freely and easily written without undue control or discipline in organization. Sentence structure is loose, and the many coordinate clauses create long sentences. Special difficulties arise from the repeated use of some words or phrases. Letters usually begin with "dear" or "dearest" (*cara, carissima*). It is difficult to know when to translate this literally or freely—"sweet," "lovely"— and when just to omit it. A minor, but typical, problem is the Italian *l'amico*. "The friend" will not do in English, but at times it is not clear how to deal with it. "My friend," "your friend," or "our friend" must be inferred or known.

On some occasions, the meaning is not clear, and the temptation to interpret or explain presents itself. Examples are the reference to Giovanni Rivetti and the rifle in letter #4 and to the mortgage crisis of letter #116.

I have tried to keep the meaning and the spirit of the original letters. At times this makes for some awkwardness, but consideration of a few examples might clarify the choice. Abele wished to reassure his father that he had plenty of money for the trip home but might have been slightly embarrassed at how much money he had put away (#188). So perfectly normal Italian *qualche decina di migliaia di lire* produces the clumsy English equivalent "several tens of thousands of lire." Yet that is what he said and what he meant, so I have left it. His vagueness was deliberate and acceptable; to translate the phrase as, for example, "thirty to fifty thousand lire" would sound grotesque or even dishonest. Similarly Abele's dissent from the customary display of mourning in letter #178 is awkwardly expressed. His explanation may have been a bit insensitive, but it certainly was sincere and heartfelt. Again I resisted the temptation to improve it. The same could be said for the repeated exhortations to be of good cheer and stay healthy or return to good health, and also the good wishes for Christmas and birthdays, which inexorably recur. They are part of the letters, and I did not wish to rewrite them.

In conclusion, I have tried to bring the story of the Sola family to life in English as best I could, without overediting or simplifications. I believe the compelling sweep of the story will more than compensate for the homely repetitiveness and occasional awkwardness.

John Lenaghan
New Brunswick, N.J., U.S.A.
Fall 1987

One Family, Two Worlds

Introduction

The Sola Family Correspondence:
A Unique View of the Migration Process

The Sola family correspondence is a rich and detailed set of documents that enables us to gain unique insight into the subjective process of migration. This Introduction facilitates the reading and use of these documents by placing them in their proper methodological and historical contexts. It explores the advantages and potential limitations of using letters to study migration, the importance of the Sola letters, the tradition of emigration within the Sola family and among the Biellesi in general, the story of the Sola brothers abroad and how their migration became permanent, Italian migration to Argentina, and finally the question of how representative the Solas were of Italian and other migrant families.

Letters and the Study of Migration

Although the historic migration of Europeans to the Americas during the century before 1930 was a movement carried out by millions of individuals, these individuals are for the most part absent from scholarly accounts of the process. In such studies, the focus is generally on society and the immigrant group; aggregate data are used to explain why the Germans, Irish, Italians, or Jews migrated from one place to another, what impact migration had on the sending and receiving societies, how migrant groups adjusted to their new environment, and so on. Occasionally some scholars include partial information on a few individual migrants.

The average immigrant as an active individual making decisions on the basis of an evaluation of the situation at hand is ignored. All too frequently the immigrant becomes a helpless victim of large impersonal structural forces such as economic cycles and labor markets. Nowhere do we gain insight into the personal motivations and ambitions of individuals or the impact of the migration experience on them. Why do the individual actors in this great drama decide to migrate when many or even most of the inhabitants from their hometowns do not? How do they choose a destination? How do they find a place to live, a job, and friends? How do they interact with each other and the members of the host society? How do they change as a result of their participation in the migration process? What happens to their traditional culture, their family and village ties, and their personal beliefs and aspirations over time?

To bring the active decision-making individual back into the migration story we need the personal records that allow us to document the subjective perspective. Sociologists studying contemporary migration have a variety of possibilities: questionnaires, oral interviews, attitude or personality tests, simulated studies, clinical studies, and participant observation.[1] These sources, however, do not exist for the historian interested in the subjective meaning of migration at the turn of the past century. Only a few written personal records—such as letters and diaries—remain.

Although the use of letters to study human behavior is not new, scholarly acceptance of their validity has varied from time to time and from discipline to discipline. Thomas and Znaniecki first demonstrated the possibilities of using letters to analyze the subjective meaning of the migration experience in their 1918 classic multivolume work, *The Polish Peasant in Europe and America*.[2] As influential as that work was on a generation of scholars, post-World War II sociologists have largely ignored or rejected its assumptions and the utility of its documentation.[3] Historians, despite such exceptions as Barton, Blegen, Conway, Erickson, Hoglund, and Kula, have exhibited a similar lack of interest in this source.[4]

However, historians and social scientists are now showing renewed interest in the use of letters to study the migration experience. Transaction Books has brought out a new edition of Blumer's important 1939 appraisal of Thomas and Znaniecki with a new introduction by the author. Zaretsky has published an abridged version of *The Polish Peasant* with a penetrating introduction. And the Social Science Research Council has established a working group that is focusing on letters among other forms of personal testimony.[5] We believe this important trend will greatly enhance our understanding of the historical migration process. We view the current work as part of the growing effort to bring back the active individual participants to the study of immigration.

Letters have unique advantages as sources for studying the process of migration. Private letters—those written for the personal consumption of a specific individual or family—served as a vital link between immigrants and families and friends back home.[6] They record the subjective observations of those who participated in the process as it was unfolding, not the reconstruction from memory of past events and feelings nor the observations of simulated or reconstructed behavior. In addition, private letters permit us to evaluate observations and comments regarding motives, adjustment, and the immigrant experience, especially when we can determine something of the history and the social and economic position of the writer and the family.

These advantages make private letters an important and attractive source for the study of migration, but potential hazards dictate that we use them with care. Blumer states the problem concisely: "On one hand, it is absolutely necessary to include the relevant subjective elements in a sociological analysis of human society, yet, on the other hand, the instruments [personal testimony] for getting such subjective elements do not allow us to meet the customary criteria for scientific data."[7]

The most important issue is to what extent and in what ways individual letters represent the broad immigrant experience. There is no question that immigrant letters underrepresent some migrants (illiterates, those who wish to sever ties with family and homeland, orphans, complete families who migrate, ordinary laborers, women, children) and overrepresent others (males of relatively high socioeconomic position who are literate and maintain ties with family and friends). Further distortion may be introduced because many more letters were written than survived and because of the selection of certain letters for preservation or publication or both.[8]

In addition to the question of their representativeness, there is the question of the accuracy and verifiability of private letters. How do we know that what the letter writers recorded is true? If they focus on public events, we can use newspapers and other traditional sources to confirm or challenge any statement, but the focus of most immigrant letters is on personal matters—and indeed that is their value. In almost all these cases we have no way of validating the specific content.

Just because of these problems relating to representativeness and accuracy, however, we do not have to reject letters as a major source for penetrating the meaning of the immigration experience. Rather we must use these sources with caution. Several points should be made here. First, as Blumer notes, "not all people who are involved in the given area of social action under study are equally involved, nor are they equally knowledgeable about what is taking place; hence they cannot be regarded as equally capable of supplying information on the form of social action under study."[9] Our concern then must be that the person who wrote the letters was informed about the subject and preferably a major participant. This does not make the letter writer in question representative, but it does mean the person had information of value to record.

Second, there are ways to check the content of letters. If we know who the letter writers were and to whom they were writing, we can use common sense to determine whether the letters make sense. Also, we can compare what one letter writer says about the migration process with what others say to see whether their comments establish certain patterns. Furthermore, we can compare what is said in letters with information gained from other sources. In other words, we can place the information contained in any given set of letters in a broad context that will increase our ability to determine its accuracy.

And, finally, we must use letters for what they can uniquely document—personal insights and feelings. Letters are important because they provide the subjective perspective on the immigrant experience. Thus, we cannot fault the letter writer who does not know the ethnic origin of the past and current presidents of the adopted country. Indeed, this information is probably not important. We want to know how the writer found housing, a job, friends in the new society and how the person perceived or felt about these experiences. If we are seeking to understand immigrants' feelings and perceptions, then letters can provide important insights. As Vecoli explains in his introduction to the autobiography of an immigrant woman, such a source "stands as a personal document against which we can test certain ideas regarding the immigrant experience. While quantitative analysis may provide answers to certain questions, there are qualitative inquiries which numbers cannot satisfy."[10]

The Importance of the Sola Family Correspondence

The letters of the Sola family merit publication because of certain characteristics that make them exceptionally accurate and informative among collections of this kind. First, we know a great deal about the actors in the drama and can therefore evaluate what they write about in specific historical, social, and economic contexts. (The family history is outlined in the next section.) Second, the collection of letters uniquely includes those of the father and mother back in Italy as well as those of the sons in Buenos Aires. We can thus understand the meaning of migration for the members of the family who remained in the sending society as well as for those in the receiving society. Third, the letters are extensive and cover a continuous period of more than twenty-one years, providing unequaled depth and continuity to the story.

Perhaps the greatest value of the Sola family letters, however, is their presentation of the universal qualities of the migration experience as it unfolded for various groups in different places at different times. Through these letters we become intimately involved in the daily life of one migrant family whose members acted out the phases of the process that, with some variation, all migrants experience. The interaction of the principal actors with each other and with the respective larger communities provides the plot in the drama.

The stage might as well have been Paterson, New Jersey, as Buenos Aires because many Biellesi also migrated there to work in the textile mills. In both these cases as well as so many others, Biella was linked informally through family, friends, and fellow townspeople with a community of Biellesi abroad. These informal personal networks provided the basis for the social organization of the migration process and influenced nearly every phase of it: the decision to migrate, the choice of destination, where to live and work, changes of residence and occupation, social life, the choice of a marriage partner.

Oreste, the oldest son of Luigi and Margherita Sola, chose Buenos Aires as his destination because his godfather lived there. When he arrived in Buenos Aires he went to live with his godfather, who introduced him to the community of Biellesi and presumably helped him get a job. When he went to Mendoza to work, Oreste stayed with Biellesi. He married a young woman in Buenos Aires who was from a town close to Biella. As a contractor he hired both his school friend as his assistant and a group of Biellesi as masons. Abele, his brother, came to Buenos Aires because Oreste was there. Throughout, the ties of family, friends, and paesani were instrumental. These personal networks, usually referred to as *chain migration*, provide a common quality to the migration process.[11]

Because the letters illustrate so well the working of the chain-migration process, they transcend the specific family, cities, and time period to which they refer. There is a universality to voluntary migration that the letters elucidate; they help us understand not just the migration of North Italians to Buenos Aires, but also the migration of North and South Italians to Brazil, Canada, and the United States, and of other Europeans to the New World. The Sola letters are, in short, a major contribution to the literature on Italian migration to the New World and to migration literature in general.

The Solas and Biella: A Tradition of Migration

The story presented in the letters links Argentina and Italy during the first twenty years of the twentieth century. Its leading characters are Oreste and Abele Sola, the sons who emigrated to Argentina, and Luigi and Margherita Sola, their parents, who remained in Italy. In its general features, the story is not different from that of millions of other families at least one of whose members migrated across the ocean. The children left for the New World. The parents generally remained at home awaiting a continually announced but frequently postponed return. Although some did in fact return, many, like the Sola brothers, never returned home while their parents were alive.

The Solas were a working-class family.[12] The father, Luigi, was chief mechanic of a large textile factory in Biella, the provincial capital of an im-

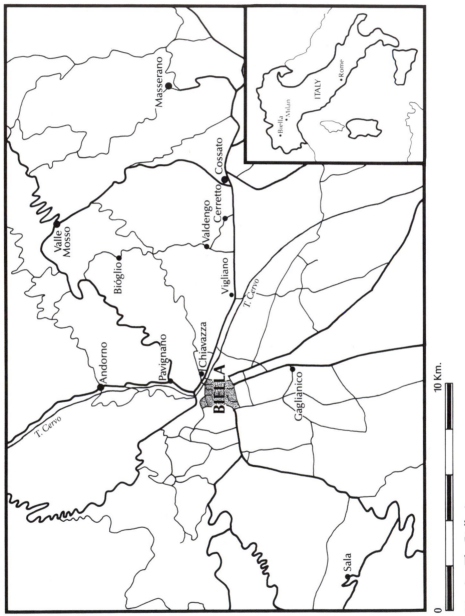

Map 1. The Biella Area

0   10 Km.

portant industrial district in northern Italy. The area of Biella was densely populated and included, in addition to the city of Biella, some eighty small towns scattered among the numerous mountain valleys, the hills, and the limited flatlands. Some of these towns had a few hundred inhabitants. Others had a few thousand. (See Map 1.)

During the years in which this story takes place, the textile industry (especially wool and cotton) expanded considerably. Although the wool industry had existed for centuries in the mountain valleys of the area, it was not until the nineteenth century that it was mechanized and achieved an important position nationally. The industry continued where it had been before, but it also expanded in the city of Biella and in the small agricultural towns of the surrounding hills and plains.[13]

The Solas were natives of Valdengo, one of these agricultural hill villages; it had a little less than a thousand inhabitants and was situated about five miles from Biella. Luigi was born in Valdengo in 1851 and spent his childhood and adolescence there. He then moved to Biella, but he maintained ties with friends and acquaintances in Valdengo, where part of his large family lived. Furthermore, he had inherited a modest farmstead and a little land there from his father.

His parents were peasants who lived by cultivating grain and grapevines on rented land as well as on the small farm that they owned but that could not by itself support them. Luigi, however, did not follow in his parents' footsteps; rather than becoming a farmer, he became a factory worker. When he was not yet eighteen, he left home with the help of relatives to become an apprentice mechanic at a naval shipyard on the Ligurian coast near Genoa. There he was able to learn the trade and to complete his training while working in various shipyards of the region before returning home to do his military service.[14]

He was in the army for four years. The only benefit he received from this experience was to improve his writing skills. After a brief period of training, Luigi was transferred to the offices of the regiment, where he served as a clerk. In this way he improved on the modest education that the few years of elementary school in his small town had given him.

Discharged from the military in 1876, Luigi worked in a textile factory in Biella and soon married Margherita, one of the young weavers from a nearby town who worked in the same factory. In local labor organizations he developed radical political convictions and in 1892 participated in the founding of the Socialist Party. Because he was an authoritative figure and an imposing example of a self-taught worker, Luigi was elected provincial delegate for his party. In the heavily working-class area of Biella, Luigi enjoyed a large following and was respected even by his political opponents.[15]

Margherita and Luigi had three children; besides the two sons, Oreste and Abele, there was a daughter, Narcisa. Oreste, born in 1883, was the oldest, followed in 1887 by Narcisa and in 1890 by Abele. The two boys pursued their studies. Oreste and subsequently Abele completed elementary school and then attended the technical/professional school in Biella, where they received a solid technical education and earned their diplomas at the age of sixteen. (See note 2 to letter #2 for an explanation of the education system.) Luigi and Margherita had planned on better occupations for their sons than that of a worker. To make this possible, the entire family was mobilized. Narcisa, unlike her brothers, had begun working at an early age in the factory in order to contribute to the family income. This was a rather common practice among the area's working-class families of that period; in general, women began working at a younger age than men. The textile industry offered employment opportunities for women, but their careers were generally seen in a different light from those of men. With marriage and the first children, women as a rule left the factory and worked at home.[16]

Contrary to most women of her position and age, Margherita continued to work after she married Luigi because they needed to support two sons in school beyond the normal age for children in a working-class family. Her salary, not high but something they could count on, must have helped guarantee that their sons could continue their education until they graduated from the professional school.

Oreste made the decision to emigrate shortly after he finished school. When he left for Buenos Aires, he was a little more than seventeen years old. Abele joined his brother in Argentina eleven years later. He was twenty-two years old at that time, and he already had worked in mechanical firms in Tuscany and Sardinia. Luigi's contacts had enabled him to get jobs there as a technician.

For both brothers—even though one was more impetuous and the other more reflective—emigration to a mythical America was the response to their aspirations of social advancement. However, the decision to emigrate was not forced on them by lack of opportunity in the local area. Biella, as we have said, was industrially developed, and at this time all of northern Italy was in a period of economic expansion.

Nevertheless, both in Valdengo and in the entire area of Biella, emigration was a widespread phenomenon in these years. From the area, people emigrated to other countries of Europe—in particular to France and Switzerland—to both South and North America, and to the European African colonies.[17] If we reduce the dynamics of emigration to a push/pull model, we face something of a paradox: The Biella area was simultaneously a staging center of emigration abroad and a focus of internal migration for those attracted by industrial jobs.

We must conclude that the widespread tendency to emigrate from the Biella area at the turn of the nineteenth century can best be explained not by the economic situation but by the fact that many experiences of emigration had accumulated over the generations.[18] Biella had a long tradition of both short- and long-range migration.

In numerous communities in the mountain valleys, emigration was almost a mass movement by the 1700s. The men—most of them bricklayers, stone-cutters, and pavers—went to work in distant regions and cities. The movement was seasonal; the sojourn to work away from home, which began in the spring and ended in the fall, was repeated year after year. The income earned from these yearly sojourns was an essential addition to the limited returns from subsistence agriculture carried out by the women, who remained at home.

An increasing scarcity of agricultural resources caused both this emigration and industrialization, which, by the end of the nineteenth century, resulted in economic success for the entire area. Dwindling agricultural resources thus stimulated the complementary development of textile production at home and the sale of labor in places far away.

The periodic emigration in this period and later in many areas of Italy and Europe explains, among other things, how high levels of population could exist over a long period of time in mountain areas even though local resources were inadequate.[19] But the extent and importance of this centuries-old seasonal migration are often underestimated. The idea that population mobility is a result of the modern age, a direct consequence of industrialization and urbanization, is widespread. In fact, however, this idea is based on an ideological prejudice, as Tilly points out; it is based on the false contrast between a modern dynamic society and a static society of the *ancien régime*.[20]

If we adopt a long-range perspective in the study of emigration, we can analyze the social process through which it spreads and identify the aspects of continuity. The seasonal migratory movements from the Biella area—as everywhere else—were based, as mentioned, on the village's social ties and personal networks. By using these ties, the men emigrated, apparently scattering at random in all directions but in reality following the invisible threads represented by the relations with their fellow townsmen. These relations were both with those who traveled every year back and forth from the destinations of emigration (by far the majority) and with the small minority of those who had settled in these destinations and often were the employers of the others. The migratory movement thus reproduced itself autonomously over the generations.

In the second half of the nineteenth century new migratory currents grafted themselves onto the existing ones. Emigration took on new dimensions both in the hilly areas—where Valdengo was situated—and in the plains, where land was good and suitable for cultivation but where the repeated agricultural crises of those years placed a growing number of peasant families in jeopardy of losing their property. Emigration also involved the textile plants of the val-

The Sola Family Tree (Five Generations)

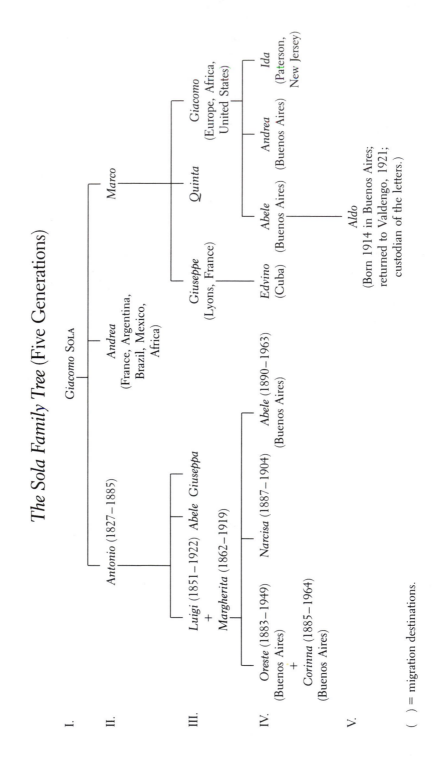

I. Giacomo SOLA

II. Antonio (1827–1885)   Andrea (France, Argentina, Brazil, Mexico, Africa)   Marco

III. Luigi (1851–1922) + Margherita (1862–1919)   Abele   Giuseppa   Giuseppe (Lyons, France)   Quinta   Giacomo (Europe, Africa, United States)

IV. Oreste (1883–1949) (Buenos Aires) + Corinna (1885–1964) (Buenos Aires)   Narcisa (1887–1904)   Abele (1890–1963) (Buenos Aires)   Edvino (Cuba)   Abele (Buenos Aires)   Andrea (Buenos Aires)   Ida (Paterson, New Jersey)

V. Aldo (Born 1914 in Buenos Aires; returned to Valdengo, 1921; custodian of the letters.)

( ) = migration destinations.

leys, where industrial development brought about a change in the labor market.[21]

In an apparently homogeneous migratory movement, distinct social groups came together and different individual and family strategies appeared. With the stimulus of changes in the labor markets and in the societies of destination, the traditional migratory currents began to change. First, in part they lost their seasonal nature because many chose to live abroad permanently. Second, they expanded to include new social strata of the population. But this new migration still took place through the strong social ties that united the emigrants among themselves and with their birthplaces.

Within the Sola family, Oreste and Abele were not the first to emigrate. (See Figure 1 for the Sola family tree.) Andrea, a brother of their paternal grandfather, traveled to many parts of the world starting in the 1850s.[22] After leasing to relatives the piece of land he had inherited, he had set off with the hope of making enough money to expand his meager property holdings in his hometown. His action was not unusual in the small community of Valdengo, where emigration was conceived of as a means to earn money either to consolidate one's position as owner of a small farm or to reestablish oneself after an unexpected financial crisis. Although Andrea left Valdengo with the idea of returning and continued to participate from afar in the events of his family and town, as is clear from his letters, he continued to travel from place to place overseas until his death. He was, he said, a "poor wanderer over land and sea."[23] He lived in North Africa, France, Argentina, Brazil, and other Latin American countries, sometimes alone and sometimes in the company of friends from Valdengo. He was a construction worker, a cook on ships, a weaver, and doubtless many other things. Letters to his brother in Valdengo, jealously guarded among the family papers, stopped suddenly in 1883. In Veracruz, Mexico, Andrea mysteriously disappeared and was not heard from again.

Luigi, the father of Oreste and Abele, had also as a young man entertained the idea of emigrating to other countries. When he returned to Valdengo after completing his military service, Luigi asked Andrea whether he could join him. Andrea, in one of his letters, discouraged Luigi: "It is best that you stay at home," he wrote with a touch of sharp bitterness; "the days of milk and honey have passed because nowhere in the world is there a field that is sown only with roses. That calmness of spirit that is enjoyed in our simple homes is worth more than all illusions of the world. It is true that the imagination promises a great deal, but reality provides very little."[24]

Even though Luigi abandoned plans to emigrate, other members of the family continued to do so. Cousin Giacomo, a peasant and shoemaker, lived alternately in Europe, Africa, the United States, and Valdengo.[25] Cousin Giuseppe, a mechanical worker, settled in Lyons, France, in 1882 and lived there with his family for twelve years.[26] He returned to Italy in 1894 because of the anti-Italian uprisings, which provoked a mass exodus of Italian immigrants from many parts of the neighboring republic. When Giuseppe returned, Luigi helped him find a house and a job in Biella.[27] The next year, Giuseppe's son Edvino emigrated to Cuba. In 1901, shortly after his arrival in Argentina, Oreste planned to join Edvino in Cuba but subsequently changed his mind. Giacomo's children also emigrated; two of them went to Buenos Aires, where they were in touch with Oreste and Abele, and a daughter settled in Paterson, New Jersey, one of the primary overseas destinations of the Biellesi.[28]

Oreste and Abele Sola—like many of their fellow countrymen—thus grew up among people who had know emigration for generations. This fact probably contributed in a decisive way to their emigration. They perceived the spatial boundaries within which it was possible to seek success through the example of past and present emigrants from the family and the local community. In their minds, therefore, geographical boundaries were much wider than those of the small area of Biella. These emigrant figures were not just mythical characters but men of flesh and bone who had lived or still lived in the same world and the same society as did Oreste and Abele. Each one was potentially a precious channel of information about the opportunities that were available in distant localities and countries of the world.

The Solas Abroad Continuing Ties with Family and Friends

Emigration was then one of the choices available to the two Sola brothers. In the context of the family and environment in which they were raised, emigration did not represent a break with their home. It is probable that the parents, Luigi and Margherita, viewed their sons' departures in this way. Oreste left at a young age. Abele was also young when he joined his brother. But in these families the departure of children barely more than adolescents from the paternal home was not an unusual event. It was considered a kind of rite of passage for the youngsters, who henceforth would have to walk alone in search of their own path. Nevertheless, the separation did not exempt the children from their obligations to their parents. For example, it did not mean—in a society in which there was no social security system for the elderly—that Oreste and Abele would evade the moral and social obligation to support their father and mother after they reached retirement age.

Luigi and Margherita retired from the factory in 1907. At that time, Oreste had already lived in Argentina for six years, Narcisa had died tragically three years before, and Abele had just finished school. Luigi submitted his resignation to the factory where he was working and with his wife left Biella to return to the ancestral home in Valdengo. They were not yet old; he was fifty-six and she was forty-five. This decision was probably made as a result of the dismissal of Margherita in retaliation for her leading role in a strike.[29] But it was also related to the fact that Abele had finished his studies; having had his diploma for several months, he could begin his life of work and no longer depend on the family.

Luigi and Margherita were now expecting support from their sons; once they retired they planned to live by cultivating the family land and from their sons' contributions. Luigi was also hoping to continue to make some money as a blacksmith. In the beginning the parents urged their sons to support them and even put considerable pressure on them to do so.[30] Both Oreste and Abele fulfilled this obligation. No one imagined that emigration and separation would provoke any tear in the web of family relations. And they were right.

It will be remembered that Luigi had also left the parental home when young in order to learn a trade. The difference between his experience and that of his sons was mainly in the distance between Valdengo and Genoa on the one hand, and Valdengo and Buenos Aires on the other. But how far from Valdengo did Buenos Aires appear to the parents of Oreste and Abele? From the letters that arrived from Argentina, the milieu into which the two Sola brothers immigrated appeared inhabited to a considerable extent by people from Biella and Valdengo. Although consisting primarily of individuals from the same area of Italy, it was a complex community encompassing different kinds of people: those who had been established in Buenos Aires for some time and those who had just arrived; those who intended to stay permanently and those who saw their migration as temporary; those who were passing through Buenos Aires because they were going elsewhere and those who were arriving in Argentina after having been in other countries. The Biellese community was complex also from the point of view of social stratification: there were poor people and those who had done quite well, farmers without a trade and "gentlemen of America," workers and artisans and important business-men, small storekeepers and entrepreneurs, those who had tried all paths and had succeeded and those who had failed.

This world was characterized especially by the fact that its members continued to maintain close relations with those who remained in Valdengo and Biella. The rapidity with which news about life in Buenos Aires spread to Valdengo and vice versa, revealed in the letters, is an indication of the continuous communication and effectiveness of ties between individuals and families on both sides of the ocean. Luigi and Margherita were astonished to learn from friends in Biella the name of Oreste's wife, who was also from the region of Biella, even before Oreste announced it to them directly.[31] The same thing occurred in the opposite direction; at one point Oreste wrote home: "I know from here as much about Biella's affairs as you do and perhaps more."[32] The letters that crossed the ocean were numerous, but as a rule they were public—that is, they were not confined to the immediate family but were shared with friends and neighbors. When in fact Luigi and his sons wanted to send or ask for information that they believed strictly private or intended for one son and not the other, they took care to mark the letter "special" or "confidential."[33]

The continual flow of people in both directions also contributed decisively to the maintenance of close relations; every year someone returned to Valdengo after a long or short migration, and every year someone left the town to embark on such an experience. The phenomenon of return migration has been studied to some extent, but it deserves thorough examination. For example, the reasons to return differed considerably; some returned because they had achieved their objectives, and others returned because they had failed. The goal of emigration could therefore be the improvement of one's social position at home and not always the search for permanent settlement abroad. Emigration could also be an experiment, one opportunity among many, for the individual involved.

If there were people who returned to the hometown, there were naturally those who left on their first emigration, and so the exchange appeared constant. From those who had already emigrated and who lived in a popular destination, the exchange was taken for granted. When Oreste, after he had lived in Argentina for several years, went to a working-class suburb of Buenos Aires to deliver greetings from Luigi to a Biellese weaver, an old companion of political struggles, he was stopped on the street by a person whom he did not know. Oreste explained what happened in a letter to his father: "[He] recognized me right off as your son because I look so much like you. We had never seen each other before, but he stopped to ask me if I was Mr. Sola."[34] Evidently it was not at all strange that on the outskirts of Buenos Aires one could run into the son of an old friend from Biella.

The distance between Buenos Aires and Valdengo is enormous if measured in miles. But when considering migration, is this a valid measure? The migratory experience of Oreste and Abele occurred within the sphere of community relations, and it was decisively shaped by them. The channels that the two brothers had utilized to emigrate across the ocean and the environment into which they were welcomed on arrival—and which mediated the impact of the new milieu—were made up of relatives, friends, and family acquaintances. From this perspective, the physical distance between Buenos Aires and Valdengo did not seem to be as important as it might otherwise have been. Both for those who remained at home and for most of those who left, the city of Buenos Aires, however distant physically, was in reality near because of the continuity of the social universe in which the emigrants found themselves when they got off the boat in America.

The Sola Migration Becomes Permanent

The migration of Oreste and Abele turned out to be permanent. But this fact emerged over time. No evidence indicates that at the time of their departures either of the sons had already decided to abandon their birthplace forever. Oreste, just as his father had done thirty years beofre, left with the intention of returning home to do his military service. When the moment arrived, however, he put pressure on Luigi to obtain an exemption for him, which in fact the father was able to do.

Oreste firmly made up his mind to seize every opportunity that he believed America could offer him. He had originally planned on moving to various countries on the continent where he could count on the support of friends and acquaintances. But for various reasons he decided to remain in Argentina; he traveled a great deal, moving from one city to another, often changing work, and even accepting the most modest of jobs. He wanted to explore the various possibilities before deciding where to settle down. After several years then, he returned to Buenos Aires, where he thought he would have the best opportunities for success. Here, where in 1908 he married Corinna, he was in fact able to improve his position greatly. In 1910, he signed a letter home triumphantly: "Your always dearer son Oreste (today a contractor on my own)." [35] In partnership with a school companion he had succeeded in obtaining a contract for a portion of a new railway line. In subsequent years he went through alternate periods of success and hard times. He was forced to abandon his construction business for a certain time; then he reestablished it. The success of his affairs would remain uncertain, but he continued to pursue his dream of making a fortune as a contractor in Argentina.

For his part, Abele had a more stable and secure life than Oreste, but for a long time he remained undecided about staying or returning. His decision to emigrate to America was difficult; unhappy with his job in Italy, he was strongly influenced by his brother's career, which at that time had just begun to be successful. However, the job that Oreste obtained for Abele in Buenos Aires—and which he never left—did not satisfy him completely. Abele was disappointed; he worked hard, but his efforts were not compensated as he expected. He even asked his father to inquire about the salary he could earn at a job in Biella, which clearly indicated that he had not yet excluded the possibility of returning. Then, the business where he was working recognized his merits. Appointed director of a new plant, Abele felt satisfied and never again thought about returning.

Luigi and Margherita, however, never considered the possibility that their sons' emigration would become permanent, although they encouraged and supported the boys' plans. When Abele indicated his desire to join his brother in Argentina, Margherita began to feel the first symptoms of the illness that would take her life seven years later. Both parents became worried and began to fear that they would never again see their sons. Oreste had been in America for eleven years, and since he had left they had never seen him. Now Abele was going away too. Nonetheless, the parents did not create obstacles for him. Luigi expressed his position on Abele's decision to go to Buenos Aires in a letter to Oreste: "Even now I would be happy if at least one [of you] were not too far away because our lives will not last very much longer. . . . But to allow the opportunity for a better life for Abele, I'll give up this wish too." [36] Similarly, two years before, when Oreste had needed a large loan to establish his construction company and had obtained it from one of his father's acquaintances, Luigi had not hesitated in vouching for Oreste with the creditor. His home and his land in Valdengo were mortgaged until the debt was settled. The existence of a mortgage on the property was revealed in a letter sent to a friend. Luigi never told Oreste about the mortgage; he only wrote, "We shall leave nothing undone so that you can be successful." [37] Luigi took a serious risk, but he was proud that he could help his son make his way in Argentina.

Luigi and Margherita's expectations reflected a conception of emigration that included return, and their behavior indicated it. Even the use that Luigi made of the remittances sent home by his sons was indicative. Oreste and Abele sent money to their parents for the purpose of helping them and guaranteeing them a serene old age without financial worries. But Luigi spent only that which was strictly necessary for himself and his wife, who had to face long and expensive medical treatments. The rest he managed wisely for his sons, behaving as if they had entrusted him with their savings until their return. Part of the money he deposited in the bank, meticulously informing them of the transactions. Part of it he used to modernize the house in Valdengo: "We have spent a fair amount of money on this, but we hope that you too will be happy to have the house fixed up a bit." [38] He then bought a small meadow, extending the family holdings if by only a little. His major effort, in his own words, was to "maintain the family estate intact." [39] In truth, it was a very modest estate: the home, composed of a few rooms, and a little more than a hectare and a half of land. [40] Nevertheless, it was an estate that he felt it his duty to protect for his sons, just as his father had done for him.

The misunderstanding about a return continued throughout the entire history of the Sola family. Oreste and Abele continually postponed from year to year the trip to Valdengo. First, it was the need not to interrupt Oreste's business and the work that Abele had just begun. Then it was the war that broke out in Europe and the hazard of sea travel. Later it was the difficulties Oreste had with his business and Abele had with obtaining a promotion. A series of external events seemed to conspire against the much-awaited visit. In reality, however, these were not sufficient to explain the behavior of the two brothers. Clearly they loved their parents and their birthplace, but these loves apparently were secondary to the pursuit of the social and economic success for which they had emigrated. The idea of success that motivated them clashed with family affections. Margherita died without the comfort of ever again seeing her sons. They finally decided on a trip to visit Luigi, but Luigi too died before they set sail for Italy.

When Luigi died in 1922, Oreste and Abele were thirty-nine and thirty-one years old. They lived the rest of their lives in Argentina. But this fact did not mean a break in relations with Valdengo. They did not sell the house nor their father's small amount of land. They entrusted the management of the land to a cousin to whom they rented it. They continued to keep in contact with him and with other relatives and friends throughout their lives.[41]

This fact explains the preservation of the letters. It is easy to understand how Luigi and Margherita would jealously guard the letters that their distant sons had sent home. When they moved from Biella to Valdengo they brought with them Oreste's first letters and throughout the years they preserved all the others. When Luigi died, Oreste and Abele, as has been said, rented the house to a cousin who kept the furniture and Luigi's numerous papers in order. During the period of fascism, when it was dangerous to have in the house political materials that the government considered subversive—such as those collected by Luigi during his life as a socialist militant—some of his papers were destroyed. But most of the rich correspondence and the family heirlooms were preserved.

Abele, who lived longer than his brother, made numerous visits to Valdengo during the later years of his life. In one of these—according to the family memory—he spent an entire night rereading the letters.[42] In the end he decided not to bring anything back with him to Buenos Aires, as may have been his original intention. Those letters, which told his story, that of his brother, and that of Luigi and Margherita, belonged to the house that had for generations been the home of the Sola family.

When this episode took place, Oreste had already died in Argentina without leaving any children, and his ashes had been transferred to Valdengo. Abele died in Buenos Aires in 1963, and the following year Oreste's wife, Corinna, also passed away. By one of the many emigrants who periodically returned to his birthplace in the never-ending cycle, the ashes of Abele and Corinna were transferred to Valdengo to be buried in the town cemetery next to those of Luigi, Margherita, Oreste, Narcisa, and the entire Sola family.[43]

The Sola Brothers: Typical Italian Migrants to the New World?

Oreste and Abele were among the millions of individuals who left Italy during the half century or so following the political unification of the country in

1871. The fact that we have so many letters spanning a period of twenty-one years written between the members of the family in Italy and Argentina means that the Sola brothers' experiences was not typical in at least one respect—it was much better documented than that of the overwhelming majority of Italian migrants to the New World. The important question, however, is were the Sola brothers typical or representative in any respects? What in their individual experiences as migrants is of significance to those interested in Italian migration and migration in general?

To answer this question we must place the lives of the Sola brothers within the context of Italian emigration and especially Italian emigration to Argentina. Between 1876 and 1925 approximately seventeen million people left Italy for destinations abroad. Some moved permanently; others, temporarily; and still others went back and forth a number of times. Italians, who had a long history of migration, as is illustrated by the story of the Sola family, were especially mobile during this period. In the 1870s the average number of emigrants from Italy was in the range of 100,000 per year. The number grew steadily until it reached a peak of over 650,000 per year during the decade prior to World War I.[44]

Although some emigrants came from all parts of Italy, they came in largest numbers from certain regions of the North (Venice, Piedmont, and Lombardy) and the South (Abruzzi, Campania, Calabria, and Sicily). Only a small number emigrated from the central area of the country. The migration from the northern regions began earliest; two out of every three emigrants before 1900 originated in the North. However, the pace of migration from the South increased after 1900; during the first decade of the twentieth century the number of emigrants from the South exceeded that from the North for the first time.

A little less than half of the emigrants went to European countries (especially France, Switzerland, and Germany) and a little more than half went overseas (especially to the United States, Argentina, and Brazil). If we examine this migration by areas of origin, however, we see two distinct patterns: Over 70 percent of the emigrants from the northern regions went to the nearby countries of Europe, while nearly 90 percent of the emigrants from the southern regions went overseas. Thus, a bimodal pattern of Italian emigration emerged during the 1876–1925 period. On the one hand, there was a continuously large although varied emigration (100,000+ per year) from the North of the country primarily to Europe. On the other, there was a later and more concentrated mass emigration from the South almost exclusively overseas and especially to the Americas.

Of the nearly nine million Italians who emigrated overseas between 1876 and 1925, eight million, or 91 percent, went to Argentina, Brazil, and the United States (2.2. million—25 percent—to Argentina, 1.3 million—15 per-

TABLE 1: *Net Immigration to Argentina by Decade, 1871–1930*

Decade	Total immigration	Italian immigration
1871–1880	85,120	37,225
1881–1890	637,670	365,570
1891–1900	319,880	201,220
1901–1910	1,120,220	452,090
1911–1920	269,090	−3,000
1921–1930	877,970	368,750

SOURCES: Argentine Republic, Dirección de Inmigración, *Resumen estadística del movimiento migratorio en la República Argentina, 1857–1924* (Buenos Aires, 1925); Associazione per lo svillupo dell'industria nel mezzogiorno, *Statistiche sul mezzogiorno d'Italia, 1861–1953* (Rome, 1954).

cent—to Brazil, and 4.5 million—51 percent—to the United States). Although the largest absolute number went to the United States, the impact of the Italians on Brazil and especially on Argentina was greater because of the much smaller total populations of the two South American countries. Because our story concerns two emigrants to Argentina, we will concentrate here on the experience of the Italians in that country.

Oreste and Abele Sola were part of a large migration that among other things dramatically changed the nature of the Argentine population. In the years between the first Argentine census of 1869 and World War I, European immigrants became a major component of the population. (See Table 1.) These immigrants were overwhelmingly Italians and Spaniards attracted by the opportunities created through the commercialization of agriculture and livestock production; the export of meat, grains, and wool; and the concomitant growth of the service sector of the economy. In 1869, Argentina had a population of less than two million, 12 percent of whom were foreign-born. During the next half century net immigration totaled nearly 2.5 million. By 1914, 30 percent of the population of nearly eight million were foreign-born, and more than half were either foreign-born or children of foreign-born.

The immigrants concentrated primarily in the eastern provinces of the country, in the cities, and especially in the leading port and capital city of Buenos Aires, where Oreste and Abele settled. As a result, Buenos Aires grew dramatically: In 1869 Buenos Aires was a town of less than 200,000 inhabitants; by 1914 it was a major commercial/bureaucratic metropolis of more than 1.5 million.[45] (See Table 2.) The immigrants exerted enormous influence in this city, especially within the economic sphere. They accounted for half its total population throughout most of the period and for approximately 80 per-

TABLE 2: *Population of Buenos Aires, 1869–1936*

Year	Total Population	Foreign- Born	Italian- Born
1869	187,350	49.3%	23.6%
1887	433,375	52.7	31.8
1895	663,850	52.0	27.4
1904	950,890	45.0	24.0
1909	1,231,700	45.5	22.5
1914	1,576,600	50.6	19.8
1936	2,415,140	36.1	12.4

SOURCES: Argentine and Buenos Aires Censuses.

cent of its economically active population. Foreign workers and owners dominated the commercial and industrial sectors of the economy and played important roles in the development of labor, business, social, and educational organizations. They also became the basis of the emerging Argentine middle classes.

The Italians were the largest of the European immigrant groups in Argentina and Buenos Aires. The Buenos Aires Italian colony comprised 44,000, or nearly one-quarter of the population of the city, in 1869 and grew to 312,000, or 19 percent of the population of the city, by 1914.[46] Throughout this period the Italian-born always constituted at least 19 percent of the population, while Italian-born and their descendants combined accounted for approximately half the population.

Three-quarters of the Italians in Buenos Aires held blue-collar jobs, but half of these blue-collar workers were skilled artisans of various sorts. Most in the remaining quarter, who held white-collar jobs, were employees in the service sector. A significant number of them, compared with their counterparts in New York and other U.S. cities of the time, however, were owners of small industrial and commercial establishments or professional contractors, as was Oreste for a time. A small number were professionals and wealthy businessmen. Upward occupational mobility was limited, but there was a slight increase in the percentage of both skilled and white-collar Italians during this period. More importantly, Italians were active in a wide range of economic protective organizations; they were instrumental in the organization of the Argentine labor movement and in the development and growth of the Argentine Industrial Union.

Italians in Buenos Aires were never concentrated in a few areas as they were in New York City; they were dispersed fairly evenly and constituted at least 14 percent of all inhabitants in every census district. There was between 1904 and 1914 a major movement of Italians toward the outlying districts of the city, where they could purchase property and live in less congested circumstances. Indeed, property ownership among Italians in Buenos Aires, which included Oreste, was much higher than among Italians in New York.

Most Italians first settled in the crowded low-rent districts in the center of Buenos Aires and then, as they accumulated resources, moved to houses they could purchase outside the center of the city. Jobs, cost of housing, transportation, and social networks were among the most important determinants of Italian settlement in Buenos Aires. Although the Italians of Buenos Aires moved frequently, movement did not always signify upward mobility. Some, such as Oreste, moved nearby to accommodate a larger family. Others moved when the opportunity presented itself to be close to family and friends. Still others moved because they were forced out of their current residence for one reason or another. Most immigrants, who worked long hours for little pay, lived in inexpensive housing close to where they worked. In Buenos Aires industry and commerce were concentrated in the central area along with inexpensive housing. As a result the Italians during the first decade of the twentieth century lived predominantly within a radius of three miles from the downtown center-city core. The growth of the transportation system, and especially a major reduction in the fares on the electric streetcars in the early 1900s, encouraged Italians to move outward. In the case of both initial settlement and subsequent movement outward, one of the most important influences was the social network. Italians in Buenos Aires settled in areas where there were family and friends from the same town. These village- and kin-based networks influenced not only residence but many other aspects of the immigrant experience, as we shall see.

The Italian immigrant community was highly developed by the time Oreste arrived in Buenos Aires in 1901, and it continued to grow stronger and more unified for some time after. The Italians started mutual-aid societies in the middle of the nineteenth century and expanded them and created new institutions with each new influx of immigrants. In addition to mutual-aid societies, several of which were quite large (3,000+ members) and influential, the Italians set up a hospital, banks, churches, a chamber of commerce, social clubs, and newspapers. Local Italian communities within Buenos Aires were based on affiliation with a particular church, local store, club, or saloon. Because the citywide immigrant community was highly developed, it was to a considerable extent able to overcome the local forces of *campanilismo* (localism) that so fragmented the Italian community of New York City and most other U.S. cities. An Italian immigrant elite linked the large mutual-aid societies with the leading Italian-language newspaper and the Italian Argentine banks, chamber of commerce, and social clubs. Not only were these institutions linked by an elite, but working-class individuals from different villages and different parts of Italy were linked within institutions such as the mutual-aid societies. We must not, therefore, lose sight of the ties of village and kin that remained strong and simultaneously influential on many aspects of the individual's life.

The letters of Oreste and Abele provide us with unique insight into the Italian community and especially the Biellesi of Buenos Aires at the turn of the century. To a great extent their lives revolved around the intertwined identifications with family and fellow townspeople from the Biella area, as we have mentioned. In fact, Italian emigration can most accurately be understood as a village-outward phenomenon.[47] The village and the specific family in question were the most important contexts in which the major decisions regarding migration were made. The decision to migrate was, as Bell points out, based on a careful evaluation of the pros and cons.[48] Oreste most likely decided to emigrate to Buenos Aires because his godfather, Zocco, lived there amidst an established community of Biellesi. Presumably letters and word of mouth indicated the job prospects. But there were other options open to Oreste in 1901. Biellesi were established in many different parts of the world, and indeed Solas were established in a variety of places as well. Many Biellesi went to Paterson, New Jersey, to work in the textile mills there, as did Cousin Ida. Cousin Edvino was in Cuba. But probably because of Godfather Zocco, Oreste chose Buenos Aires as a destination. Once Oreste was in Buenos Aires and decided to settle there, it was natural for Abele to join his brother. Nevertheless, Abele first worked in Tuscany and Sardinia before he decided to go to Buenos Aires.

From the letters we get some sense of the Biellesi of Buenos Aires. We are given no clear idea, however, of when and how the community was first established. Oreste's great-uncle Andrea had been in Buenos Aires before the 1870s, but perhaps he did not stay because no Biellesi were there at that time. Clearly, however, the community was in existence well before 1900. How much before is difficult to determine. Zocco, about whom we know little except that he was Oreste's godfather and an old friend of the Sola family, was well established in Buenos Aires by 1900 and obviously had been there for some time. He was probably in the construction business, as is suggested in letter #28, and was an influential member of the community of Biellesi, to which he introduced Oreste.

The letters make it clear that the network of Biellesi was extensive, active, and influential in the lives of its members; they provide many bits of information on those coming from and going back to the Biella area and on the use of the network for friendship and support. Zocco introduced Oreste to the Biellesi in Buenos Aires and helped him get a job. When Oreste went to Mendoza, he stayed with friends from Valdengo, and he talked constantly during the early years of visiting friends in Peru or Cousin Edvino in Cuba. When he married, he married a woman from the Biella area. When he started his business, he hired a friend from Valdengo to assist him and a number of workers from the area. The best friends of Oreste, Corinna and Abele were two families from Biella, the Pellas and the Sassos. They also saw a good deal of Cousins Abele and Andrea and their families. Messages were hand delivered from the parents in Valdengo and vice versa. Information traveled back and forth rapidly so that members of the network knew a great deal about other members in both Buenos Aires and Biella.

The network was so active that at times it seemed to intrude too far into its members' private lives. Oreste, for example, complained about busybodies and those from Biella who expected support from their fellow villagers. In addition, the network limited the activities of its members in the sense that it was not tied into the larger Italian network of Buenos Aires. Oreste seemed to prefer the newspapers from Biella to those from the Italian community of Buenos Aires. Only once did he mention an Italian mutual-aid society, and then he indicated no particular attachment to it.

The Biellesi were active in Buenos Aires, but how large was the community, where was it located, what did its members do, what held it together? Precise and complete answers to these questions are impossible, but the letters provide some useful information on these subjects. Physically there seem to have been at least several centers of the community: one in the center of town in the area of Calles Rivadavia and Rio Bamba, where Zocco lived until he returned to Valdengo in 1907 and where Oreste lived from March 1901 to February 1914; another in the area of Puente Alsina, on the edge of the city; and a third in Belgrano, where their friend Luigi Fila (letter #118) lived. The communities certainly numbered in the hundreds and perhaps in the thousands with most Biellesi probably living in the Puente Alsina area and in Belgrano, where the primary employment was in nearby textile mills. The occupations of those in the Rivadavia/Rio Bamba community were varied; they included unskilled and semiskilled laborers, artisans, some small and medium businessmen such as Oreste, and white-collar workers such as Abele. The communities seem to have been held together by personal ties. The letters do not mention institutional affiliations, although it is possible that other Biellesi besides Oreste, Abele, and their friends were members of unions, mutual-aid societies, or clubs. The Biellesi in Paterson, New Jersey, were active in the textile strike of 1913. Perhaps too the Biellesi working in the textile factories near Puente Alsina and in Belgrano were united in a labor union or organization of some kind.

This returns us to the issue of how representative or typical Oreste was of the millions of Italians who migrated to Argentina. Clearly he was better educated than most, which is one of the reasons we have the letters in the first place. Beyond his education, however, is much that is typical of the emigrant/ immigrant experience—not that all migrants acted in the same way, but many did. The informal network among the Biellesi was a major influence in his life. His drive for economic success, his purchase of property, his financial ups and downs, his initial intention of migrating temporarily, his talk of a return that in fact he never made, and his commitment to support his aging parents were also typical of many. Oreste may not have represented all Italian immigrants in Argentina, but his life as described by the letters duplicated much of the general process through which all immigrants went.

The Sola Letters

Our selection includes 208 of the 351 letters that are still in existence. (Photograph 1 reproduces one of these letters.) The collection covers a period of twenty-one years—from August 1901, when Oreste arrived in Buenos Aires, through November 1922, when Luigi died in Valdengo; it contains all the letters Oreste and Abele wrote home—respectively, 107 from August 17, 1901, to October 12, 1922, and 100 from June 11, 1912, through October 12, 1922—4 letters from Corinna, and the first drafts of letters that Luigi sent to his distant sons. The 137 letters of Luigi and 3 from Margherita do not cover the entire duration of the correspondence. Some of these letters were unfortunately lost or misplaced. They begin with July 1908 and are interrupted the first time in September 1909. The pattern continues from then on with the result that we have letters from the following periods: August 1910 to March 1911, February 1912 to April 1914, June 1915 to June 1916, September 1918 to June 1919, and finally October 1920 to March 1922.

The frequency with which the letters that are in the collection were written varies considerably, as Table 3 shows. Obviously some letters are missing; nevertheless, those available give us some interesting information regarding frequency. The parents were constantly complaining that Oreste did not write enough, but we have no indication that during the periods for which we have letters they wrote much more than did the sons. Also, there were more letters when something new or special happened. For example, Oreste wrote more than a letter a month during his first seventeen months in Argentina, a letter every two months during the next two years, and only a letter every four months during the subsequent two years. Similarly, Oreste's success as a contractor in 1910, the arrival of Abele in 1912, and the death of Margherita in 1919 rekindled interest for a time and resulted in more frequent letters.

The selection presented here includes 70 letters from Oreste, 58 from Abele, 4 from Corinna, 3 from Margherita, and 72 from Luigi for a total of 207. To this an additional letter of Abele, written to his cousin of the same name (Giacomo's son) after his father's death, has been added and concludes the story. The letters have been put in chronological order and divided into nine chapters in order to permit the reader to follow the unfolding of events in this family autobiography: Seeking Wealth and Adventure (1901–1903), Mak-

TABLE 3: *Frequency of Letters between Argentina and Italy by Year*

Year	Letters included in book		Letters not included in book		Total letters sent		
	From Argentina	From Italy	From Argentina	From Italy	Argentina	Italy	Both
1901 (5 months)	5	0	0	0	5	0	5
1902	8	0	6	0	14	0	14
1903	4	0	2	0	6	0	6
1904	5	0	0	0	5	0	5
1905	3	0	0	0	3	0	3
1906	1	0	2	0	3	0	3
1907	4	0	2	0	6	0	6
1908	3	4	1	0	4	4	8
1909	3	4	2	2	5	6	11
1910	7	2	5	4	12	6	18
1911	5	3	4	0	9	3	12
1912	13	12	3	8	16	20	36
1913	10	9	2	9	12	18	30
1914	8	3	1	3	9	6	15
1915	11	10	5	3	16	13	29
1916	4	3	5	10	9	13	22
1917	8	0	4	0	12	0	12
1918	6	5	3	3	9	8	17
1919	8	10	10	1	18	11	29
1920	4	0	9	7	13	7	20
1921	6	7	6	13	12	20	32
1922	7	3	6	2	13	5	18
Total	133 ⟍208⟋ 75		78 ⟍143⟋ 65		211	140	351

ing It in Buenos Aires (1903–1907), Marriage and Family (1908–1910), Oreste Becomes a Contractor (1910–1912), Abele Joins His Brother (1912–1913), the Impact of Economic Crisis (1913–1915), Italy Joins the War (1915–1917), the Death of Margherita (1918–1919), and the Impossible Return (1919–1922).

In order to make space, we have eliminated some unessential passages from

Buenos Ayres 17 Agosto 1901

Carissimi Genitori

Dal giorno 5 del corrente mese che sono giunto,
sto in ottima salute come pure i miei due compagni
appena arrivati ci siamo fatti condurre all'indi-
rizzo del padrino Focis il quale poi ci fece conoscere
vari di Valdengo che da vari anni risiedono in America, e tutti dal più al meno se la passano bene
qui la lingua è il Castilla, molto simile allo spa-
gnuolo, ma però non senti uno che la parli dapper-
tutto dove vai sia all'albergo che sul lavoro tutti parlano
il piemontese o l'italiano, anche quelli delle altre
regioni ed gl'Argentini stessi parlano l'italiano
questa città è bellissima, v'ha un lusso enorme
che le strade che qui si dicono calle sono selciate
con legno di madera che è durissimo o sono in cemento
liscio come il marmo, e perfin troppo secché i cavalli
a sei tiram che quelli delle vetture che qui corrono sempre
scivolano e non è raro in un giorno vederne cadere
venti e più, vi sono dei palazzi oltre il bello, all'odo
sopra piani, se al più ma con degli ornamenti
in tutta Torino non trovi uno eguale, il palazzo
più bello è quello del serbatoio dell'acqua potabile, cos-
truito dagl'inglesi, è qualche cosa di sorprendente sino

Saluterete tanto la famiglia Ripetti Giovanni
fratelle compreso l'Pii, Genio, Tilio, ecc.
famiglie Mello Laurise Cesere, la Pina e Ilde
Ismardi, ecc. insomma tutti quelli e
forse si ricordano di me.
Ricevete anche voi un supremo e affettuoso
bacio ed abbraccio dal vostro sempre
                              affz.to figlio
                                 Oreste

Quando mi farete sapere vostre notizie
                 Calle Rivadavia N.º 1982
                         Buenos Aires

Forse avrete riceventi i saluti da Ferrini Pietro
fatto perchè ho impostato le sue lettere qualche
ora prima e dev'essere partita su un'altro
vapore, e questa ritarda sino ad oggi o forse sino a
mercoledì.
      Salutatemi tutti gli amici che solo do-
mandano di me
      Ciaooou   Oreste

Photograph 1.   One of the original Sola letters (#1).

those letters that we do present. We have systematically omitted the ritual for-
mulas that recur at the beginning and end with little variation throughout the
correspondence. The formula "We are always in excellent health and we wish
you the same" or "We have received your very dear letter with the greatest
pleasure" begin every letter. And the formula "Receive dearest parents so
many kisses and a heartfelt embrace from your affectionate children" or "Accept dearest children our warmest kisses from your loving parents" conclude
each letter. Also we have for the most part eliminated the greetings that were
sent to friends and relatives and that came just before the concluding formula.
These greetings vary a lot from the simple—"Give our best to all our friends
and relatives" And "Our relatives are fine and send you their greetings"—to
long lists of persons—"Many greetings from your friends over here and say
hello for us to those over there. And Tirisin, what does he have to say? And
how is Riccardo? All our greetings to Carmelina and Gino, to Maria, to Car-
linet, in short to all those who remember us."[49]

Moreover, we have omitted most of the references to letters sent and received. These references for the entire duration of the war (1914–1918) were
extensive and detailed. The shortage of mail ships and the attacks by German
submarines that resulted in frequent and considerable delays prompted these
references. One example should be enough to make the point clear: "Your last
letters are from November 3 and 21, 1917, and January 1, 1918. We have not
received a card from Oropa, which you say you have sent. Our last letter is
from November 30, which you have received. In your letter of November 21
you say that you have received our last of September 3. Surely you have also
received our letter of October 1 with postcards since you mention it without
giving the date in your letter of November 3. This is good to know because up
to now by good luck not a one has gotten lost."[50]

Finally, we have omitted most references to internal Italian politics—the
affairs of the Socialist Party (of which Luigi was a local leader), the debate on
Italy's joining the war—to military operations during the war, and to political
considerations in general in Argentina and in Europe. We have judged these
to be of secondary interest for the readers of this book. However, such passages
appear with some frequency in only the latter part of the correspondence
(1915–1922). The greatest portion of the letters retains an intimate, family
character.

The children's letters were always collectively signed even if only the first
one listed did the writing. To avoid confusion, we have put in parentheses the
names of those who did not do the writing. In this sense, a letter which concludes "Your affectionate children Oreste, (Abele, and Corinna)" is in reality
to be considered a letter of Oreste alone. And one that concludes "Your dear
children Abele, (Oreste, and Corinna)" is to be assigned to Abele alone.

As for the letters of the parents, it was almost always Luigi who wrote in the name of both. The only three letters signed by Margherita that were found among the first drafts are from 1908, 1909, and 1915, and all of them are included in our selection (letters #35, #39, #126). In the notebook that contained the first drafts of the letters, short pieces in her name appear later. Considering the severe illness that afflicted her, Luigi must have done the writing, perhaps as she dictated, and only one copy was sent to the children.[51]

The letters that arrived in Buenos Aires from Valdengo were always addressed to both children and to daughter-in-law Corinna, but the first listed was of the greatest importance because the letter was considered to be addressed especially to him or her. Generally this was so because the parents wanted to answer a letter written by the first listed or because they wanted to pay particular attention to some individual—to Oreste because he was the head of the family in Buenos Aires or because he had not written for a long time, to Corinna because she was ill. This custom was dropped only in exceptional cases, such as the confidential letters that were addressed to one person only and that were responded to with equal confidentiality and signed individually.[52]

The normal amount of time for letters to travel between Valdengo and Buenos Aires at that time was between twenty and thirty days. Every now and then, however, the long-distance dialogue between parents and children was influenced by the vagaries of the postal service—letters that crossed in mid-ocean or were lost, questions and answers that overlapped and piled up. But this immigrant family autobiography continued to play itself out in an intelligible and coherent manner until the death of Luigi resulted in the sharp and painful interruption of the letters. The termination of the letters in 1922 brought down the curtain on the story of the Sola family.

Notes

1.   *Herbert Blumer,* Critiques of Research in the Social Sciences *(New Brunswick, N.J.: Transaction Books, 1979), pp. xxiii–xxviii.*

2.   *William I. Thomas and Florian Znaniecki,* The Polish Peasant in Europe and America, *edited and abridged by Eli Zaretsky (Urbana and Chicago: University of Illinois Press, 1984).*

3.   *Ibid., pp. 29–47.*

4.   *H. Arnold Barton,* Letters from the Promised Land: Swedes in America, 1840–1914 *(Minneapolis: University of Minnesota Press, 1975); Thomas C. Blegen,* Land of Their Choice *(Minneapolis: University of Minnesota Press, 1955); Alan Conway, ed.,* The Welsh in America: Letters from the Immigrants *(Minneapolis: University of Minnesota Press, 1961); Charlotte Erickson,* Invisible Immigrants *(Miami, Fla.: University of Miami Press, 1972); William Hoglund,* Finnish Immigrants in America, 1880–1920 *(Madison: University of Wisconsin Press, 1960); William Hoglund, "Finnish Immigrant Letter-Writers: Reporting from the United States to Finland, 1870s to World War*

I," in Finnish Diaspora II: United States, ed. Michael G. Karni (Toronto: Multi-cultural History Society of Ontario, 1981), pp. 14–31; and Witold Kula et al., Writing Home: Immigrants in Brazil and the United States, 1890–1891 (New York: Columbia University Press, 1986). See also Louis Gottschalk et al., The Use of Personal Documents in History, Anthropology and Sociology, Bulletin 53 (New York: Social Science Research Council, 1945).

5.   Blumer, Critiques; Thomas and Znaniecki, Polish Peasant; and Vincent Crapanzano, Yasmine Ergas, and Judith Modell, "Personal Testimony: Narratives of the Self in the Social Sciences and the Humanities," Items 40, 2 (June 1986):25–30. See also Josephine Wtulich, "Introduction" in Kula, Writing Home; and Emilio Franzina, Merica! Merica! (Milan: Feltrinelli, 1979).

6.   Erickson, Invisible Immigrants, p. 3; and Marsha Penti-Vidutis, "The America Letter: Immigrant Accounts of Life Overseas," Finnish Americana 1 (1978):22–40.

7.   Blumer, Critiques, pp. xiii–xiv.

8.   Erickson, Invisible Immigrants, p. 6.

9.   Blumer, Critiques, pp. xxxi.

10.   Rudolph J. Vecoli, "Foreword," in Rosa: The Life of an Italian Immigrant, ed. Marie Hall Ets (Minneapolis: University of Minnesota Press, 1970), p. x.

11.   Samuel L. Baily, "Chain Migration of Italians to Argentina," Studi emigrazione (Rome) 19, 65 (March 1982):73–91.

12.   Most of the information on the Sola family is found in the private documents and papers held in the Archivio Dr. Aldo Sola, Vigliano, Italy. Additional information was furnished directly by Dr. Sola.

13.   Numerous studies on Biella and on the economic history of northern Italy exist. See, for example, R. Tremelloni, L'industria tessile italiana: Come è sorta e come è oggi (Turin: Einaudi, 1937).

14.   In the archives of Dr. Sola there are nineteen letters sent from Luigi in Liguria to his parents in Valdengo between 1869 and 1871. These letters are part of a larger collection that includes all the correspondence that Luigi sent home during his military service.

15.   P. Secchia, Capitalismo e classe operaia nel centro laniero d'Italia (Rome: Editori Riuniti, 1960).

16.   F. Ramella, "Famiglia e lavoro industriale in alcuni distretti piemontesi tra Otto e Novecento," Storia urbana 17 (1981):81–101.

17.   The results of extensive research on emigration from the area of Biella to different destinations abroad, produced and financed by the Sella Foundation, will be published by Editrice Electa, Milan.

18.   R. C. Taylor, "Migration and Motivation: A Study of Determinants and Types," in Migration, ed. J. A. Jackson (Cambridge: Cambridge University Press, 1969), pp. 99–133.

19.   J. P. Raison, "Migrazione," in Enciclopedia Einaudi (Turin: Einaudi, 1981–1984), 9:285–311.

20.   C. Tilly, "Migration in Modern European History," in Human Migrations: Patterns and Policies, ed. W. H. McNeill and R. S. Adams (Bloomington: Indiana University Press, 1978), pp. 48–72; and Taylor, "Migration."

21.   On the social changes that were caused for the textile workers, both at home and

at work, by the transformation from proto-industry to the factory system, see
F. Ramella, Terra e telai *(Turin: Einaudi, 1984).*

22.   *The archives of Dr. Sola contain interesting letters from Andrea written be-*
tween 1858 and 1883, including sixty letters generally addressed to his brother Antonio,
who was Luigi's father.

23.   *Letter from Andrea to Antonio, 25 January 1860.*

24.   *Letter from Andrea in Rio de Janeiro to Antonio, June 1877.*

25.   *This information was provided by Dr. Sola, whose paternal grandfather was*
Giacomo.

26.   *Giuseppe was Giacomo's brother. The two brothers were nearly the same age as*
Luigi, their cousin, but neither of them shared his socialist ideas.

27.   *Following the assassination of Sadi Carnot, the president of France, by an Italian*
anarchist, Italian immigrants in Lyons and other regions of the country were con-
fronted with a wave of xenophobia. See P. Milza, Français et Italiens à la fin du XIX
siècle *(Rome: Ecole Française de Rome, 1981). In relation to this situation, there is an*
interesting document of Giuseppe Sola's in the Archives Départementales du Rhône,
Lyons. The document refers to a letter of September 1894, sent from Biella and ad-
dressed to the French authorities, which lists all the family furnishings hastily disposed
of at the time of the crisis. Giuseppe asked for compensation but was turned down (4 M
340, Dossiers d'indemnisation des dégâts).

28.   *In the 1880s, New Jersey was a popular destination for weavers who emigrated*
from Biella. Most were employed in silk factories in Paterson and in Passaic. Interesting
documents on this emigration are preserved at the American Labor Museum, Botto
House, Haledon, New Jersey.

29.   *The development and conclusion of the strike at the large factory in which Mar-*
gherita worked is documented in the local socialist newspaper, Corriere Biellese.

30.   *Letters #32, #34, #36, and #38. For a discussion of how much the boys*
earned and how much they sent home, see the Appendix.

31.   *Letter #32.*

32.   *Letter #27.*

33.   *Letters #124, #144, and #157.*

34.   *Letter #24.*

35.   *Letter #50.*

36.   *Letter #68.*

37.   *Letter #51. The mortgage of Luigi's property is mentioned in a letter to a friend*
that is in Dr. Sola's archives.

38.   *Letter #36. For a discussion of how much the boys sent home and how large the*
"estate" in Italy was, see the Appendix.

39.   *Letter #157.*

40.   *The house consisted of two floors with three rooms and a kitchen. In addition,*
there was a barn with stalls, pigstys, a chicken coop, and a hayloft. Around the house
was a small garden, a vineyard, and a small field, to which was added the land ac-
quired by Luigi with his sons' money. Most of this information was contained in a
"Convenzione d'affitto" drawn up in Valdengo 11 November 1895 between Luigi and
the person to whom he had rented the property. The "Convenzione" is in Dr. Sola's
archives.

41.   *This information was furnished by Dr. Aldo Sola, who is the son of the cousin to whom the house in Valdengo was rented.*

42.   *Dr. Sola remembers this event.*

43.   *Dr. Sola buried the ashes of Abele and Corinna.*

44.   *Data for the following section comes from Commissariato Generale Dell'Emigrazione,* Annuario statistico della emigrazione italiana dal 1876 al 1925 *(Rome, 1926).*

45.   *James R. Scobie,* Buenos Aires: Plaza to Suburbs, 1870–1910 *(New York: Oxford University Press, 1974).*

46.   *Samuel L. Baily, "Chain Migration"; "The Adjustment of Italian Immigrants in Buenos Aires and New York, 1870–1914,"* American Historical Review 88, 2 *(April 1983):281–305; and "Patrones de residencia de los italianos en Buenos Aires y Nueva York: 1880–1914,"* Estudios migratorios Latinoamericanos *(Buenos Aires) 1, 1 (December 1985):8–47.*

47.   *Samuel L. Baily, "The Future of Italian American Studies," in* Italian Americans: New Perspectives in Italian Immigration and Ethnicity, *ed. Lydio F. Tomasi (New York: Center for Migration Studies, 1985), pp. 193–201.*

48.   *Rudolph M. Bell,* Fate and Honor, Family and Village *(Chicago: University of Chicago Press, 1979).*

49.   *Letter #82.*

50.   *Letter of 1 March 1918.*

51.   *Letter #126.*

52.   *Letters #124, #144, #157.*

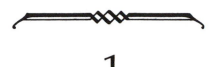

1

Seeking Wealth and Adventure (1901–1903)

Oreste Sola arrived in Buenos Aires on August 5, 1901, and for the next twenty months pursued with mixed success his quest for wealth and adventure. His first letter reflected the wonder and enthusiasm of any tourist reporting home on his distant travels; in it Oreste dwelled on the size and beauty of Buenos Aires as only a draftsman could. Although Godfather Zocco had taken him into his own house, presumably helped him find work, and introduced him to the Biellesi of Buenos Aires, Oreste was eager to move on. He chose as his destination the rapidly growing interior city of Mendoza, in part because his good friend Secondino Miglietti's sister and brother-in-law (Cichina and Carlo) lived there and in part because an employer offered to pay his way. He lived with Cichina, Carlo, and Luigi Ferraro, a native of a small town near Biella, for more than a year. Secondino joined the group for seven months but then returned to Italy.

The search for wealth was not productive at this point in his career. Although he said things were better than in Italy, Oreste complained that he was working as a laborer and "they don't pay me as I want" (#3). He noted there was some unemployment in Mendoza and that he was only earning "a bare living and with difficulty at that" (#4). Ever the optimist and believer in American opportunity, he concluded: "Still I am not losing heart ever. I have been through a good period at first, then an excellent one, and now I am in a third one that is very tough. But I'll get back on my feet. We are in America" (#4).

The search for adventure was somewhat more rewarding, although not completely so. Oreste did see many new places and strange things—for example, a puma and a guanaco (#10). He also rode horses for hours and hours on the pampas. His desire to travel and see the world—to visit his friend Berretta in Peru or Cousin Edvino in Cuba—was frustrated, however, because he could find neither Berretta's address nor someone to travel with him.

Oreste's world was circumscribed largely by a network of family and fellow Biellesi. He was obviously concerned about the welfare of his family and paid special attention to his brother, Abele, and sister, Narcisa. Nevertheless, he was a negligent correspondent and constantly apologized for not writing frequently. It is not hard to understand why Margherita, so far away from her oldest son, worried, and why Oreste in turn tried to reassure her that everything was all right.

In Buenos Aires and Mendoza, Oreste associated primarily with friends and relatives from the Biella area. Zocco was the center of this network, but it extended to many others in Buenos Aires, Mendoza, and a few additional Argentine cities. Although he wrote home that he had learned to read and write Spanish within six months of his arrival (#8), Oreste did not mention an Argentine friend until more than four months after that, and there was no indication that the friend was at all close (#10).

As strong as the ties of family and town were, Oreste was not eager to return home. He mentioned such a possibility in general terms probably to placate the family, but his main interest was in Argentina. His good friend Secondino, however, was a classic case of the returnee: He missed his wife, his health was of concern, and he had a job back in Valdengo (#11). The chapter closes with Oreste traveling from Mendoza to several other Argentine cities in search of work.

Letter 1

Buenos Ayres, 17 August 1901

Dearest parents,

I have been here since the 5th of this month; I am in the best of health as are my two companions. As soon as we got here, we went to the address of Godfather Zocco, who then introduced us to several people from Valdengo who have been in America for some years and all are doing well more or less. The language here is Castilian, quite similar to Spanish, but you don't hear anyone speaking it. Wherever you go, whether in the hotel or at work, everyone speaks either Piedmontese or Italian, even those from other countries, and the Argentines themselves speak Italian.[1]

This city is very beautiful. There is an enormous amount of luxury. All the streets—they call them *calle* [sic] here—are paved either with hard wood or in cement as smooth as marble, even too smooth since the horses, tram horses as well as carriage horses, which run here, keep slipping constantly. It is not unusual to see twenty or more of them fall in one day.

There are some buildings beautiful beyond words, only five stories high, six at the most, but with ornamentation the equal of which you won't find in all of Turin. The most beautiful building is the water reservoir, built by the English, and, what is surprising, it is all marble for half its height but with certain small columns sculpted and decorated with exquisite workmanship. The other half of it is also enchanting; it occupies 10,000 square meters.

The piazza Victoria (Plaza de Mayo) is also beautiful, where all around on two sides there are only banks. They are of all nations: English, French, Italian, Spanish, North American, etc., etc. On another side is the government building where the president of the Argentine Republic resides. He is Italian, Rocca by name, the third Italian president in a row who sits on the Argentine throne.[2] There is also the railway station of the south, which is something colossal. With workshops, offices, and the station itself it will cover one million square meters. Now they are at work on a government building for the Congress (Parliament). The architect was an Italian, as is the chief contractor, who is supervising all the work. It is a job which in the end will cost more than 700 million lire. It will occupy an area of a block which is 10,000 square meters and will be surrounded by a square, which, along with the building, will constitute an area of about 100,000 square meters. This work will be better than the first [the railway station], but perhaps I shall not be able to see it finished.

All of this is inside the city, but if you should go outside for a few hours, it's worse than a desert. You only find houses made solely out of mortar, with only a ground floor and a door you have to enter on all fours. Outside you don't see a plant; everything is desert. The plains stretch as far as the eye can see; it takes hours on the train before you come to the mountains. There are a few tracts of land, sort of green, where they may let a few horses loose to graze. Here they let the animals go out no matter what the weather might be. Here you can't find a rock, though you pay its weight in gold for it. All the ground is black like manure, thick and muddy. When it doesn't rain, it gets hard, and if you try to dig, it shoots out as if it were rock.

The food here is pretty good, but it doesn't have much flavor. This is true for all Argentina.

All the guys here are jolly as crazy men. In the evening when we get together before going to bed we split our sides laughing. They would all like to go back to Italy, but they don't ever budge. Perhaps I will do the same. Here we eat, drink, and laugh and enjoy ourselves; we are in America.

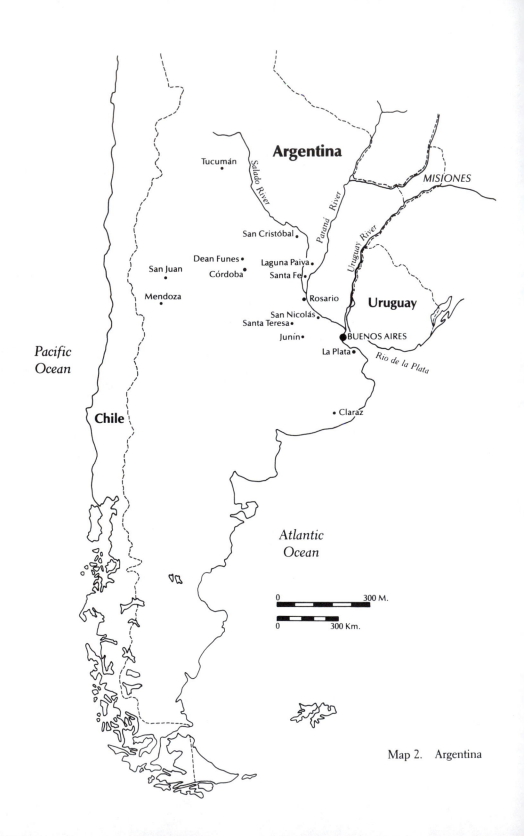

Map 2. Argentina

Goodbye. You too should be happy as well as Mom that I am in America. Give a kiss to Narcisa and another to Abele. Tell him to study hard, that one who studies and is knowledgeable is greatly respected and sought after here.

Take one last loving kiss and hug
from your always loving son,
Oreste

1.   *He does not speak or understand Spanish and therefore does not realize that Spanish and Castilian are the same thing. Although 25 percent of the total population and an even higher percentage of the adult population of Buenos Aires was Italian-born, and therefore the Italian language was indeed spoken in many places, Oreste obviously exaggerates when he claims that everyone speaks it.*
2.   *Oreste is in error here. The president to whom he refers, Julio Roca, was Argentine not Italian. The preceding president, José Uriburu, also was not Italian. However, Carlos Pelligrini, president from 1890 to 1892, was the son of a French-Italian father from Savoy.*

Letter 2

Mendoza, 18 September 1901

Dearest parents,

I am still in good spirits and happy that I am in America. I am now at Mendoza instead of Buenos Ayres. I didn't like Buenos Ayres too much because you don't get good wine there; and then every day the temperature changes twenty times, and I was always chilly. Otherwise it was fine.

One day I got the idea, knowing that Secondino's brother-in-law and sister were in Mendoza. Since the boss advanced me the money for the trip,[1] I made up my mind to come here, where you see nothing but hills and mountains in the distance, like at home. You drink very well here; the wine costs half what it does in Buenos Ayres and is pure and delicious. I am living here with Carlo and his wife and a man by the name of Luigi Ferraro from Chiavazza, who has been here for seven years traveling around in America. There are few people here from Biella, but there is no shortage of Italians. I still haven't learned a word of Castilian because, everywhere you go, they speak Italian or Piedmontese.

I am better off here than in Buenos Ayres. I am only sorry to be so far from my friends—they didn't want to come—and from Godfather and the rest.

This city is ugly; it never rains even though it is close to the mountains. I have written a friend to send me the address of my schoolmate Berretta, and I might just go and see him in Peru; it takes four days or more on the train. From Buenos Ayres to Mendoza takes two nights and a day on the railroad without ever changing trains or getting off. The longest stop is a half hour. In the entire journey you don't see a plant. [There are] two or three rivers about

400 meters wide. They are all in the plain, so calm that you can't tell which
way the water is going, and yet they flow on in an imperceptible way.

Throughout the journey one meets only horses, cows, and goats, none of
which have stables. On the rail line you don't see a house for three hours or
more, and everything is like that. The first night an ox was sleeping on the
tracks; the train hit it so hard that it knocked it for a distance of more than fifty
meters. It gave a long bellow and then died. There are also ostriches in great
number. You find carcasses of other animals who have just died; the owners of
these vast tracts don't go looking for them. They leave them there to rot as
food for the vultures, which are abundant. All of Argentina is like that. From
Mendoza it take fifteen hours by mule to get to Chile. My trip cost me more
than thirty scudos.

Everyone, Carlo, Cichina, and Luigi, give their regards to you. Tell Secondino to come and see America, to drink and eat and travel.

Time is pressing since I have to work every evening until ten. I work at
home after work.

You should write me at:

> El Taller del Ferro Carril G.O.A.
> Mendoza

Goodbye everybody. Kisses to Abele and Narcisa. Tell Abele to study hard
and to learn to work. Send him to the technical schools;[2] I imagine he has
been promoted. Goodbye, Mom and Dad. Be in good spirits as I am.

Yours always,
Orestes

1.   *The government of the province of Mendoza and many individual employers
made a major effort to attract European immigrants during the two decades preceding
World War I. It was not unusual for an employer to advance money to pay for the trip
from Buenos Aires to Mendoza.*
2.   *The Italian educational system of that period started with four obligatory years
of elementary school. Beyond that the student could choose one of two paths: five years
at the* ginnasio, *which was followed by three years at the* liceo *and then by the university; or three years at the technical school followed by either three years at the professional school, which both Oreste and Abele did, or four years at the technical institute,
which opened the way to the* politecnico.

Letter 3

Mendoza, 13 November 1901

Dearest Father, Mother, brother, and sister,

This morning Secondino arrived as you had already indicated he would in
your letter of 14 October. He had a very good trip, and he made everyone

happy to see him healthy and cheerful—as we are, Carlo, Cichina, and Luigi. He gave me the trousers which you gave him to bring me and the letter written by Dad and Narcisa.

I have been here in Mendoza for about three months, and I am happy that Secondino is here now too. But I don't plan to stay fixed here. I would like to go to Peru with Berretta or to Cuba, where dear Cousin Edvino is staying, since I know that those who are there are doing well now. It wouldn't be bad here except you aren't sure about employment or about anything, especially for the type of work I do. So you can't even be sure of staying in one place. Before leaving I am waiting to get the address of Berretta.

I thought that I could send something; instead I had to make some purchases. Be patient. I think of our family conditions too often to be able to think of anything else. Excuse me if I have been slow in writing. It's because I hoped to get a particular job, and I wanted to let you know. I was waiting for the decision of the company. The job went to another, also Italian, with whom nobody could compete. But let's leave the subject of work because here there are so many professions and so many trades that you can't say what you are doing. Today it's this and tomorrow it's that. I tried to go into the construction business for myself, but it didn't work out. So much effort and expense. Now I am doing something else, and I shall change again soon.

My friends as well as Godfather are still in Buenos Aires. They are fine and want to be remembered to you. I receive news (from Buenos Aires) almost every week.

Pardon me, dear parents, brother, and sister, if I am sometimes slow in writing. It is not that I forget, quite the contrary. Only please don't reproach me the way Narcisa does because, if you knew how painful these reproaches are to us here, especially when they come from the family, you would not believe it. I shall try to write more often.

Narcisa asks me for postcards, Abele for stamps. I cannot satisfy anyone since they don't sell illustrated postcards here even though there would be many beautiful things [to show], like, for example, the ruins of Mendoza of 1860 caused by the earthquake, which often happens here six or seven times a year.[1] If it is a special earthquake, you seem to be in a boat, rocking like at sea. But if it gets a bit strong, you have to lie down so as not to fall. Some attribute it to the various volcanoes, mostly extinct however, which are in the mountains here. Others say it is because of the huge storms of the Pacific meeting the winds that come from the Atlantic. However, no one can verify it.

From what I make out from Dad's letter, he says that he was planning to send me some clothes when I get established here. Excuse me, dear parents, your sacrifices are already excessive. Now it is my job to pay them back at least in part, and I shall do everything possible to that end. But excuse me, I am old enough now to earn my bread. I beg you not to be offended about this. If later I shall be in a position to, I shall send you money and everything. But for now, first of all, I have clothes to wear. I have already purchased here two suits and four pairs of trousers. So don't be upset then. Rather, I repeat, as soon as I am able, I'll see that you get something. Now I cannot; it has gone badly for me before I got started. When I shall again be the way I was in the beginning—but I don't know when because here [in] America [things] can change from one day to the next—you will have some repayment.

I have received your newspapers and bulletins, letters and all, because the telegraph and postal service here is something very precise. I was very pleased to get them. I read also in the bulletin of the professional school that they are asking for the address of members who are living outside the country. If I should send it and then, before publication, I should move, I would be in the same situation I was before. Also they want you to indicate the kind of work you are doing for publication in the bulletin because it will be, I believe, an issue with all the graduates of the professional school, and I can't tell them that. I change from one day to the next. At that moment I was a draftsman second grade in the workshop of the Trans Andes railway. It is a direct railway to Chile now under construction. But I am not doing it anymore because the section that the four of us were assigned to work on has been finished.

Now I am working as a smith and various things for the Great Western Railway of Argentina. But since they don't pay me as I want and I have to be first a blacksmith, then work as a planer, then at the lathe, I don't like it. At the first other job that comes along, I'm off. When I find something better, I don't want to work as a laborer for low wages anymore.

I am very sorry to hear that Grandmother is sick. I hope that this too will pass and that by the time you get this letter she will be long since cured.

I got a card from Nicodano from Sardinia. If I come to Italy, I too shall try to go see that part of the world. Since you ask me who still has my books, there is Orazio Rosazza, who has got the *Three Musketeers*, two volumes unbound. Cesare (Lucci) Ferreri has *Quo Vadis*. Ezio Barbero from Pavignano has the chemistry book. I don't think there are any more of them. If it has not been lost, there was in the box in the buffet a booklet where all the books which were loaned out were listed.

Your most loving son and
brother,
Oreste Sola

1.   The earthquake to which he refers occurred on March 20, 1861. It destroyed the entire city of Mendoza and killed much of its population.

Letter 4

Mendoza, 25 November 1901

Dearest ones,

A few days before this letter you will have received another written on the day of Secondino's arrival; a few days later he received some newspapers which indicated that you were on strike.[1] I understand that in this season such a big strike will be very distressing. I, however, right now absolutely cannot, for the moment, help you in any way. If I had been able to get that damned construction job, I assure you I would have "hit the jackpot."[2] From one day to the next another bit of bad luck could come my way; but everything is in doubt, there is then no certainty nor prospect.

Now they are coming here every day on the emigration train, about 600 persons a week. They are then sent out of the city in great numbers; but many remain, and we are beginning to see some unemployment but only in a small way. It's just that working in such conditions you only earn a bare living and with difficulty at that. If I have bad luck, I'm not staying here any longer. I want to go to Cuba with Boffa and the rest since Berretta doesn't answer. Nothing is certain however. The ideas come in crowds, but the execution is just miserable. Still I am not losing heart ever. I have been through a good period at first, then an excellent one, and now I am in a third one that is very tough. But I'll get back on my feet. We are in America.

Be patient then. I too am aware that Mom is working at night, that you are working on Sundays, etc.—things that don't happen here. Here in every profession and everywhere you work nine hours a day and only 'til noon on Saturday. You don't work on Sunday nor after midday meal on Saturday, and you get more respect. When you ask for some improvement in pay, the owners don't say that they will show up with a rifle and fire at the first one who makes trouble, as the famous Giovanni Rivetti used to say.[3] Here, if they don't want to give it to you, they look into it, they review it; but generally they give it to you, and all this without unions or anything. They are capitalists who are more aware; that's all there is to it.

Think always of your loving son who is in America, always in good spirits, even when things are going badly for him.

Oreste Sola

Secondino, like me, is always in good spirits, and we are always together. He sends you his warmest greetings and so does Carlo's family. Secondino would like you to say hello to his wife if it is not too much trouble.

1.   *Oreste is referring to the major strike at the Biella textile factory in which Luigi and Margherita worked. The strike, which ended in defeat for the workers, was provoked when the owners increased the work load without increasing salaries.*

2.   *The Italian phrase is* fare l'America. *This phrase was used frequently to describe immigrant success or "making it in America."*
3.   *Giovanni Rivetti was one of the owners of the Biella textile factory in which Luigi and Margherita worked. Given the size and importance of the factory, Rivetti's conduct greatly influenced that of the other owners in the entire area.*

Letter 5

Mendoza, 19 December 1901

Dearest parents, brother, and sister,

Here in a little while we shall have the grape harvest. The grapes are very plentiful; there are peaches and every other kind of fruit by the armload, but the sun is too much. The heat is beyond words, and to think that we are at the foot of a mountain range.

Soon it will be Christmas. I think that when you get this letter, you will have had a good holiday and begun the new year even better.

I imagine Grandmother will have recovered by now. Give her my warmest greetings, as well as my uncle and cousins and the others who ask about me.

I suppose the strike has been settled, but, as I foresaw from the first newspaper account, with a defeat like that of the railway workers of the Economic Railways.[1] Never mind! One step at a time.

For me the desire to go somewhere else is still very keen; I can't find anyone to come with me.

Our friends in Buenos Aires and Godfather are still fine, and they will continue to be so since, when I get their letters, they are always in good spirits. At least in this way we are always together, though more than 1,200 kilometers separate us. Similarly, I hope you will always be in good spirits and keep on being so.

I hope that Abele will be at his studies; make him study hard, and read. Narcisa is sure to be good. You are all always in my heart, and I am always thinking of you.

Secondino and Carlo's family send you their greetings.

I don't have anything else to say since there is nothing new. Just now they were making preparations and maneuvers along the highways and all over because war with Chile was feared, but now it has all passed. Better that way since we would have been the first if it had come. We are right on the border.

Keep up your spirits and think always of your distant son who thinks of you with love.

Oreste

1.   *The Economic Railways was a streetcar company that operated in Biella in that period.*

Letter 6

Mendoza, 13 January 1902

Dearest parents, brother, and sister,

As usual my health is still the very best, and there is no lack of good spirits. We are spending days in real American style. The worst is just that you live in uncertainty about a job, but then here it is nice to make a change sometimes.

I learned from Godfather that Pella, the son of the woman who is a tobacconist in Cerretto, has arrived in Buenos Aires, along with someone else, whom I don't think I know. I think they have both found work. I know Pella has since Zocco has already told me so; he didn't say anything to me about the other guy.

My schoolmate and shipboard companion, Guelpa, has gone to Montevideo in Uruguay. Godfather and Crivelli wrote me this, but from Guelpa himself I have no news yet. I imagine he is doing fine as usual. Crivelli, according to what he wrote me, left for Italy on the 4th day of this month. I don't know why for sure; he gave me a lot of reasons, but I don't believe a one of them. He will be there the last days of Carnival. I don't know whether he will be coming to Biella. I have given him my greetings for you, nothing else because I wasn't even sure if he was leaving. If he comes, you will see him.

Last week I received your letter with the newspapers. This morning I received no less than twenty-two items, newspapers and letters. They came from just about everywhere.

My shipboard companion as well as Godfather Zocco are in good health, and they give me, and you, the news about Irma's wedding. Here too Secondino and Carlo's family are in good health, and we are spending carefree, happy days together. All of them ask me to give you their warmest greetings.

Your always loving son,
Orestes

Letter 7

Mendoza, 27 January 1902

Dear parents, brother, and sister,

At this time of the year we are having the grape harvest. There is fruit of all sorts, and the grapes are extremely plentiful. There is a kind of peach which is just incredibly big, larger than the head of Abele, and everything is cheap. Every day a train comes from a nearby town, S. Juan, with thirty to forty or more freight cars loaded with fruit and vegetables of all sorts, which are then sent on to Buenos Aires. What is almost completely lacking here are apples, which are sold at a very high price because of their scarcity. Peaches, pears, and an endless supply of other fruit make up for them. They are so plentiful here that they are used to fatten pigs.

You must not think that I am doing badly, as you tell me in a letter written on Christmas day, which I received a few days back. It is just that I have the desire to travel. I want to see the world—everywhere—while I am able. I don't know for sure—Pierino wants to come to Mendoza. If he comes, after a few months we will go off for somewhere else. My friend Guelpa has gone to a small town not far from Buenos Aires. Godfather is fine and in good health, as are my other friends.

I should like to know whether my membership has lapsed in the alumni association of the professional school. Let me know. I don't have the receipt; perhaps I lost it. Have you continued to pay for the books which I was getting in installments? Let me know. Please do not lend out any unbound books because they are likely to get torn. Tell Abele to study (hard). As for me I am studying Spanish and English in the evening, the latter of which someone is teaching me who has traveled in twenty-three countries and also Australia. I am also studying the design of railway cars.

Tell Narcisa to work and learn well; tell Abele to study hard and to read tirelessly, to buy books, ones on instruction by De Amicis and similar writers.[1] Tell Mom not to work so hard and that, if I did not have to make some purchases myself, I would like to help her very much.

Stay healthy and in good spirits. And as for yourselves take from your far-away son, who loves you from the bottom of his heart, the warmest kisses and hugs.

Yours,
Oreste Sola

1.   *Edmondo De Amicis (1846–1908) was one of the most popular Italian writers of the time. He was a socialist whose political essays and books were widely circulated, but his novel* Cuore *was most popular and gave him a permanent place in the history of Italian literature.*

Letter 8

Mendoza, 13 February 1902

Dearest parents, brother, and sister,

In Mom's letter, which gave me great pleasure, it seems that she is afraid I am suffering. Get these doubts out of your head. The air here is good; we eat steaks and grilled meat every meal just like eating potatoes at home. In this season we are fine here. Only now that I have some experience [here], I should like to see something of another place; I have a desire to travel through the world. Here there is an enormous grape harvest; as usual it will last into May or more, even to June.

I hope Grandmother will now have recovered completely since the illness has already lasted a long time. Give her my warmest regards, and also my cousins and uncle.

Please, do not worry about me so much, I am fine here—that goes for Mom especially. Here I lack for nothing. We are in America, and so everything is available here.

I saw the grade that Abele, that little devil, got, and it is pretty poor. He has got to read and study a lot. So then try to make him get his brain together. As for Narcisa, I imagine she is happy and healthy too, just like me. Tell her that I am always singing and whistling. Now I am reading and writing Spanish and am learning Catalan songs. I shall turn myself into Tamagno[1] at the very least.

My dear ones take the finest kisses from your son and brother,

Oreste

Pardon the bad writing. It's so that it could still go out tonight since there are trains only three times a week. And at times, if you miss one day, the delay can be eight or ten days.

I just this moment received the newspapers you sent me. Goodbye.

1.   *Francesco Tamagno (1850–1905) was the greatest Italian tenor of the time. He made a series of triumphal tours abroad and in particular to Argentina.*

Letter 9

Mendoza, 14 April 1902

Dearest parents, brother, and sister,

Here it's still the same as in my previous letters, grape harvest and nothing else.

From your very dear letter I learn that my very dear friend Ermanno Guala came to Biella for several days on his vacation. It would have been a pleasure, more than I can say, to have seen him. I imagine you will have given him my address, and he will write me.

Carlo Cravello and Bic are working as weavers at Alsina in Buenos Aires. Luigi Fila is there too, but I don't know whether [he is] in the same factory. Guglielmo and Paolo are working here in town for a Piedmontese. We are always in good spirits and spend the evenings and holidays together.

Secondino, at his wife's urging, will leave for Italy within a few months. We are getting a big laugh out of this brief campaign of his since he gave the impression of wanting to stay down here forever. As far as that goes I am not saying anything. If I come back, I shall come back before leaving for the army.[1] But then there is time.

I don't have anything else to say.

Your far away son and brother,
Oreste

Pardon the bad writing. Guglielmo is here waiting for me. Bye.

1.   *He is referring to the Italian army here. Immigrants were not subject to conscription in Argentina.*

Letter 10

Mendoza, 15 June 1902

Dearest parents, brother, and sister,

It's always the same with me here. The weather is already getting cooler; the mountains are covered with snow. Here in the city, however, you don't see it. It is a surprising sight sometimes when a train comes from the Cordillera loaded down with snow. The cold weather here is not like it is at Biella; it's like the spring there, only there aren't those beautiful green fields and trees and busy gravel roads.

Here all the roads are dusty; one who has to go several kilometers outside of town can skip at least three meals.[1] Here it is very much the custom to go on horseback; you don't see anything else out there in that immense desert where the trains go more than half a day without coming on a station. That is the one pastime that I like: to ride at full speed for hours and hours.

The animals of the desert suffer badly from the dryness, and some years they die by the thousands. Almost all of them are rotting corpses, and if you come across one of them while you are riding your horse, I can tell you that if it's after dinner, you throw up at once. The horses here hold up for entire days at a gallop without seeing any food or water at all.

The other day I went with another friend of mine, who is half-negro, way out toward the foothills of the mountain range, on horseback, of course. Where there is no train you go on horseback or in a carriage. We came across a small lion, not a real lion, but it looks very much like one. I don't remember the name, only they are big like work dogs, with tawny hair. We went after it, but since they are small, it disappeared in the midst of these small thorn thickets, as if into a fortress.[2] These animals are rare since they eat chickens, geese, and so forth, which are here in enormous numbers, worth forty centavos each, and turkeys too. And therefore they are getting killed.

You can see other animals; there are ostriches—the local youths ride some of these, but if they get irritated, they can even take your eyes out. They are fine animals; they eat anything, even stones. They lay huge eggs but not very tasty. With one of these a person is good for an entire day. There is another animal, the guanaco; that's what they call it here. It's like a calf, but it has a face more like a camel, kind of reddish, and it's always puffing up its cheeks. When you run across it or it catches sight of you, it always runs back and always spits at you. They are docile and gentle. They have a long neck, they are well-proportioned, [and] they run a great deal.

There are also innumerable cows and oxen scattered about. Many other animals are around about here, but none is fierce or dangerous.

These are my diversions. Secondino and my other friends generally prefer something else. Within a few months Secondino will be coming back up there. Guglielmo, Paolino, Secondino, Carlo, Cichina, and their children give you their warmest greetings.

I am leaving off now because Guglielmo is waiting for me for a game of boccie.

A thousand kisses from your son
and brother,
Oreste

Bye—keep in good spirits.

1.   *Because one eats so much dust.*
2.   *The animal he refers to here seems to be a puma, which is the same thing as a cougar or a mountain lion.*

Letter 11

Mendoza, 15 July 1902

Dearest parents, brother, and sister,

Today on the two o'clock train Secondino Miglietti will leave for Buenos Aires, headed for Biella. He will bring this letter and will be able to tell you all about me since he has been my fellow lodger all the while he has been in America. He will be in Biella by the middle of August; he will get there at a good time, for the fair. As for me, if I come, I shall come for another one, that of 1903.

Secondino has made up his mind to come back up because he was unable to put aside much money here and because it had been his intention to have his wife come down here too. He now realizes that this is inadvisable. As a result he is the one who is going back. He also suffers from rheumatism. In these regions its effects are much stronger, and you can lose your health entirely. The certainty of a job at the warehouse finally made him resolve to return.

I know you will give him a good welcome and that will make me happy. Give my warmest greetings to my cousins and to Grandmother, who has been suffering from such a long illness.

Lots of kisses from your always
affectionate son and brother,
Oreste

Letter 12

Mendoza, 17 October 1902

Dearest parents, brother, and sister,

In the last letter but one you told me about the efforts that Signor Ormezzano would make on my behalf. They were faint and distant. You must not put too much confidence in these American travelers. It is not because of this that I wish to think badly of him. Quite the contrary. First of all I don't know him. It's a disease that everyone has—promising. The execution then is left to his own inclination. By this you will already have grasped that I haven't gotten anything from him. But even if I had received some news from him, I would not have moved with great speed. You have to find out first.

Now I can't complain about anything here, even though I am not rich. And as for your concern to send me something, I thank you for it. I am sure that it will have been some unpleasant news from someone that has misled you in this way. Answer him without pretending anything since he didn't know what I had and have in my pocket. If for some people things are not going well, for others they are not going too badly. That's enough for this matter since I can imagine that you will have gotten a load of ideas into your head on this subject. What I am saying is just don't worry so much. I am always in good health, and I am not afraid. Perhaps in another year or so I'll come home, and we shall see each other.

Godfather and all the other friends here are in excellent health. Guglielmo and Paolino give you their warmest greetings. Like me they are always in good spirits.

For my sake keep in good spirits and stay healthy.

Lots of affectionate kisses from
you son and brother,
Oreste

Letter 13

Santa Teresa, 28 November 1902

Dearest parents, brother, and sister,

I did not write to you any sooner because I did not know where I would be stopping. I am now here in this small country town in the middle of the plains in the province of Santa Fe. But I won't be staying here long. Within two or at the most three months I'll go to Santa Fe or Buenos Aires. So I suggest that you do not write me at this address because it takes too much time (two months) for the letter to get to me, and it might turn out that I would not be here anymore.

I left Mendoza to get another view of the world. My friends Paolino and Guglielmo are still there, and everything I get they will send to me.

When I left Mendoza, I went to Junin. From there I went to San Nicolás to visit my travel companion, Giuseppe Guelpa, and we had a few pleasant days together. He may return home in January or February.

From S. Nicolás I went to Santa Fe, thinking that I would visit Ferrara. Instead he had gone to Rosario, where, however, I did not find [him] because I didn't have any addresses. I asked about that certain Ormezzano, but no one knows him, and then too there are no electric trams in Rosario. It is a very beautiful city, just like the others, Santa Fe and San Nicolás, all three on the right bank of the Paraná River. In Santa Fe it is very beautiful, and sometime in the future I am going to go there. It is a very beautiful view; you see the city of Paraná on the other bank. There is a very beautiful huge iron bridge over a sharp bend of the Paraná River. It is two kilometers long with (I don't remember) eighty-three or ninety-three supporting piers. It is huge. Sometime in the future I shall take a closer look at it.

I imagine that Abele will have begun his studies again and that he will continue to do well and that he will be doing the second year of the technical school.[1]

In another letter I shall write at greater length; now I have to work like a martyr for a company since I undertook a job on my own account.

What I recommend is that you do not write me until I give you a regular address, and if by chance you do write, send the letters to Zocco's address in Buenos Aires.

> Your always more loving son and
> brother,
> Oreste

1.   *See letter 2, note 2.*

Letter 14

> Santa Fe, 13 March 1903

Dearest parents, brother, and sister,

I had written you from Santa Teresa in the south that I was staying there. It's about a month now since I finished my work in that area, and I have come back here to Santa Fe, where I had been for a few days in November of last year. But the city is absolutely dead; there is no business at all. Today or tomorrow I am going to leave here. I will go to San Cristobal. I don't know whether I shall stay there. If I do not stay, I am going right on to Tucumán, where at this time there are big work projects.

Here in Santa Fe I would have a job, but it doesn't suit me and so that is why I am going on.

Mom's nasty illness pained me very, very much, but I took consolation knowing that she had improved a great deal and that she was expected to get well soon.

I am happy that Grandmother is with us, or at least with you, if she likes it better that way.

I imagine that Abele is doing well with his studies, at least you said so in your last letter, and that Narcisa is working eagerly.

> A most affectionate kiss and a
> hug from your loving son and
> brother,
>   Oreste

2

Making It in Buenos Aires (1903–1907)

Oreste returned to Buenos Aires in March 1903 and on April 7 started to work as a draftsman for a firm that was constructing the new Argentine Congress building. This marked the beginning of stability and success that continued for some time. "I assure you that I am tired and have had my fill of traveling," he wrote his family. "Since I have a good job, I have a firm desire to stay put" (#15). In 1907 he secured a second job working for the National Senate to take care of the heating and ventilation of the Congress building (#27). With two salaries he did rather well: In letter #30 he spoke of owning two pieces of property and of his desire to build a house.

Financial success brought with it some unforeseen consequences. His relationship with his family changed in June 1906, almost five years after he arrived in Buenos Aires, when he first sent money home and promised to try to support them (#26). Where formerly they had sent him money and clothes, now he was sending them money. The parents in Italy were becoming dependent on the immigrant son in Buenos Aires.

In addition, financial success seemed to have changed Oreste's attitude toward his fellow Biellesi. The network continued intact even when Godfather Zocco returned to Valdengo in 1907 (#28). Various friends and acquaintances still came and went, and hometown contacts remained important. His friend Caucino, for example, who arrived in the winter of 1905 and returned to Italy in May 1906, fit the pattern of the *golondrinas*, the swallows who went to Argentina each year to harvest the crops during the Argentine summer and returned to Italy to harvest the crops during the Italian summer (#25, #26).

However, Oreste had negative feelings toward some of the Biellesi: "There are few people here whom I know really well, especially from Biella," he explained to his parents; "it's not that I dislike them; rather, when they every so often come upon lean times or are out of work, they attach themselves to you, on the pretext of being fellow townsmen, . . . and they think you have an obligation to support them" (#22). He continued by giving specific examples of such types. Oreste was also concerned about the busybodies in Biella and Buenos Aires prying into other people's business. In another letter he warned his parents: "Dearest parents, do not listen to the words that others write you. I keep to myself, and when I meet someone, it's not my custom to make myself known. My close acquaintances are few, and no one knows my affairs" (#20). We can only surmise why privacy was so important to Oreste, but it is clear that if no one knew how much money he had, no one, including his parents, could make demands of him when he said he did not have the resources to help.

Changes seemed to take place within the family as well. Oreste wrote less frequently, probably indicating less interest in matters at home. Only an event of major importance, such as the death of Narcisa (#19), temporarily changed this pattern and rekindled the immediacy and intensity of family relationships that characterized the earliest letters. The idea of returning home remained vague except in response to his obligation to the army, and when he got out of this obligation, returning became even more distant (#15, #17, #24, #28).

Finally, the theme of monotony is introduced in this chapter. In May 1905, for example, when he had not written for four months, he attempted to explain why: "But my life is always the same, and I don't ever find anything to fill up two lines. Perhaps you will say that a young man like me, who has studied at school, should know how to put together a letter, at least to his parents, the people dearest to him. But since I can't ever find anything to say, since nothing ever happens here, there is nothing left but to say that I am in good health" (#24). This same theme is repeated frequently (#25, #27, #28).

Thus, settling down and getting two good jobs brought many rewards, but it also created some problems.

Letter 15

Buenos Aires, 3 May 1903

Dearest parents, brother, and sister,

As you will see from the heading, I am once again in Buenos Aires. Yesterday evening, while I was visiting Godfather Zocco, he showed me Dad's letter, indicating that you were already thinking ill of me because for some time now I haven't written. Actually you are not far wrong.

I am fine here, in excellent health; business is also good. As I had written you from Santa Teresa, [it is just] that I had to keep on the move. I left there toward the end of February and went straight to Santa Fe, where I had to take a job with a French railway firm. I worked a few days, but then, since Frenchmen and Italians don't get along with each other, I went on my way. The next day I left for San Cristobal (San Cristoforo). I stayed there for only three days since they are still all negroes,[1] and I headed straight for Tucumán, where I had an excellent job. But since there is malaria in that area—they call it *chucho* (*ciucio*)—and at that time there was also smallpox, and it seemed to be spreading, I got scared and took off again. I would have liked to go to Bolivia, but since I was rather far away from the big cities, it was not convenient for me. So I headed for the capital. Almost two days and three nights on the train. I assure you that I am tired and have had my fill of traveling.

Now for about a month I have been here and have been employed in the work on the *Congreso Nacional*, which is under construction; the work will last at least a half dozen years. I am doing very well here, and if I did not have to do my military service, I would stay on to the end. That would be of great advantage to me.

Meanwhile for this year I am not coming to Italy to be in the army. Since I have a good job, I have a firm desire to stay put until next year so that then I would do only one year of military service.

In a few days I'll pay a visit to the Italian consul, just so that I won't be declared a draft dodger, though I have time up to the age of twenty-six. For this year then, unless something special happens, it will be difficult for us to see each other again. I had come here to the capital with the intention of coming back home, but since I have hit the mark nicely, it's better that I stay here.

The day before yesterday we celebrated May Day, but there wasn't much of a crowd however. We talk a lot about the celebrations in Italy. Some time ago Sasso arrived, and he gave me news about you. . . .

I imagine that Abele will be making progress in his studies and that soon he will become a Marconi or something like that [and that] Narcisa will continue to work and to sing. I'll accompany her from here. [I imagine that] Mom will be in good health, as well as Dad, and so you will last a hundred years, just as I think I will keep on going.

All our fellow countrymen here are in excellent health. Zocco and my travel companion Pierino give their regards to all of you.

Keep in good spirits and stay healthy, and don't worry about me so much. I manage all right wherever I am.

Best and heartfelt kisses and hugs from your ever-affectionate son and brother,

Oreste

Zocco is giving me a note that I am enclosing with this letter. He says hello to you.

1.   *It is not clear exactly what he is referring to here. There were blacks in Argentina at the time, but there were many more mestizos, or mixtures of Europeans and Indians. He could be referring to either one or both.*

Letter 16

Buenos Aires, 5 June 1903

Dearest parents, brother, and sister,

I wrote you about a month ago in answer to a letter of yours in which you were already thinking ill of me because for some time you had no news of me; a few days later I received a note from Zocco, who said you had received news of me and that this put your worries to rest and brought peace to your heart. I have already said on other occasions don't worry so much on my account—I know how to come out all right—and don't be afraid that I am suffering from poverty. No, I am not swimming in wealth, but I am perfectly able to take care of myself.

I am here still together with Godfather Zocco. I am still employed at the same job; I like it and I'm doing fine there.

Last week Federico, from Valdengo, was here in the capital; I had met him in Santa Teresa. He left right away after a few days because the work in the fields has to start up again now that the harvest of corn is over—it was very plentiful. Antonio Pella, who had been in Italy a year ago, has also left for the fields but those in the southern area. He has taken a job in those parts, and he has gone to finish it up. He may not come back to the city for the entire year.

Zocco is still the same: He eats, drinks, and plays the glutton. We live together, and the life that he leads is also mine.

For some time I have had running through my head the idea of perpetual motion. I have purchased the paper to make the calculations and drawings, and, within three or four months, if not sooner, I'll tell you if I have been a total ass or something like it. For now there is still nothing new.

For a while now we have begun to feel the cold here. It doesn't freeze though. It's an extraordinary event for it to freeze here, and it never snows either. But on some days a biting wind blows off the pampa plains that stings your ears and even your nose. But it's never cold the way it is at home. Here businesses like restaurants never close their doors, neither in summer nor in winter.

Taking a close look at your letters, where every now and then Abele puts in his two cents worth, I note his handwriting (and spelling) is terrible; and if he is like that in other things, he's got to be a real donkey. And in composition he is not doing well either. He should read, and a lot. If he were Spanish, I would send him a trunkload of books for every taste.

I imagine that Narcisa has now turned into a fine young woman, and that she will always be industrious, and that Grandmother is still with us. On one occasion I sent you some papers. If it took less time for them to get there, I would send more of them often. But it takes twenty-two to twenty-five days or even more. And they are very old when they arrive, and [the] news and politics are out of date.

So then stay in good spirits, and if I am every now and then slow in writing, don't think ill of me. Imagine that you see me, healthy and in good spirits, singing (with that beautiful voice, which I still have just like it used to be—or worse).

> Take a fine loving kiss from your
> beloved and unforgettable son
> and brother,
> Oreste

In case I did not send it to you in my last letter of a month ago my address is the same as my first one.

> Calle Rivadavia 1982
> Buenos Aires
> Argentina

Letter 17

Buenos Aires, 25 August 1903

Dearest parents, brother, and sister,

The day before yesterday I received a package of newspapers and a postcard of Biella from Abele. It is a pleasure, and I like reading the Italian papers. *L'Asino* and *L'Avanti* are for sale here too; *L'Asino* is even like an Argentine paper.[1]

Last week I was at the Italian consul for the business about conscription. After a very long discussion (about three hours), he ended up by telling me that of necessity I would have to present myself before the end of March of next year. Otherwise I would be declared a draft evader and accordingly subject to the full force of the law.

The only way out of this dilemma would be if we can claim that Abele is unable to work or, rather, subject to illnesses which make him unable to work or endanger his health. And this might just be possible since he is blind in one eye. If you want to try to make inquiries from a lawyer and then have Abele have a medical checkup, perhaps I shall be able to save myself from military service. If not, either in March or afterward I shall come back up there. If you will do this, write me, and you will be doing me a favor.

Paolo Stellino from Valdengo arrived less than a week ago. He is here in Buenos Aires and is fine and in good spirits. We are together with other Biellesi; Luigi Botta, the cousin of Linda from Valdengo, has also come to Buenos Aires. We almost always spend the evenings together.

Here I am the same as always; I am fine and am still working at the Congress. In another one of your letters I shall be anxious to learn the result of Abele's make-up examination. Tell him to study.

Paolino, coming from Mendoza, has told us about the bad earthquake, which you will have read about in the daily papers. We laugh and pass the time as cheerfully as possible.

Other than that there is nothing new here. Zocco asks to be remembered to all of you. Stay happy and in good health. Your always loving son and brother,

Oreste

1.   L'Asino *and* L'Avanti *were well-known socialist newspapers.* L'Avanti *was the official paper of the Italian Socialist Party, and* L'Asino *was a satirical paper.*

Letter 18

Buenos Aires, 24 May 1904

Dearest parents, brother, and sister,

True it has been some time now that I haven't let you hear from me, and this has depressed you, and perhaps you have thought ill of me. Yes, you are even right to do so. I have been too negligent, but don't think that I have forgotten you, quite the contrary. True, you can always find the time to write a letter—and there is time—but, believe me, the work at the office is so boring, spending the entire day drawing lines or writing, and that is even worse. It makes you so tired when you are finished with work that you don't want to do anything but relax or go for a walk.

For some time now I have had to work overtime, and from the beginning of the year up to last Saturday I worked nights too and in the morning before the regular hours. Believe me I was so fed up with it that, when coming home, I would sit down at the desk with the intention of writing you, just looking at the sheets of paper; I would leave them there and say, "Tomorrow for sure," and so the days went by.

For so much work I expected better pay, but it doesn't matter: I took this past week off. I had permission. I took the opportunity to visit all the small towns around Buenos Aires, but they don't have anything to compare with our hills and mountains. Here everything is flat. When you have seen one town, all the others are the same, laid out on a grid like the new cities. The houses are low, only a very few have two stories. In short, nothing beautiful. The best thing is the banks of the great Paraná River, completely lined with tangled trees, with its calm muddy waters; they are never rough but smooth as a billiard cloth. There are some cattle which always come to drink and which graze on the always-green banks, formerly the home of crocodiles and *chacares*.[1]

Buenos Aires is always the same. Everywhere there is construction and modernizing. They say that for twenty years there has not been so much work going on as today. The explanation for this is in part this year's abundant harvest. The land is the only profitable thing in these parts.

A few months ago there was the election for the presidency, but the outcome is still not certain. There were also the elections for the senators from the capital and the deputies, where for the first time in South America a socialist won. He is Alfredo Palacios, a man of great energy and well regarded even by his political opponents. At the first meeting at which he was present, he raised a protest about those murdered by the police on the First of May; three were killed, and quite a few were injured, about 200. Such incidents, however, are frequent in these republics, and here no one pays much attention to them.

All our friends over here are in excellent health and hope that you all are too.

Keep in good spirits, and if sometimes I am negligent in writing, don't worry about it, don't think I have forgotten you because you are very close to my heart. Tell Abele, that little devil, to study, and study hard.

Don't worry so much about your loving son and brother, Oreste, who loves you always and wishes you well.

Oreste

1.   *This is a misspelling of the Spanish word* chacaras *or more commonly* chacras, *which means small isolated farms.*

Letter 19

Buenos Aires, 9 July 1904

Dearest parents and brother,

I don't know what to think; I don't know what to say. I often come home from work in the evening deep in thought with my head resting on the palm of my hand, going over the days spent at home, the laughs I enjoyed with Narcisa, when we sang together, and all the good things that were and now are nothing but memories since Narcisa is here no longer.[1] Believe me, getting news like this, when you are so far from your dear ones, is an immense sorrow. Here, where no one can give you comfort, where you are alone, there is nothing left but to think about it, to let yourself go in tears, closed up in a room where no one might bother you.

I got the news of her death on St. John's Day (24 June) in the morning while I was getting up; the postman gave me his usual "good morning." It was an enormous blow; it seemed that everything went dark, as if in an eclipse, and that sleep had come over me. I sat down, and resting on my drawing table with the sad letter, I lowered my head between my arms. I got up at once as if awakened with a start and let my sorrow pour out in tears. I wept, and weep again at the thought that if I come back home, though I have the consolation of you, my dear ones, Narcisa, my dearest, beloved sister will be missing, and that I shall never see her again.

Then on St. Peter's Day (29 June) I got Abele's letter, a sad confirmation of the previous one. Poor Abele, you saw our dear sister right up to the end; for me three years have now gone by, and I never would have thought that I was not to see her again, poor Narcisa.

Several days before I had received a note from unhappy Dad, where he told me about the sad illness that in the end tormented Narcisa. Shortly afterward, when I stopped at the main post office, I picked up two registered letters from Armando Rivetti in which it was also discussed. Why, in his second letter he even said that we would probably not lose our dear Narcisa in view of the successful operation. I shall write an answer to my dear friend, but now I lack the will; I am melancholy and sad. Next month I shall send you, my dear ones, my picture. Right now it is still too cold, and the sun hardly ever shows itself.

I have sent you two of my pictures—taken with a camera—of me in the office with my two work companions. I don't think that you have received either these or the accompanying letter since I have had no word about it.

As for pictures of you, I have that very nice one of Narcisa, which I have had elegantly framed, which I now hold in greater value as a memory; [I have] the small ones of Dad and Mom, but they are gradually getting faded; [I have] one of Abele that is more or less the same and another one, the first I received from you. I am keeping all of these with loving care.

You complain of my long silence. It is true that I have been very negligent, but you are not out of my mind for a minute. Many times I sit myself down at the desk to write you, but, not knowing what to put in it, I postpone it and send you a greeting on a postcard.

Some days after Abele's letter I visited Pella from Cerretto, who, as he was telling me his news from home, told me that his sister was going to be married. Thinking that I had not yet heard the news from you, in the manner of a true friend he gave me the *Corriere*[2] to read, the one that told about the last day of Narcisa's existence. What a difference between the one piece of news and the other! Since I too had been thinking that one day Narcisa would have become a bride and mother and with her nice manner and her heart would have made a family worthy of you and of her brothers, I became even sadder, and leaving my friend, I came back home in a pensive mood and once more by weeping gave vent to my grief over the tragic event.

When I think of dear good Mom, who did so much to save Narcisa, the thought saddens me at the pain of the loss; the pain will have been even greater for her [Mom], since she [Narcisa] had become a companion to her. Poor Mom, who has done so much for us, to see what would have been the best companionship and comfort disappear. Thinking about it splits my heart in two.

You complain that I had not even a word of comfort for Uncle Giacomo. That isn't true. I have written; perhaps you have not received the letter.

I'll stop writing now because every time I refresh the memory of the tragedy which has touched us, I weep and feel bad.

I know that this letter of mine, which will arrive in about a month—that is, three months after the tragedy—will do nothing but open up for you the wound that had begun to heal, and, instead of being a consolation, it will increase your sorrow.

Farewell. Ease the pain of your grief as much as possible since we can apply no cure for it. And you, Abele, be good and studious. Now that you are the only one left at home, don't make our dear parents angry, be obedient to them, and try, by applying yourself to your studies, to be a consolation to them who do so much for you.

Your ever more loving son and
brother,
Oreste

1.   *Narcisa died in Biella on May 29, 1904, after a brief but painful struggle with cancer. She was seventeen years old.*
2.   Corriere *and* Corriere Biellese *were distributed in various localities abroad especially where emigrants from the town resided. Luigi Sola was one of the founders of the* Corriere Biellese *in 1895.*

Letter 20

Buenos Aires, 28 August 1904

Dearest parents and brother,

The more I think about it, the less I can make head or tail of it. Only today have I taken from my eyes the handkerchief which dried the tears at the loss of Narcisa, and here is a new blow.[1] Perhaps destiny is persecuting us.

It is impossible to imagine the feeling that came over me as I read those lines written by Abele because Dad was unable to. I thought about it, and I didn't believe it. It seemed to me that I had just dreamed it. I reread those pages several times; I read the newspapers, and in each one I took in the tragedy. I really can't understand it all. If it were true that a god exists, and that he punishes only the bad, you could call these events mistakes.

It is sad for a son, when all these high hopes are placed in him, not to be able to help his parents and not even in cases as sad as this. Believe me, it makes my heart weep. Believe me, dearest parents, nothing causes more anguish than not to be able to repay one who has done so much for me. I understand the reason for your request. I am not refusing out of stinginess, nor for any other nasty motive. Believe me, it's because I cannot, because I don't have anything; I am barely standing on my feet.

Perhaps some ignorant idiot, minding other people's business, will have written home that I am living like a lord, and this will have come to your ears, and you will have asked him for news of me. But believe me, no one knows, and since I have been in America, no one has ever known either how much I earn or how much I have in my pocket, nor do I ever say either what I am doing or where I work. Dearest parents, do not listen to the words that others write you. I keep to myself, and when I meet someone, it's not my custom to make myself known. My close acquaintances are few, and no one knows my affairs.

As for this famous "source" others have already had the occasion to pay him their thanks. People who take an interest in the affairs of others and don't know how to manage their own. I am not mentioning his name because I have no desire to repeat it yet another time. Believe me, dearest parents, don't ask for or listen to information from others because they don't know.

Don't think that I have said this as a pretext to begrudge you my help. No, if you thought so, I would be offended. It's just that I know that a certain person over here, whom you know, takes pleasure in other people's affairs. So, don't think that I am being mean. For me it is absolutely an impossibility [to send you money], but I shall make every effort I can. If Abele is a good student, after he has done the three years at the professional school, if he studies mechanics, I should like to support him in his studies at the Zurich Polytechnic, which even here is very famous.

I spend my time here the same as always: I work, and in my time off I go for a walk now and then, and at home in the evening I study or read. This is what hurts my budget. Studying, in this country, is fantastically expensive. Since there are no science books in Castilian, and the few that there are are awful, you have to turn to ones in other languages, which cost a lot even having them sent to you directly.

I have delayed answering your letter because I wanted to send you my picture. But the photographer, heavily in debt, said goodbye to his business and took off. A good reward to whoever finds him. So, I am stuck with the portrait that is only on the glass negative, and it will, who knows, be sold at auction along with a thousand others. That's the way things are in America.

I am, however, enclosing one of those which you should already have if the letter has not been lost. I am with two of my companions at work in front of my desk. I am the one with the longest mustache.

I have high hopes that Dad will have recovered by now and that the next letter I get will be written by him again. To dear Mom, who has sent me the newspapers, I shall give in return something from here.

I am waiting to hear in the next letter about Abele's exams.

Your very loving son and
brother,
Oreste

1.   *Oreste is referring to a work-related accident to Luigi that was reported in the* Corriere Biellese. *Apparently it was not too severe since it did not keep him out of work for long.*

Letter 21

Buenos Aires, 4 October 1904

Dearest parents and brother,

For some time now I haven't let you hear from me. I don't want to give you any reason to think badly of me; I am getting back in touch.

It is a pleasure to read that Dad is getting better very rapidly and that he will then recover completely. Poor Dad, take heart. They say life is a pleasure; I don't think it is for everyone.

Mom, ever sweeter, sends me a small picture of Narcisa, the sister whom I have always loved and who, tragically, is no more. Thanks, dear Mom, I shall put this picture with the others. Every day I shall look at it with the others of you, my dear ones, and I shall revive for myself the memory which is always growing.

I am enclosing in this letter a picture of me, taken by the son of my boss one day at work. It's a shame that he has broken the negative so that he can't make a better one of it. I wanted to go and have my picture taken at a place that was a bit more elegant, but now that I am dressed in mourning I am not going. I didn't turn out too well because I was caught by surprise, but, more or less, that's the way I am.

Life in Buenos Aires is always the same. We are beginning to feel the heat. There is never anything new. A tremendous amount of work is going on in the construction of houses.

In the newspapers here I read about the tragedy which occurred in the Sella factory a few days ago.

Your always more loving son and
brother,
Oreste

Letter 22

Buenos Aires, 6 December 1904

Dearest parents and brother,

Failing to keep my repeated promises, I have not written you for some time now. But I haven't ever forgotten you for one moment; I was anxious to hear the results of Abele's make-up exams. I am delighted to know that he has succeeded in getting the technical degree, which I also got from the newspapers from home. I think he will now be more attentive to his studies; now that he is a young man, he will devote all of his good sense and intellect to his education.

I note the pleasure you got from receiving that small picture of mine, which didn't turn out so well. In a little while I'll send you a much better one. I would have had it taken by now, but I keep putting it off. I don't know why even myself; I am just a bit negligent.

A few weeks ago I went to visit the family through which you sent me the socks and the embroidered handkerchiefs, for which I thank you from the bottom of my heart. But don't go to a lot of trouble; I lack nothing here. The entire family sends you its warmest greetings, especially the young woman whom you had bring me the stuff.

On another occasion I'll go visit them; they live quite far from the center of the city, about twelve kilometers, and the trip is quite nasty, especially when it rains. I got a lot of news of Biella, and so I spent a very enjoyable and pleasant evening with them.

Dad asks me whether I have visited Boggio; honestly I don't know who he is. There are few people here whom I know really well, especially from Biella; it's not that I dislike them; rather, when they every so often come upon lean times or are out of work, they attach themselves to you, on the pretext of being fellow townsmen, even if you have never seen them before, and they think you have an obligation to support them. I have not ever acted negatively to anyone, but since in this country there are people absolutely without shame, when they meet the guy who is obliging, they want nothing so much as not to work. It often happens that those who introduce themselves either directly or who have been sent by another are peasants. Here in the city they can do nothing but be a porter in a factory or a laborer in the construction industry, work that pays very little considering the cost of living. And so you always come across them—worse than broke, they are in debt. If then you advise them to go work on the land out in the provinces, it's like insulting them. They are afraid that once they leave the city, they will certainly be lost.

There was someone sent here by a very good friend of mine because he was fed up with supporting him, since the guy didn't want to take the job that my friend himself had offered him in his own house. He sent him to me so that I could put him to work as an office boy. He was too stubborn; he couldn't even adjust to this. And then they were going to give him regular pay, and he would have had an eight-hour day since the draftsmen employed in Buenos Aires work only six, at the most seven hours a day. I supported him for a month, eating and sleeping in a restaurant-inn, where he could also have been the waiter. Unable to get out of it he accepted the job. After two days he disappeared. A good reward to whoever finds him! Others, less tricky, show up every day.

Don't think I have said this because Dad is asking me whether I have seen Boggio, whom I don't think I know. It's only that I would not want the sort of guy I have just been talking about to show up on me. People who know a trade can easily find work and even get paid pretty well, whatever the trade is. The day laborer, however, has very lean pickings unless he can adjust to the work in the country.

What I really would have liked would have been to know on what steamer the girl was coming, the one whom you asked to bring me the stuff. When you arrive in a new city, you want to see it all at once—this is the greatest pleasure that the foreigner has. I would have done beautifully as a guide since her father, who has been here only for a short while and is always out, is not acquainted with this huge city.

Tell Abele to study so that he will get a lot out of it.

My Godfather gives you his affectionate greetings.

Your ever beloved son and
brother,
Oreste

Have a good Christmas holiday and a good end and beginning of the year.

Letter 23

Buenos Aires, 25 January 1905

Dearest parents and brother,

I have had your letter for some time now, from which I see that Grandmother is seriously ill. I hope that by now she will have recovered completely. From what I read Mom has really given up hope, and she tells me that if I delay a bit more my return home, I won't find anyone left. Poor Mom, I understand her distress; I too think often about it, but I don't know how to find any cure for it. Mom thinks that this latest illness will now take Grandmother from us, especially considering her already advanced age. Really I don't know what to say to this.

Grandmother is no longer so young, and we will have to expect fate's decision; true it is sad, especially in a house where one misfortune comes so suddenly after another. The more I think about it, the less I can make head or tail of it. That's the way destiny is; resignation is the only solution. It is hard to think that we must suffer without remedy, but unfortunately we can't change it. I had held off answering your letter in the expectation of some new report on Grandmother's health, but since I got no more news at all, I don't know whether I should be optimistic or the reverse.

From Mom's letter I see that Abele is going to the professional schools.[1] I hope he will study hard and do himself proud. If he shows that he is eager to learn, I believe I can pay for his support at a more advanced institution than mine from my earnings here. For within a couple of months I expect to be getting paid better, and then I shall also be able to be more grateful to you.

Your always more loving,
Oreste

1.   *See letter 2, note 2.*

Letter 24

Buenos Aires, 18 May 1905

Dearest parents and brother,

It is now a very long time that you haven't heard any more from me, in spite of the promises I made to be more diligent and punctual in answering your dear letters. But do not think or fear that this means I have forgotten you. Quite the contrary, every day, every evening when I get back to my own small room, I think of you. Many times I stop reading or studying in order to write you. I begin the letter, but then, who knows, I start to think; I stop for a moment to try to give you some news from here. But my life is always the same, and I don't ever find anything to fill up two lines. Perhaps you will say that a young man like me, who has studied at school, should know how to put together a letter, at least to his parents, the people dearest to him. But since I can't ever find anything to say, since nothing new ever happens here, there is nothing left but to say that I am in good health. But since, as the proverb says, no news is good news, I let it drop. I go back to my book or the compass or my pencil. And always thinking of you I go on with my studies or reading.

For almost a month I have been at Puente Alsina, where there are some textile factories and some families from Biella are living. I went to say hello to Mom's friend who had sent me her greetings. The entire family gives you their best; yes, they are perhaps a bit late, but still they are good-hearted. In this town I have met several friends of yours, Dad, who remember you with affection and pleasure. Why, one recognized me right off as your son because I look so much like you. We had never seen each other before, but he stopped to ask me if I was Mr. Sola. Explanations followed, and he gave me a great welcome. Among the others I met Festa and one other person whose name I don't remember, just as I can't remember the first man's name. Festa is your friend from the famous event of '98.[1] We spent the entire afternoon together talking about Biella and its environs, and about the people of Biella, especially you, dear Dad, whom everyone remembers with pleasure. From them I got the address of your dear friend Fila. The next Sunday I went to visit him. I even spent the entire day with him and his son, who has now become a man. Both are fine and say hello. Fila himself especially begged me over and over again to give you his special greetings. In a few Sundays I'll go back and visit them. He told me he was going to write you.

It's been some time now since I have been to see the consul. After I had heaped all kinds of abuse on him because he would not give me an enlistment certificate of the third category,[2] I succeeded in getting him to do it for me. I think that now it will be all right over there too [in Italy] since they are sending off from here to Biella, I don't know to whom, and from Biella then they will send me the necessary document, etc. This was the fourth time now that I showed up there. The first two times I was always polite; the third time I began to shout. This last time then I was already fed up, so I threatened to unmask their excellent service in the newspapers of the capital and to take my case to higher authorities. That was enough for him to send me to get two witnesses, who are from Biella, for my signature. Now I think that within a month at the most I'll have everything in order.

Your ever more affectionate and
dear brother and son,
Oreste

1.   In 1898 the Italian Government violently repressed the popular agitation and strikes caused by difficult economic conditions. At the major culminating demonstration in Milan the army shot into the crowd. Hundreds of socialist and anarchist leaders were arrested. Luigi Sola and thirty-two of his companions were arrested in Biella but were released a few months later.
2.   An enlistment certificate of the third category excused the individual from military service except in a national emergency such as war.

Letter 25

Buenos Aires, 11 October 1905

Dearest parents and brother,

For a long time now I haven't written you, but I am always thinking of you. I had already received several weeks ago that last dear letter of yours; then yesterday I got several postcards from Abele, who tells me that he had made a fine excursion up into the mountains. Good, you have to enjoy yourself too, and this kind of sport is the favorite one for me too.

I see from your letter that Mom has become one of the victims of the Rivetti strike.[1] I already knew about the strike and other movements in the Biella area from the *Corriere*, which is sold even here. From the papers here I also saw that there has been an exceptionally severe storm. The largest paper has reported that there were hailstones weighing 900 grams. If that is true, it must have been really extraordinary.

My friend and companion Rinaldo Caucino, "the giant," arrived a few months ago. He stayed a while in Buenos Aires, but now he is at Rosario di Santa Fe. We are keeping in touch.

I was at the consul's this morning to see if my papers had arrived yet. He told me that they had been delivered on the 23rd of August to the subprefect of Biella for a decision. I was able to verify this myself from the books and letters of the ministry.

From what I see in the newspapers they are putting together a steamship company whose ships will make the crossing from Buenos Aires to Genoa in thirteen days at a very low price. If this should already be in place by the time of the Milan Exposition, it might turn out that I would make a trip over for two or three months.

Life here in Buenos Aires is always the same; there is a tremendous amount of construction work. The workers took advantage of it and have managed to get an eight-hour day at a pay that varies according to the trade. The average is four pesos, but no one works for less except the unskilled laborers.[2]

I am cutting back expenses in every way so that I can help you, and I think that by the end of the year I'll be able to send you something. But don't get your hopes up.

I am happy about Abele's promotion, and I think he will keep up the good work in the years to come. And if I shall continue to do well, I think I can support him in his future studies.

He asks for my judgment on what subjects to study. I should say mechanics, and if there is also a course on electricity, to study it too, as well as mechanics. But the thing that is really necessary for a good engineer is to know how to draw and write well, even *very* well.

Your son and brother,
Oreste

1.   *Oreste is referring to another strike at the Rivetti textile factory in Biella, where Margherita worked. The owners locked out the workers and thus forced them to accept the owners' conditions.*
2.   *For a discussion of earnings, see the Appendix.*

Letter 26

Buenos Aires, 12 June 1906

Dearest parents and brother,

I always promise to write you, and I never do it; I don't know why. I remember you all always; I would like to be close to you, and when I think that now [it is] almost five years since we have seen each other, it seems a lot. I wanted to come home on the occasion of the Exposition, but it is not a suitable time now. I am trying to get another technical government post, one that would leave me time to continue to devote myself to the job I now occupy, and so I could earn quite a bit.

My friend and companion Caucino embarked on the return voyage a month ago. Since, according to what he said, he will come back, I gave him the job of getting me some books. I also left him a letter with my greetings and 100 lire for Abele if he is good and studies for his semester grades, as he promises in his last letter. He can use them as he wishes at the Milan Exposition.

I am enclosing with this letter 300 lire; it's not much. Within a few weeks I'll send you some more, and if the appointment goes well for me, I'll keep it up.

I would like it if from your trip to the Exposition you sent me (I am giving this job to Abele in particular) the catalogs of the machines that the different firms, of all nations, have on exhibition. You will get many free, especially brochures and price lists. [If] it should be necessary to pay for them, I would send you the money for however much it might be (within limits however).

I went to Pierino Pizzoglio's house to get the stuff that Mom took the trouble to send me. I thank her so much, but I don't want her to go to a lot of trouble.

Your always more loving son and
brother,
Oreste

Letter 27

Buenos Aires, 3 May 1907[1]

Dearest parents and brother,

Many, many times I sat down at my desk to write you, but I didn't bring myself to do it. The reason for this was to avoid repeating the old story of hopes and expectations. Now that I know I have succeeded, here I am back with you.

As you see, after such great and tremendous efforts I have succeeded in becoming an employee of the government, in the service of the National Senate. I hold the position of the technical chief (chief technician) in the Congress (Parliament). I constantly have to deal with deputies and senators. I am getting indigestion from politics, something that doesn't agree with me at all. I am, however, still holding the job I had before, so I am two employees, but they aren't ruining my life. In the government position I have the responsibility of taking care of the heating and ventilation of the Congress, as well as all the other piping installations, like gas, hot water, sewers, and cold water. In the job which I already held I do the computations for the work on the part of the firm which is constructing this very building.

I am sending you through the Bank of Italy 200 lire, and I shall try to do the same every month. And if at any time I should get anything in addition, you will share in it.

I am sure that Abele will study hard and will become a fine young man.

My companions Violetta and Cravello paid me a visit. They are employed outside of Buenos Aires in the provinces.

Life here is always the same; it's rather monotonous, but if you want, you can also enjoy yourself.

Guglielmo Motta left two weeks ago. I think he will have brought you greetings.

One thing I ask of you—more than that, it would be a tremendous favor. That is, I don't want anyone to know how I am doing here, whether or not I am making money, whether I send you money or not, etc. If they ask about me, tell them I'm fine. If they are coming here, give them my address. I know from here as much about Biella's affairs as you do and perhaps more. I take no pleasure in any advertising. Don't take offense at this. This is the way it is in America among serious people.

Your son and brother,
Oreste

Zocco sends his greetings.

1.   *Written on paper with the letterhead "National Senate."*

Letter 28

Buenos Aires, 8 August 1907

Dearest parents and brother,

You ask me in your last letter if I have received the discharge papers you sent me. I was sure that I had already informed you that I had. I am very happy about it; thanks.

You speak to me about Abele; you would like him to come join me here. I am of the opposite opinion. I should prefer, now that I have a reasonable position, that if he studies hard, he should go on with his schooling, so that he could go to the university and get a degree as an engineer. If this seems best to him, I shall be able, and I will make every effort I can, to send you 250 lire every month and if possible even something more. I think the expenses for his education won't go beyond 150 francs a month. I think Turin is the city with a good university that is most moderate in its living expenses, but you can select some other place. It is, however, always better in the big cities because the best professors are there. It's a big thing to have the degree, though often one might know less than those who don't have it. He could select at his own pleasure the field where he has the most inclination for study, either as a civil engineer or a mechanical or electrical engineer. I don't know how the fields are divided in Italy. I would like it if you gave me an answer about this. If you are in agreement, and he too, he could at once get himself ready for the exams.[1] I think that he will have done well in those that he took recently, as Dad promised me.

I have learned of the arrival of Guglielmo Motta and Zocco, whose wife, from what I have heard, is seriously ill. If you see them give them the warmest greetings from me, and ask Zocco if he has the desire to come back here now that the two Houses (Senate and Deputies) have approved the construction of the diagonal roads and of the Congress Square (*piazza del Congresso*). I think it will be several years before the job begins.

In another letter toward the middle of the month I shall include the promised sum of money.

Last month the sociologist Ferrero was here.[2] He gave eight lectures, or to put it better he gave eight classes, in Roman history in a theater in the city. I was there for all of them; they were mobbed, and he was, as he deserved, greeted with great applause. I had the good luck to have a box seat free of charge, for the prices were a bit too high. Now he is on tour through the provinces, and I think they will be trying to get him from all around in the neighboring countries. All the theaters of our capital are working always at full capacity in spite of the very high ticket prices.

The monotonous life that we lead here goes on, and only when a foreigner comes and entertains us with concerts or lectures do we get a break from it.

Your loving son and brother,
Oreste

There is something I forgot. In Dad's last letter he said that you two would like to retire because you are tired of the long, hard work. You are right about that. If that which I can send you will be enough to live on, I wish you a well-deserved rest. Here in America in the great firms and companies, when a man has worked constantly for so many years and has contributed to the success of his particular employers, even though the law does not compel them, they give him a little something by way of a gift. Though it is not enough for a pension, at least it helps a lot. Dad, couldn't you quite politely go up to them and, when you say hello to the Rivettis, have a try at it. It might work. I know that they are tough back there, though they aren't exactly open-handed even here. Nonetheless there are times when, if they are at all considerate, it can be worth the trouble.

Oreste

1.   *In order to go on to the university, which for an engineer was the* politecnico, *Abele would have had to take new exams to bypass the technical institute. See letter 2, note 2.*
2.   *Guglielmo Ferrero (1871–1942) was a sociologist, novelist, and historian of ancient Rome. Later, as an opponent of Mussolini, he left Italy. He became a professor of history at the University of Geneva in 1930.*

Letter 29

Buenos Aires, 4 September 1907

Dearest parents and brother,

The last letter which I got from Dad asked me for 1,000 lire for the purchase of various things, farm implements especially and a cow. Right off I began to laugh to myself thinking of the naiveté of your request with its explanation. But then I thought: I don't know why, wanting to retire from one job, you would dedicate yourself to another. I believe that with the money that I can send you, you will be able to live, I don't say on easy street, but at least in peace. For the moment I could not satisfy your request since I too have to collect more than 2,500 lire, which they don't ever pay. My idea would be for you to spend your time strolling about those beautiful towns, even living in Valdengo if you don't choose Biella. But the idea of undertaking labor in the fields, I can't swallow it. You, Dad, will be able to read your newspapers, write comments about them, etc., and expect to be a candidate for something or other, etc. Mom will sing happily and knit socks. Abele, however, will have to study, and hard. I think this would be the most restful thing that you should set about doing.

Within a few days I hope to get a letter from you telling me whether Abele intends to continue his studies and where he will go. I imagine that he will be an earnest student and will know how to make a good impression on his new professors.

I am enclosing in my letter a check for 200 lire.

Your loving son and brother, Oreste. So many, many kisses.

Letter 30

Buenos Aires, 21 November 1907

Dearest parents,

Yesterday was my birthday, and I celebrated it the best I could, but I would like to have seen you. First of all I am astonished at the decision on Abele's part, and you agreed with him in your advice, not to go on with his studies. I have found no good reason for this decision, contrary to my advice. You, and he, say it was not to be a burden on me. But believe me, dearest parents, for me it is no burden at all. I could also send you the sum of money for the completion of his studies, but I would have to sell a fine piece of property, which every day is going up in value and on which, if all goes well, I will want to build a house for myself. Abele excuses himself for not wishing to continue his education, saying that he would like to help the family. Then he goes on to give me a summary of his expenses, and it turns out to be slightly less than his income. And then I don't think a salary of eighty lire is very tempting at all. The career that is open to anybody is not always altogether prosperous. Tomorrow I shall answer his letter sent to me from Grosseto.[1]

Another thing that astonishes me is the blacksmith shop that you want to set up. To stop on one side to start up on the other is in my opinion the same thing all over again. As to the field you want to buy, I am of the opposite opinion. Much, oh much better is to invest the money in property here, where the return is certain, and it is going up in value every day. I have bought two pieces, and for one they have already offered me half again as much as the purchase price. I am not selling it because it will still go up in value, and greatly.

I repeat then that which I had said in another letter, that when you retired from the factory, it was my firm intention that you set about leading a peaceful and free life, touring a bit through the cities of Italy and through the lakes. So then I don't share your ideas. I am enclosing in this letter a check for 200 lire. I think that, instead of helping toward the construction of a workshop, they [the lire] should go for a trip on Lake Maggiore or somewhere else.

As for putting some money aside for me, dear Father, don't think of it. I am offended when you say it; think of how you can live the best way you can.

Your son,
Oreste

Goodbye, Mom; today is the first day of my twenty-fifth year in action. If you see him, say hello to Zocco for me.

1.   *Abele was employed, through a friend of Luigi, in a company in Grosseto, Tuscany. It was his first job.*

3

Marriage and Family (1908–1910)

In February 1908, Oreste married Corinna Chiocchetti, a native of Gaglianico, a small town near Biella. He was twenty-five and she twenty-three. The focus of the letters for the next year and a half was on marriage and the real and anticipated consequences of this new relationship for the family. Oreste began by rather casually announcing he was about to get married and would introduce his bride—he did not mention her by name—to them when he returned home. In this and subsequent letters there was some question about whether the parents would attempt to interfere, approved of the marriage, or would continue to receive financial support from Oreste. An important new dimension in this chapter enables us to understand the nature of intrafamily relationships: It includes letters from the parents, generally written by Luigi, to their son in Buenos Aires; these letters provide firsthand the perspective of the parents. As the family members dealt with the consequences of the marriage, the busybodies who appeared in the previous chapter reemerged, and Oreste once more reminded his parents to maintain secrecy at all times.

Margherita was obviously delighted with having a daughter-in-law and especially with the prospect of grandchildren. In two simple, touching letters, filled with misspellings and grammatical mistakes, she conveyed her love for Corinna and her hope for a grandchild (# 35, # 39). The letter, she says, is "to show you that if our son chose you from everybody for his companion, we too will love you like a daughter. . . . You have filled the spot in our heart left empty by our poor Narcisa" (# 35). But the possibility of a grandchild was uppermost in her mind. "For us," she explained in the same letter, "the love from you two is enough, but if then you would make us grandparents—oh, with what joy we will love our grandchildren. Just thinking about it brings tears to my eyes." Corinna did become pregnant but lost the child (# 37).

The letters of Margherita to her daughter-in-law nevertheless made Corinna very happy; Oreste noted that "Corinna wept with joy [when she read the first letter]; she kissed it so many, many times. She gave it to everyone who comes to visit us to read. At night she would keep it under her pillow" (# 37). Marriage also produced a new interest on everyone's part in exchanging photographs (# 40, # 44).

The question of returning to Valdengo became an important issue with marriage and the possibility of a grandchild, especially for Luigi and Margherita. Luigi explained that they had fixed up the house and opened up two rooms in the basement. "When you come home with your wife," he continued, ". . . you will be happy to find your room well prepared and provided with everything necessary" (# 36). In his answer to this letter Oreste noted that when Luigi "said that he had had two more rooms built in the house, Corinna said right off, 'They will be for us when we go for the Exposition'" (# 37).

Nevertheless a certain tension within the family regarding money and support became apparent. Luigi pleaded with Oreste not to forget his parents since "we cannot do without your continued help" (# 32). A month later he thanked Oreste for the help but made it clear that he needed more: "Thanks to your help we hope to manage quite well. Without it we would have to live from hand to mouth" (# 34). Oreste apologized for his failure to carry out his promises. "It is not because of stinginess or carelessness; it's just that I can't come up with anything more" (# 33). It is worth noting that Oreste seemed to be sending many more postcards at this point, probably because a postcard could not include a check.

Yet all in all the marriage of Oreste and Corinna produced happiness in the Sola family.

Letter 31

Buenos Aires, 19 February 1908

Dearest parents,

Your last letter cheered me up a lot to know that you have finally settled in Valdengo. I think that you will be happy there, remembering me too sometimes.

Things are almost always the same with me; the only thing new is that I am about to get married. In another letter I shall send you my picture and one of her, and when I come home, I'll introduce her to you. I don't think you will try to hold things up, as parents are often accustomed to do with their children, because in my case it would be the same [anyway]. I shall keep the same relationship with you that I have had up to now, and every month I'll still send you the same amount as I do now.

I have not received any more news of Abele. I believe he will do well. I will write to him in a few days because he may not have received my other letter.

Stay happy and in good health; the countryside will still be a little gloomy because of the excessive cold weather, but then the beautiful season will come.

Your affectionate son,
Oreste

Letter 32

Valdengo, 6 July 1908

Dearest son Oreste,

I do not know what to think. Must I think poorly of you? I cannot because I know too well the kindness of your heart. Must I think well? I am hesitant because since the 20th of March I have received no more letters from you.

I received the two illustrated postcards that you sent the 16th of April in which you promised that you would soon write me a letter. To everything you write I have always responded with the same plea in regard to us. We are always anxious to receive your picture with your wife, whose name we still do not know. We are waiting for the day that we will embrace both of you here with us. We hope it will not be far off.

One thing that I must tell you and that has not made us too happy: We knew in Biella a good part of your affairs, what you earn, and that you send us 200 lire a month, and who your wife is.

Nothing wrong with that if you had also told us the name of your wife, then we could affirm that which the others are saying; instead we must, with displeasure, remain ignorant about that which less concerned people know about your business.

With this we do not intend to reproach you. Only to urge you not to be too expansive with others who can make all kinds of remarks.

We keep repeating our plea to remember us, that in the conditions that we are in we cannot do without your continued help, and as you know, we are in debt to Cousin Carlo for 2,700 lire.

We are convinced that with your marriage you will have had to pay for some special expenses, and so you will have had to suspend the usual enclosure of money to us, but we hope that you will not forget us.

Word has gotten back to us that we were opposed to your marriage because we wanted you to marry the one we wanted. Whereas you yourself can verify the contrary because first of all we still don't know who your bride is and, in our answer on the subject to your letter in which you said you were going to get married, we expressed the hope that she be healthy, honest, and industrious—and nothing more.

So then this accusation that they are making against us is nothing more than someone's malicious invention.

We are very unhappy about it.

We hope that this letter will cross with one of yours responding to some of our wishes expressed in our previous letters.

We especially need your help and good news of your new phase of life in the harmonious company of your young wife. We are waiting with open arms to welcome her here with us in your company.

We urge you to write often and give us news because we feel terrible when you are slow in writing.

If it were not too far away I would like to come visit you since it has been such a long time since we have seen you, and if you delay so much, we might perhaps borrow money, and one or the other of us will come visit you. Would you like that? Several days ago we got a letter from Abele. He is doing fine; he's happy.

Your loving parents

Letter 33

Buenos Aires, 19 July 1908

Dearest parents,

Please excuse me if since the month of this past March I have not written you at all, nor shown any life in my promise to write you. Here is the reason.

The Argentine government is far from prompt in its salaries; they can even fall behind by years. Only this month, after many protests, which leave them cold, have they paid us for November and December. As for the months of 1908, they are not even talking about them yet. However, toward the end of the year, when they start to deal with the proposed budget of 1909, I think they will have to talk about that concerning 1908, which has remained at the mercy of the individual ministers. I have spoken with some deputies, and it looks as if they will try to intervene on my behalf.

I have delayed so much because from one day to the next one kept hoping for a solution. But now we have all resigned ourselves to the situation, and we wait. For many, almost all, who have no other resource than their government money (not everyone can hold two jobs!?) life is a bit grim, and they are scraping by on the strength of borrowing.

The salary I get from the firm working on the Congress enables me to live with security enough, but now in part because of the increase in the cost of living, and in part because of our private affairs, and then you must realize that now I am a man with a wife to support, everything slips away without any big expenses.

Please excuse me then if so much time has gone by since I have carried out my promises. In the months to come, until I am able to get my full salary from Congress, I shall send you about 100 lire a month. I know it's not much, but for now bear with me, dearest parents, and don't think badly of me in your hearts. It is not because of stinginess or carelessness; it's just that I can't come up with anything more. I'll send it to you then all at one stroke at the start of next year. In the meantime I am enclosing in this letter a check for 400 lire.

This week I have sent you two postcards which you will get a few days before this. I sent the same to Abele in Sardinia;[1] tomorrow I'll write him a letter, giving him the news in detail. I am glad that he has found something better. I think he will be able to do what he has to and become a man. Traveling a bit from one region to another will stimulate him, and so he will gain a lot of things that will be useful to him. It is, however, necessary for him to study, to study always and hard.

Today it is five months that I've been married, and I do not regret it at all. She is sweet; she talks to me often of you and Biella (she hasn't be here long and still misses it). She takes care of the house—and all the domestic tasks—efficiently and with good taste. I am delighted with her. In the evening we enjoy a laugh together, and sometimes we go to the theater or to a concert. On Sundays, if the weather is good and not cold, we make an outing outside of town with different couples we know, and so we spend the time contentedly. She is eagerly looking forward to the Exposition of 1911 to see her own dear ones and you, for whom she makes my affection grow every day. As to any new addition, she gives no promise of one so far, but there is no hurry. Next month I'll send you our pictures, long since promised. Count on it.

Enrico Ferri landed yesterday; he came for a lecture tour.[2] I saw him last night at about eleven at an Italian club (l'Unione e Benevolenza[3]), which today celebrates its fiftieth anniversary. He seems to have aged a lot; perhaps the cash he will take home will rejuvenate him. He has a contract for 200,000 francs a month and all expenses paid. I have taken a subscription for the first eight lectures. If there is anything interesting, I'll send you the newspapers. I am sending you one, in Italian, the one about his arrival.

Accept, dearest parents, so many, many kisses from your loving son and his wife, who looks upon you with the same respect as I do. One more big kiss for Mom from my wife.

Bye. Keep in good spirits.

Your dear son,
Oreste

1.   *Unhappy with his job in Grosseto, Abele was successful in finding a position with a company in Carloforte, Sardinia.*

2.   *Enrico Ferri was a leading Italian socialist politician and intellectual.*
3.   *The Unione e Benevolenza was the oldest and largest Italian mutual-aid soci-ety in Buenos Aires. It was founded in 1858 and in 1908 had a membership of approxi-mately 5,000.*

Letter 34

Valdengo, 11 August 1908

Dearest son Oreste,

Nothing is more agreeable than receiving something you have wanted so badly. Yesterday evening as I got back from Novara, from the regular session of the Provincial Congress,[1] I had the supreme pleasure of your longed-for and expected letter.

We thank you so much for the 400 lire that you have sent us. It came at a very good time because we had need of it. As you say that for now you can only send 100 lire a month, it is possible that will be enough for us if no un-usual expenses pop up. It is always a great pleasure to hear of your excellent health in the company of your young wife, and we hope that she always will be good company for you; that is the finest thing in life. And since a long time still separates us (until 1911!?) from being able to embrace the two of you, we would like a picture of you both; and we need to know from you her name and that of her family so that we could at least make their acquaintance, inviting them sometime here to our house, until the time when we can all see each other together.

Today we got the letters you sent us. The special joyful welcome given to our excellent Ferri in those distant parts of yours gives us great pleasure. An honor for him and for Italy.

We are spending a good part of our daily life in farm work, as much as we can do. I am doing some work in my trade here at home.

The crop looks promising, and we hope that it continues so. Only it costs a lot to have the work done by day laborers, considering the heavy increase in wages for farmworkers.

Thanks to your help we hope to manage quite well. Without it we would have to live from hand to mouth.

We hope that you will not have to lose any of the money owed you by that government of yours and that you will be able to put yourself in a position to help us.

Your loving parents and parents-in-law,
Bye.

1.   *Luigi had been for some time a provincial delegate from Biella, elected on the Socialist Party line. The Provincial Congress met in Novara, the capital of the province.*

Letter 35

Valdengo, [no date, 15–28 September 1908]

My dear daughter-in-law,

Pardon me if right off I take the liberty of treating you as if you were my own daughter—that is, giving you the intimate form of address.[1] It's to show you that if our son chose you from everbody for his companion, we too will love you like a daughter, and if you will be able to make him happy, being a good companion to him, you will have no reason to complain about us. On the contrary, you have filled the spot in our heart left empty by our poor Narcisa.

Love our dear Oreste then, and think of us as nothing other than parents who will love you as if we were the ones who gave you life.

For us the love from you two is enough, but if then you would make us grandparents—oh, with what joy we will love our grandchildren.

Just thinking about it brings tears to my eyes. Be happy then both of you, and you, my dear Corinna, don't worry about those rumors. We already love you very much. Do your best to make Oreste happy and don't think of anything else. Your mother, Margherita, my dear Corinna, will have a real affection for you just like your own mother, and you, I hope, will feel the same way toward me. My dear children, my heart is so happy that I would like to go on writing to you, but all I could do would be to say over again that I love you so very, very much.

Well then, crown our happiness soon by giving us a fine little baby. I embrace you and kiss you with special love, our dear Corinna.

Your loving mom,
Margherita

Dear Oreste, I ask you to give this to my dear daughter-in-law. I hope you won't be jealous. A kiss from your parents, Mom.

1. In Italian, unlike English, there are two forms of address for individuals: the formal and the personal, or intimate, forms. Margherita is explaining her reason for using the personal form.

Letter 36

Valdengo, 25 October 1908

Dearest son, Oreste,

All Saint's Day is coming soon. As usual we shall go to spread flowers on the graves of our dear Narcisa and dear Grandmother at the Biella cemetery. You too, along with your young bride, please remember, far away though you are, our dear ones who are no longer with us. Now that your birthday is coming soon we send you our most affectionate good wishes for happiness and health in the company of your dear Corinna.

I must really explain to you that the 400 lire will be very useful for the purpose of paying for part of the masons' work on the house. You will, of course, remember how the house was laid out. We have had the two upstairs rooms in back finished. We have opened up two windows in the basement and made it liveable; it has been changed into a room where one can be warm and have good light in the winter. We have taken out the furnace, and in its place we have gained a bit of useful space (for wine vats now).

We have spent a fair amount of money on this, but we hope that you too will be happy to have the house fixed up a bit.

When you come home with your wife—we are anxious to embrace both of you—you will be happy to find your room well prepared and provided with everything necessary, in addition to [finding] the house in good condition.

The crops have turned out quite well. Only a few weeks before the grape harvest there was a storm that caused a lot of damage. For the rest we can be happy.

We are still waiting for the picture of you with your bride that you promised a long time ago.

Your parents and parents-in-law

Letter 37

Buenos Aires, 4 December 1908

Dearest parents,

In spite of all my promises I am always late, and it looks as if I am neglecting all that I intended to do in your case. Do not think so, my dearest parents; I am doing everything I possibly can for you, who have done so very much to earn my love. Unexpected events have compelled me to fall behind again this time. But at the beginning of the new year it is expected that everything will be in good shape and everything will begin to go at full speed.

For the same reason I have failed to give you news of myself because I feel as if I have fallen short of an obligation. Don't let this make you think that I am forgetting you or hold you less in esteem. No, the memory and love of you are constantly growing in me, especially now that it has been sharpened by my beloved Corinna.

I have received two letters from Dad, and Corinna got one from Mom. You can't imagine the happiness and pleasure that Mom's letter brought us. Corinna wept with joy; she kissed it so many, many times. She gave it to everyone who comes to visit us to read. At night she would keep it under her pillow, and when she would wake up in the morning, she would get it and reread it. Corinna loves you a whole lot, and she is anxious to see you and embrace you (in 1911).

While I am writing this, she is looking for a greeting card to send you. She had already wanted to write you earlier, but since I had not done so, she was shy about it.

I regret that I have to tell you that an heir, whom we had planned for well, has been lost. It was, however, nothing serious. Preparations are under way for another and with better success.

A few days after I wrote to Abele, I was very pleased to get a long letter from him. I have not yet answered him, but in these next few days I shall take the time for him too. I am pleased that he is doing better; I think that he will be intelligent and quick to learn. In my letter I asked him what he was able to handle best or at least what he felt himself most inclined to. I have been waiting for his answer for the purpose of telling him whether he should come over here with me, but I have not yet got an answer.

For the coming year I have already been listed in the budget with a salary of 200 pesos (440 lire). Add to that the salary from the firm working on the Parliament building, equal to the first, and I shall then be in considerably better financial condition, considering that I shall have to collect almost all of my government salary for this year.[1]

It gave us great pleasure and we laughed at the same time reading Dad's last letter. When he said that he had had two more rooms built in the house, Corinna said right off, "They will be for us when we go for the Exposition." Your letters bring us a world of happiness. We spend the evenings talking about them.

About what I tell you in my letters, especially concerning private affairs, I sure hope you will always keep quiet.

When you get this letter, you will already be in the Christmas holidays or at the end of the year. I, and my wife as well, give you our best wishes for complete happiness, absolute good cheer, and a world of joys.

Your beloved son,
Oreste

I forgot to tell you that on the 20th of November, the day of my twenty-fifth birthday, we spent a splendid holiday in the company of some friends. I had just two days before received Dad's last letter with his best wishes for the day; it made me much more cheerful than usual (and I never lack for good cheer), and we had a great time. Corinna became rosier than usual and was even more vivacious; that evening she was a flower for our fine group of friends.

Contrary to the goal I set myself for these holidays, I am unable to send you 150 lire, which you will now be late in getting. I kept waiting from one day to the next since they said that the government would pay, but it was not true.

Bye, keep in good spirits.

Oreste

1. *For an estimate of Oreste's financial situation, see the Appendix.*

Letter 38

Valdengo, 19 January 1909

Dearest son Oreste,

We have spent the holidays of Christmas and New Year in good health.

We received the money order for 150 lire that you sent us, for which we thank you very much. At the same time as your letter we also received two cards with holiday greetings, one for each, sent to us by your and our dear Corinna. They convinced us all the more of the love you two have for us, so we anxiously wait for the day when we can embrace and kiss you both with joy. Your sincere generosity in helping us was a great pleasure. Last year we spent quite a few hundred lire, as we have told you in other letters, to do some of the things the house needed and to prepare living quarters with a bit more room for everyone, for the time when we will be able to have the joy of seeing you and embracing you all together here at home. We hope soon, at the latest 1911. We have managed here as best we could. However we must honestly say that our existence depends on yours. This is not to reproach you if you don't completely achieve all that you have promised yourself and set as a goal. Taking into consideration that you have set up your own house and family and the delays in collecting your earnings. . . .

We learn with no pleasure of the loss of our grandson to be, but the hope of a return match and subsequent victory cheers us up. And when it will happen, it would be our joy to be able to have him with us since he will cost a great deal there. If you are willing to send him along to us, and perhaps Corinna too, we would be delighted to have them. We are very glad that you have also written to Corinna's family, and they are all quite happy about it. We will invite them some time soon to our house to strengthen among us all the ties of affection: ours, yours, and yours and Corinna's.

Abele has written us for the Christmas holidays. He has sent us a box of Tunisian dates. He is fine; he says he has written you and is waiting for an answer. I see from your letter that you will have done so by now. As far as ability goes he is not lacking. [As far as] goodwill and intelligence, he is very quick, so much so that the Cosimini gentlemen of Grosseto are very unhappy that he has left them. Where he is now, they are happy to have him.

Although we would prefer that he stay where he is, at least until you come home and he will have passed the draft age, we do not want to stand in the way of his joining you, even very soon, if you have some good prospects for him.

We are always the same here, in good health; it is a bit cold, not like where you are. We hope that you too and Corinna are doing well. There is some news I must share with you. Your cousin Abele, Giacomo's son, has decided to leave in three weeks on the French ship *Italie* for Argentina. We will give him your address. We are sure that you will be glad to see him after so many years.

Always remember your very loving parents.

Luigi and Margherita

As far as secrecy about our affairs goes, rest assured. We have had to confirm only as much as others were saying. This was for the sake of our dignity and yours.

Letter 39

Sent to Buenos Aires with Cousin Abele
March 1909

My dear children,

I am taking the opportunity of Cousin Abele's arrival over there to send you, Oreste, a dozen handkerchiefs and you, Corinna, a scarf. I don't know whether you will like it; I selected it according to my taste and the way things are in fashion here. What I am sending is not very much; I would like to have done more, but since I have to depend on others, I didn't want to be indiscreet.

In any case I hope that you will accept with good pleasure the little that I am sending you. Let it be like a pledge of the great affection that we carry for you, especially for our dear Corinna. An hour doesn't pass but that our thoughts fly to you, and even now I am getting the nest ready for the future child since we hope that you will not deny us the joy of coming to give birth here with us.

You don't know how much the thought cheers me up that I too will at last · be a grandmother and that I will be able to clasp in our arms the son of my children. Yes, my Corinna, I love you already so very much that in my heart you have now taken the place, as if you were my dear and ever-lamented Narcisa. But in the future I shall love you twice as much if we can call the new child our own, since Dad will be crazy about him, if you plan to send her [Corinna] back in time [for the delivery], since we would be extremely jealous that someone else might see the longed-for small creature before us. Wouldn't you give me this pleasure? And you, my adored Oreste, rest assured that your bride will be treated like a queen and, as far as loving her goes, we already love her very much.

I'll stop writing now. Dad sends you so many kisses, and I embrace you with all the love in my heart. I am your mother.

Letter 40

Buenos Aires, 1 March 1909

Dearest parents,

I have not answered you sooner because I was too busy; there is, however, always time for a letter. Instead I sent you some postcards. I am enclosing some more of them with this letter.

Now that I've got married, I have another address, which is that of my new residence, where from now on you should send me your letter. It is *Rio Bamba 253*.

I have sent some postcards to Abele. I think he will have received them by now, and I am waiting for his answer. Tomorrow, according to the notice in the newspapers, my cousin and friend, Abele, will arrive. I shall go welcome him on board ship.

I had heard that Zocco had planned on returning to Buenos Aires. I don't think that will turn out to be true. If you see him, give him the warmest greetings for my part.

I am enclosing a check for 200 lire.

My wife, Corinna, is always thinking of you. She has placed your photograph next to her bed, and before going to bed she gives you a kiss and talks to me about you. The memory and the affection [for you] unite us in a strong love.

The tragedy which fell upon the two Italian cities made a great impression here.[1] Everywhere subscriptions for contributions have been offered; they have done very well. It has gone beyond a million lire.

You keep asking me for a photograph, but you don't ever send us one of you that is worth the effort. Before the end of the month I think I shall send you ours. You will then be in our debt to do the same.

This very evening I am writing Abele, and I expect I shall have an answer.

Your son Oreste, in company with my [sic] better half, Corinna, greets you and kisses you with enthusiasm.

Bye. Stay happy and healthy.

Because of cash problems I am sending you today this letter, which I should have mailed last month.

I have received the greetings from the new arrivals and the lovely gift sent by Mom to Corinna and me. Thanks, a thousand thanks. Corinna is delighted with it, and she has already shown it to everyone. They all think it is in exquisite good taste.

Your son and daughter-in-law,

Oreste (and Corinna)

3 April 1909

Bye.

1.   *On December 23, 1908, an earthquake destroyed Messina and caused a great deal of damage to Reggio di Calabria. Some 60,000 people were killed in the disaster.*

Letter 41

Valdengo, 18 April 1909

Dearest son Oreste,

Since 16 January we have received no letters from you. The 16th of this month we did get two more nice postcards where you let us know that by means of Cousin Abele you have received the small gift. We hope that you will do your best to set him up with a job; he needs it.

As we already told you, even when we were still at Biella but had made up our mind to come home to Valdengo, we had complete confidence in your help whereas you suggested we stay at Biella. We more than counted on the money you promised, which would have been more than enough; but with the consideration that it would not have kept coming over a long period, we decided to come home so that we would not spend so much and to put aside a little in reserve in case your help, for unforeseen reasons, might be sharply reduced. We had already foreseen that should you marry, your help would as a result be reduced. But we had the hope that the reduction would not have come so soon.

As you will have learned from other letters, the money you sent last year has been spent to fix up the house. We are convinced that you will have had a lot of expenses setting up house with your wife. For us it is a joy that you are married and that it is going well. Our preceding letters can bear witness to our wishes. We don't know whether your situation permits you to promise us anything. We would just like to know what we can count on. We hope that you won't be offended that we speak this way. Be patient with us.

Here we are working on our small plot of land as much as we can. It is very hard work because we are not used to it and are old, though in pretty good health.

We keep hoping that the day will come when we can embrace you along with your wife and tell you directly all the things you don't say in a letter.

We have heard nothing from Abele since 21 March. We hope that you too will write him and that, like good brothers, you will keep in constant correspondence.

In the expectation of some clarification from you, we send you our warmest kisses, in the company of dear Corinna, and we beg you always to remember your aged parents.

Your loving parents

Letter 42

Valdengo, 1 June 1909

Dearest son, Oreste,

In his last letter Abele tells us, concerning his coming to join you, that he had written you on the subject. We are still of the same opinion as we have already told you. He should wait until you come home (1911, isn't that right); however, we do not wish to stand in the way if this might be his big chance.

I have a task for you on behalf of a friend here. Carlo Pella wants to know if the Bank of the Province of Buenos Aires still exists. He has left with them an account book in the name of Quinto and Carlo Pella, entered in ledger 174, page 1441, with a balance of 2,048 pesos as of 9 June 1890 plus the interest up to the present.

The friend in question, the heir of his brother Quinto, who died recently, wants to know if the bank still exists and to give the power of attorney to you to draw out the above-mentioned balance. In case the answer is yes, he will send you the account book with the appropriate power of attorney, and he will pay for your services.

Your loving parents

Letter 43

Buenos Aires, 12 August 1909

Dearest parents,

I am always negligent in the same way; I promise the world, and then for one excuse or another I don't ever carry out my promise. For some time now I have been meaning to write you. I have, however, sent you some postcards which I think you will have received.

I wanted to give Dad an answer about the money deposited in the Bank of the Province of Buenos Aires. I was unable to go there in person because of the hours of the bank and my heavy workload, which I couldn't let go. So I am not in a position to give an answer on this topic. I think, however, that at this point you are not going to get anything out of them. The reason is that some time ago a demand for payment was made by the depositors, and they reached an agreement as best they could.

In truth I have not written you at all, or rather have not answered sooner, because I really didn't have the time for it. I had been working for about three months on the project for a huge building, the Post and Telegraph Office, the anticipated cost of which comes to fourteen million pesos (note that the peso is worth 2.2 lire). The bids in competition for this enormous construction have been presented just today, and they were opened this very day at 4 P.M., five minutes after the passing of the deadline for the competition. It looks as if the construction firm for which I have done so much work has a good chance of winning the contract. If that should be the case, I can assure you that things will go pretty well. But I am not getting my hopes up too high about it.

I received a very sweet letter from Mom with the date of 4 July. Corinna wept when she read it; she loves you so much. About all that she told us in the letter we here don't know anything, about the operation, the leg, and what all. I think I understand what the problem is, and infections are very dangerous, especially in those areas.

Now, however, I am sure she will have recovered and will be cheerful the way she always was when I was home. Oh, how well I remember it!

I am still waiting for an answer from Abele, but it doesn't come. I think he wants to get even with me. Fine, I'll wait.

I am enclosing in this letter a check for 500 lire.

Your loving Oreste (and Corinna)

Letter 44

Buenos Aires, 9 December 1909

Dearest parents,

Every time I hear from you, Corinna weeps with joy; she loves you so much, and she rereads your letters over and over again by herself.

The other evening I went to see Cousin Abele and his wife; they are fine, including the baby girl. I also saw Pantelin's daughter, her husband, and others of Biella, all in perfect health.

I thank you from my heart for the gift you sent us, but it wasn't necessary to go to such trouble. An even more heartfelt thanks to Mom for the good choice; Corinna is very pleased with it and shows it to everyone who comes into the house. She wanted to try the beautiful stockings on at once, calling my attention to their fine workmanship and high quality. In the near future we too will try to send you something to reciprocate in part.

Corinna, and I too, are in perfect health; we are always in good spirits and

Photograph 2. The formal, professionally taken photograph of Oreste and Corinna promised in letter #44 and sent in a letter of January 9, 1910, not included in our selection.

happy. Because of the heat, which is pretty oppressive, on Sunday we go into the country or along the islands of the Tigre. It is picturesque scenery, a little Venice (very little in magnificence, but very, very great in area covered).

I am enclosing in this letter two small photographs taken of me these past few days. I am with Guala, Sig. Lavino from Valdengo, who is also traveling on the *Mafalda*, Emilia, and Corinna. [I am also enclosing] two others, one of me and another one of Corinna. I had wanted to send with this letter the pictures taken of us together and individually, but the photographer doesn't ever have them ready because of the excessive amount of work he has. Be patient, for they are sure to be ready for the next letter.

I should like to have one of you together or individually, but well done so that I can frame them the way I keep—and with the greatest respect—those of Abele and dear Narcisa.

I hope Mom will now be recovering from her sickness, but she must be very careful and not wear herself out with housecleaning.

I am enclosing in this letter a check for 200 lire. I thought, and it was everybody's expectation, that the Besana firm would have succeeded in getting the job for the Post Office. Instead things went badly, and I was badly disappointed. But it doesn't matter; I shall still keep at it just the same.

I am enclosing two postcards for each of you. At the same time I am sending others to Abele, as I do every time I write to you. I don't know, however, whether they will go unanswered. Since he has been in Sardinia, I have received only one letter. I had written him to come here, but I haven't ever gotten an answer.

When you get this, it will be Christmas; I hope you spend the holidays in complete happiness, the way we spent my birthday, and I am pleased that it was so well remembered by you.

Best wishes from the very depths of my heart, and from Corinna as well, for lovely holidays and thousands and thousands of happy years to come. Corinna would like to add her thanks for the gift and her best wishes for good holidays.

Oreste

Dearest Dad and Mom,

I am happy to call you this, and I think you will feel the same toward me, even though you do not know me, but I love you the same as my Oreste does. I am always thinking of you, and every day at the table we talk about you with pleasure.

Accept, my dearest ones, my most sincere thanks as your daughter, happy with the gift you sent us on the occasion of the very day that was celebrated by us with rejoicing. Some time in the near future I too will remember you [with a gift]. Accept also from your daughter Corinna loving good wishes for a merry Christmas, and good end and beginning of the year, and for so very, very many others to come, always blessed and happy.

Your daughter,
Corinna

Letter 45

Buenos Aires, 6 March 1910

Dearest parents,

We received a few days ago your dear letter in response to our photograph and to the 200-lire check that I sent you in January. Sorry that I could not do the same in February because of various concerns of my own.

Enclosed with this I am sending you a letter for Sig. Carlos [sic] Pella and a receipt for thirty lire for the expenses I met in concluding this business for him. Give it to him if he pays you. If not, you can tear it up. I am also enclosing a check for 150 lire.

Every time we get one of your dear letters Corinna weeps with happiness. She rereads, and has me reread, the same letter several times. Now she wants us to take a new picture to send you since the first one gave you so much pleasure. We will do so but in a while. Our friends and fellow townsmen, whom I see every so often, are all doing fine, and they say hello to you.

I would like it, as I have already said on other occasions, if you would not let anyone see the letters I send you from here, nor [speak of] my affairs with you—under no circumstances. People who get news from there tell me about things I would not like them to know. The same for the postcards and photographs that we send you; keep them just for yourselves. If someone wants to see them, let them come to our house. I don't want to hurt your feelings with this, but there are things I would very much like to be kept quiet, especially because they don't concern anyone else.

While it is cold over there, we are dying of the heat here, but now it has cooled off a bit and is more comfortable.

I have also sent the same picture of us to Abele, and I am waiting for an acknowledgment of it. Perhaps tomorrow I'll write him too.

Your beloved and loving
children,
Oreste (and Corinna)

Letter 46

Buenos Aires, 9 April 1910

Dearest parents,

With this letter I am sending you a magazine from here which has some pictures of a Mendoza *bodega* (winery), simply to show you the importance of viticulture, which is constantly growing in this country. Whereas, as I remember, when I was back home, they said that in America one didn't drink wine because there wasn't any. On the contrary, it is one of the best products here. And I, so as not to let our traditions go, always keep at home some bottles from here, even old ones, in with the Barolo, the Valtellina, Polcevera, Falernian, Champagne, etc. I assure you [they have] a very refined taste. After the Tokay I find the white wine of San Juan among the best. Corinna also likes it, especially if it is good. We are, however, always very temperate, one well-tasted sip and that's all. We are a perfect couple.

As of the day before yesterday, the [7th] of this month, it's seven years that I have worked in Buenos Aires for the Argentine government and for the Parliament firm. I am happy that I have performed my job well, and I am always thanked for it, as at this time of year.[1]

I am enclosing with this letter a check for 200 lire. I think that in the near future I shall be able to make up the months I have lost in my arrangements with you.

It is beginning to cool off here, and we are comfortable. We are very close to the celebration of 100 years of independence, and there is a lot of work on all sides, both here in the capital as well as in the farthest village from the center of the Republic. You can't find good masons for less than six pesos (twelve to thirteen lire) a day, and on certain occasions you have to pay the unskilled laborers almost the same price. This is the reason why I kept urging Abele to come and join me. But that he wanted to wait until he had drawn his number really makes me laugh. He has lost an opportunity to make several thousand lire. Well, I won't send for him again—that's for sure. We see that however much the governments in America advertise in Europe, people are too stupid and timid. They think they will come here and have to fight with the Indians. But when you get to Buenos Aires, you see at once that you are in one of the largest, most beautiful, and modern cities. It's enough to say that to cross it from one side to the other in either direction takes at least an hour and a quarter by electric streetcar. Its fourteen kilometers on one axis and seventeen on the other. Imagine a Biella of such size, and starting from Piazzo [the Upper Town] you get all the way to Lessona.

For the rest, life here is monotonous and rather cold. Nothing happens to change the usual humdrum routine. You see everything, you talk about it, and it goes by.

I'll write Abele tomorrow. I sent him, as I did you, some newspapers and postcards with the Andes tunnel.

Stay cheerful and happy, always remember your son Oreste and Corinna, who love you so very much and find joy in you.

Bye.

1.   *He is referring to the bonus customarily given at this time of year.*

4

Oreste Becomes a Contractor (1910–1912)

On May 25, 1910, Argentina celebrated the one hundredth anniversary of its independence from Spain. Oreste was not very interested in the centennial celebration itself, but he was fascinated by the Exposition that took place shortly thereafter, and he was to benefit from the widespread construction and growth that accompanied it. In three letters (#47, #48, #49) he described the Exposition and his and Corinna's visits there plus his splendid observations of Halley's comet.

We are introduced to the main focus of the chapter in letter #50: Oreste was awarded the contract to build the railroad from Santa Fe to Dean Funes. He began work in September 1910 with 57 workmen and soon had increased the number to more than 100. The ties of family, friendship, and village contributed to the success of this project. Oreste hired his old school friend Secondo Cravello as his chief assistant, and he summoned a team of nine Biellesi from Buenos Aires to work as masons. Perhaps most importantly he arranged to borrow some of the money for the project from his father's friend, Carlo Pella of Cossato, and to have his father serve as guarantor for the loan. Luigi and Margherita were supportive of their son, but they were "afraid that something bad may happen to you out in that wild place where you are" (#53).

Corinna, who remained in Buenos Aires while Oreste got established in his new job, joined her husband in December 1910. Her letter (#55), enclosed with one from Oreste, provided the kind of vivid detail that supported Luigi and Margherita's image of where their son worked. "Life is full of sacrifices," Corinna told them, "since there are no conveniences. We live in a railway car. . . . There is nothing here. . . . What I find strange is how come there are no cows nor milk and the countryside is dry. . . . There are dead animals everywhere; . . . it's like being in the desert. The only human beings you see are the men who work for Oreste. You can't believe how it is unless you see it" (#56). Corinna was uncomfortable and a bit bored, but she endured this life for a year in order to be with Oreste.

Many of the themes we have encountered in previous chapters reappear again: Family ties were strong and important; money was of major concern on both sides of the Atlantic; Oreste did not write often and apologized for his negligence; Oreste was concerned about maintaining secrecy especially with regard to financial matters; and Luigi and Margherita kept trying to induce Oreste and Corinna to return home. The chapter closes with Corinna returning to Buenos Aires and Oreste instructing his parents to write to him in the future at his old address in Buenos Aires because the construction project was nearly finished.

Letter 47

Buenos Aires, 3 May 1910

Dearest parents,
There is still a tremendous amount of work going on because of the Exposition, which is now at hand. They are constructing an enormous number of buildings and offices. There are also projects for the railway system and the enlargement of the port, and more.

I have written just now to Abele, regretting that he did not come when I first called for him. So he lost a good opportunity, which may be slow in coming again after the Exposition since they always leave behind a sort of economic crisis.

Three days ago we got your last dear letter. We see that you are devoting all your efforts to fixing up the house. Corinna, every time she reads about these things, gets very happy and looks forward with pleasure to the day when she will be able to embrace you there. What *I* suggest to you is not to spend money uselessly but rather to enjoy it as best you can and in so doing you will have made me happier.

I have received a letter from Carlo Pella, whom you also had told me about in your last letter. I shall respond to him next week since the listing of these shares is not until Friday. It's better to wait a few days since now that they have to pay the first coupon, the shares will have to have gone up by at least four or five points from when I wrote you. In any case I shall try to do the best I can for Sig. Pella's affairs. As soon as the sale has been completed, I shall send the money directly to him, along with the newspapers giving the price of shares on the exchange for that day.

Corinna, who is always cheerful and happy, is always occupied in rereading your letters and postcards. She has made a nice album of them, and it seems to her that you never write soon enough. She always thinks of you with the greatest pleasure and rejoices to receive your dear letters.

Cool weather is beginning here; the theater season is starting up too. Corinna has now made a beautiful new dress and looks like a Madonna. She is also filling out a bit more.

A few days ago, when I got your dear letter, we sent you some illustrated postcards with stamps made especially for the Exposition.

They show scenes and people of these days; they are very handsome except for the printing, since they turned out blurred.

Your loving children,
Oreste (and Corinna)

Along with this I am enclosing a check for 200 lire.

Letter 48

Buenos Aires, 15 July 1910

Dearest parents,

This month I have delayed in sending you this letter because I wanted at the same time to send Sig. Pella the answer concerning his certificates and the corresponding amount. It has been impossible for me up to now because of an accident which happened to the person who bought the shares for me. In a week, however, I feel sure that I will be able to finish off everything that should already have been resolved.

I am enclosing in this letter a check for 200 lire.

I am astonished that Abele has never written to me again.

A few days ago Signora Quinta Stellino from Valdengo left here. She had been to visit me along with her son who lives here. She may come to see you to bring you our greetings.

Corinna, who always thinks of you with great affection, is getting stouter every day. She is plump and ruddy; she is in good spirits, singing all day long.

You've been asking me for news of Halley's comet, which you did not see. Here it was seen constantly and brilliantly; every day you could see the tail getting larger and longer. Corinna compared it to something incredible. The day or, rather, the night the tail passed over the earth, it wasn't visible in Buenos Aires because it was cloudy, and it was really the only day to see it there. But since I was in the northern part of Santa Fe Province, I had the chance that very night—and others before and after—to observe its real magnificence and grandeur. Imagine a brilliant nucleus the size of the sun, shining with the brilliance of the fixed stars, cut in half as in the case of the setting sun, and a tail getting wider, white, but transparent, so much so that the stars above could be seen through it. It got so long that it passed through half of the hemisphere or, rather, further than the point from which it was observed, as in this sketch,

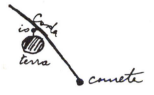

and it was the size of the Milky Way or even larger. In truth I never thought I would see such a spectacle. Here there were even many people who, out of fear of the end of the world, stayed up all night for several nights. After this passing, you could still see it toward evening as it got dark, but it was much reduced in size, and every day it kept getting smaller until it disappeared. Now it's already like an ancient legend; no one thinks about it any more.

The news here consists of all the big receptions that the European governments are giving for the future president, [Roque] Saenz Peña; the enormous expenses caused by the centennial celebrations—they were so great they don't want the public to know about them; the new law restricting the anarchists and the emigrants;[1] and the Exposition, which is going to be a flop. They talk about everything in an uninvolved way, as if they were things that didn't concern us.

We are enclosing in this letter three nice illustrated postcards, and we are sending one to Abele.

Your children who always think
of you with so much love,
Oreste (and Corinna)

When you write to Abele please ask him if he is getting my postcards. Every month, when I send them to you, I send them to him too. Thanks. Bye.

1.   *He is referring to the Ley de Defensa Social (the Law of Social Defense), which prohibited foreign-born anarchists from entering the country, propagating their ideas, or holding public meetings. On June 26 a bomb exploded in the empty Teatro Colon, and an anarchist was accused. Within forty-eight hours the National Congress passed the law.*

Letter 49

Buenos Aires, 2 August 1910

Dearest parents,

We are living in perfect harmony here, always happy and cheerful.

I am enclosing in this letter a check for 200 lire. It is intensely cold here, but the weather is dry and clear.

For two Sundays now we have been going to the Exposition, which has just opened. It's a splendid way to enjoy oneself, as well as being educational. I keep Corinna walking from morning to evening, right up to closing time. In two entire days we still haven't managed to see all of one section, and there are five: Railways, Industry, Agriculture and Animal Husbandry, Health, and the Arts. It will be with us for at least three months. Corinna has a good time, even though she doesn't understand; she makes us laugh with the explanations she gives of certain objects and machines. And then we eat at the Exposition and enjoy ourselves; we get home after midnight and sleep peacefully.

In another letter I'll write you with the details of some of the exhibitions they have put on; they are very worthwhile.

Along with this letter I am sending in its case an album with twenty-five views of the city. They were carefully taken and turned out well. It's a record of historical value. A framed picture can be made of any one of them.

I'll write Abele tomorrow, from whom I am still waiting for an answer. I'll also write Sig. Carlos [sic] Pella of Cossato since I have completely settled his account.

Your children,
Oreste (and Corinna)

Letter 50

Laguna Paiva, 11 September 1910

Dearest parents,

As you will see from the heading, I am no longer in Buenos Aires since I have taken on the project for the construction of a railroad to go from Santa Fe to Dean Funes. I had my eye on this project for quite a while, and in August they awarded it to me. I have already been at it for two weeks, and the project is a very promising one. For now Corinna is still staying in Buenos Aires at the old address, but she will come to join me if later on I have more comfortable living arrangements, for it is the desire of us both never to be separated.

The day before yesterday I got your dear letter, which had been forward to me by Corinna. I am pleased to hear that you are well. From Abele, however, I haven't gotten anything for more than a year.

Coming back to the subject of my new residence, which I'm sure will astonish you, I'm doing very well. I am camped on the banks of the Rio Salado, where the dams are being built for the bridge. Right now I have fifty-seven workmen, but in a little while there will be many more. There are also some Biellesi with me, all masons, who came especially for this.

In your last letter, of 10 August, you spoke to me about the Pella business. I am sending with this some documents for him and a letter. Would you please deliver them to him since I don't have the address with me here? I forgot it in Buenos Aires.

For this project I have undertaken, for which I have as my chief assistant and friend an old school friend Sig. Secondo Cravello, I need a certain amount of capital, at least until I collect the first installment of the payments. I can't put together the entire amount since some thousands of pesos are required (25,000). So I am turning to Sig. Carlo Pella, since he has such confidence in me, to put together the above-mentioned sum, which is absolutely necessary so that I don't have to resort to debentures or [ask for] payments in advance. I should not like to do this since it would be bad business, considering the way and the people who have helped me to get this enterprise under way.

With the sale of his shares I collected 2,891.40 pesos for Sig. Carlos [sic] Pella. I would go into debt to him for this sum with the promissory note I am enclosing here, for which, however, I need your signature as guarantor. I don't think you will have any problem with this task, especially since you may count on it for sure that it is a safe enterprise. In case, however, Sig. Carlos [sic] Pella should raise objections in regard to this, I shall send him the amount at once, through the mail, as I tell him in the letter which I am sending along with this.

For this affair I am asking Sig. Pella for two years' time, with interest of seven percent paid in advance annually. I am enclosing this amount here for you. Would you deliver it to him, and get a receipt to send back to me if he agrees. As far as your thinking the amount I am asking for is outlandish or inflated, don't worry about imaginary problems. Count on it! It will be a sure thing and will be decisive for my future.

I don't think you will find any disadvantages in all that I have spelled out, neither you nor Sig. Pella. Should this, however, not be the case, as I said before, we will finish up the business as if nothing had been requested. In that case though I should like Sig. Pella to return to you or me the letter which I am sending to him here enclosed.

So then I am waiting for your answer in this regard, as well as that of Sig. Pella, whom I thank so much for the confidence he has shown in me.

Tomorrow I'll write Corinna. I think she will send you some postcards the way we did when I too was in Buenos Aires. In her last letter, with which she forwarded your letter to me, she complained a lot about my absence, and she wants me to send for her at once.

When you write to Abele, tell him that I am not writing to him anymore, at least not until I have received an answer or at least a postcard in return for all the letters and cards I have sent him. If he had listened to me, it would certainly have been much better. At least I think so.

Your always dearer son
Oreste (today a contractor
on my own)

As usual I am enclosing a check for 200 lire with this letter. *N.B. Don't say a word to anyone about what I mention here.*

Letter 51

Valdengo, 8 October 1910

Dearest son Oreste,

Thanks so very much for the money order.

This morning my friend Carlo Pella came here; I was at Cossato yesterday to see him, but I didn't find him. He accepted your proposal completely. He is very satisfied with the interest that you have paid him. He will write you today or tomorrow.

As to the capital we agreed that should he need anything before the due date, he would come to me and we would reach an agreement. In the meantime you are free to make use of the entire sum. We are keeping all of this absolutely secret. On Monday we are going to Biella together to cash each of our checks. I am returning to you the receipt for the interest that Pella has signed. I signed the promissory note that you left for him; there's no problem.

For us it is a pleasure that you are launched on an enterprise that we hope will bring you good fortune. We shall leave nothing undone so that you can be successful.

If it won't be convenient for you to send us money so often, please consider your own interests, and we will try to do without until you can send it without difficulty.

On Thursday from Biella we sent a postcard to you and another to Corinna. You will be getting them soon.

As far as Corinna's staying in Buenos Aires until you can find comfortable living arrangements, until you can have her come stay with you, if you and she would like, it would be our great pleasure and joy for her to come stay with us.

A few days ago we got a letter from Abele in which he says he got a letter from you: "Oreste has written, but he still doesn't answer my question about his coming home. I keep insisting [about this]."

Since it seems that he is not especially satisfied now, because they aren't giving him a raise in his salary (150 lire a month), and he is free from conscription, in accordance with our wish to see the two of you together next year at home, he would like to come join you.[1] This is the reason he says he keeps insisting on his question.

It's a mystery to us: He says he writes you and you don't get it, and vice versa. Perhaps someone is intercepting the letters? We can't understand what's going on.

In any case, since we see you have turned to a friend to have him help you in your project, could you perhaps profit nicely from Abele's help? Or could you get him some employment, even in Buenos Aires, that pays fairly well? We would write him to come home and then leave for over there. We beg you to write us at once how you feel about this.

Dearest son, wishing you the most fortunate advancement and the very best health, we send you our kisses with love.

Your loving parents

1. *The parents are hoping that Oreste will come home and bring Abele back with him. They want the brothers at home in 1911 and then Abele can go to Argentina.*

Letter 52

Estación Altor del Chipion, 28 October 1910

Dearest parents,

You won't find the place I'm writing this from on any map of Argentina; I am the first one to construct a home in this place. Eleven days ago I began the station; it's 114 kilometers from Santa Fe. I am in the middle of the pampas; the nearest town (if you can call it a town) is forty-seven kilometers from where I am.

The work is going on at full speed; I already have more than 100 workers spread about in the construction of roadbeds and stations. They are all working happily, and with their wages they save a good deal. I have here a team of nine Biellesi; they came from Buenos Aires summoned by me. They all work together with others from various countries. It's completely cosmopolitan here, and they all get along well with each other.

Working at this pace I think that I shall have completely finished everything within two years, and then life will be easier since the work that is being done is bringing a good return, noting that the masons working here earn no less than twenty lire a day and their expenses are very small in proportion [to their earnings].

This week the director-in-chief of engineering of the State Railways came to inaugurate the line. We made the trip together, in a special train and in the company of the director of the Laguna Paiva–Dean Funes line. He [the director-in-chief] appeared to be happy with the works I constructed, and he congratulated the director [of the line], who passed it on to me. This was quite a comfort to me. It will, however, be an even greater pleasure when I begin to collect part of the sum for the project, which is already building up to a size-able sum. But this won't be until near Christmas.

In November I think Corinna will be able to come join me since two rail-way cars will be granted to me, whereas now one has to live in tents. Corinna waits for nothing but the day that I go to get her or that I send for her to come. She even writes me that if I delay, one fine day I'll see her show up here. We love each other so much.

I don't know what feelings you will have had about the letter where I asked Sig. Carlos [sic] Pella if I might borrow the sum he had entrusted me to col-lect. Don't be alarmed; I turned to him because I had observed the confidence which he had shown in me, and he will be sure to get back the sum loaned to me along with the interest before the agreed-upon time. I am sure Sig. Pella will have raised no objections in this regard, but if he should perhaps be against the plan I have worked out, I shall return his credit at once.

I am sending you, or better to say that Corinna will be sending you, a letter of mine with 200 lire. I was unable to send it last month because I was too far away, where there are neither towns nor means to send on registered corre-spondence since we don't have money here and it is necessary to go to Santa Fe for what is necessary. Indeed I am sending this money on to you from Buenos Aires by means of Corinna so as not to reduce too much my deposit here in Santa Fe.

Would you give my warmest greetings to Sig. Carlo Pella; I owe him a lot of gratitude, and I shall know how to be thankful to him. I am also waiting for a response from him on this question.

Your beloved son,
Oreste

Letter 53

Valdengo, 30 November 1910

Dearest son, Oreste, and Corinna,

We were anxiously waiting for news of you from the wilderness where you are now, but we did not expect the money order for 200 lire this time since you had many obligations, as you had said in another letter. If you have need of it to carry out your enterprise, please stop sending us money for a while; we certainly won't hold it against you.

It gives us the greatest pleasure to hear that you are doing well and making a good impression on the authorities over there, and that all your workers are happy and industrious.

As I told you in my last letter, if it should be inconvenient for Corinna out there, it would be a great pleasure if she would come stay with us, at least until [you have] a bit more convenient place to stay.

We beg you to send us often news of yourself and of Corinna because it always makes us feel better. And we are afraid that something bad may happen to you out in that wild place where you are.

Abele is now at Cagliari, working for the same firm.

With our best wishes for good holidays, and a good end of 1910 and a good beginning of 1911.

Your loving parents,
Bye

Letter 54

Santa Fe, 20 January 1911

Dearest parents,

Please excuse the long time that you haven't heard from me and that I don't carry out what I promise. The lack of time and the enormous distance to get to a post office often prevent me from carrying out that which is most sacred.

I imagine, and I hope, that you both are in excellent health, like me and Corinna. Since Christmas day she has been out here with me, and she is happy to be at my side. I made a quick trip to Buenos Aires to get her, and so we have now left that residence for good.

When you meet Sig. Pella greet him warmly for me. I would like to write him, but I don't have his address with me since I came here just for some purchases. Before the year is out I shall settle the business with him.

The project is still going well; indeed it looks as if now there will be greater momentum, and so much the better.

I am enclosing a check for 500 lire to make up for the time I missed.

Your always more loving son,
Oreste

I am stopping here because Corinna too wants to add in her own hand her sentiment of regard for you.

N.B. I still haven't heard from Abele.

Letter 55

[Enclosed with 54]

Dear Mom and Dad,

I am happy to be back with my beloved Oreste again. He came to get me a few days before Christmas. I am fine here as to health, but life is full of sacrifices since there are no conveniences. We live in a railway car that Oreste had them fix up as living quarters. Every time he has to go some distance to check on work in progress, it gets coupled to the train and we're off. So you see it's a nomadic life just like the gypsies. There is nothing here; you don't see anything but animals of all types and birds in great numbers.

What I find strange is how come there are no cows nor milk and the countryside is dry because it hasn't rained in a long time. There are dead animals everywhere because the water of the rivers is salty and there is no grass in the fields; it's like being in the desert. The only human beings you see are the men who work for Oreste. You can't believe how it is unless you see it. But it doesn't matter to me at all, and I am happy to be with him even in this desert, which looks like a sea made of earth, because I love him so much. Dear Mom, I am enclosing a photograph of me taken before I left. [Now] we expect a nice one of you two.

> Your daughter-in-law,
> Corinna

Letter 56

> Valdengo, 10 February 1911

Dearest son, Oreste, and Corinna,
    A few days ago we learned from the Pella family, since Ermanno Guala had been to visit them, that Corinna has come to stay with you and that you had gone to get her over the Christmas holidays.

We also know that Armando Pella has taken over your house in Buenos Aires.

We are very happy that Corinna is with you. As we had said, it would have been a pleasure for us if she had come home here with us rather than to stay alone in Buenos Aires.

We hope that you are in excellent health as we are and that your affairs are going well.

We have recently heard from Abele. He's fine; he is in Cagliari, as I told you in my last letter. We are waiting for a letter of yours about his situation.

We have to give you some bad news. On the 5th of this month Corinna's father died. We were unable to go for the burial because we found out about it too late.

The entire Stellino family has left for Buenos Aires.

> Your loving parents

It's cold here—6 below zero [centigrade]. We are keeping cool!
> Bye

Letter 57

Valdengo, 15 February 1911

Dearest son, Oreste, and Corinna,

We received your very welcome letter today; we were so anxious to get it, to know if you really were together.

We don't know how to thank you for the 500 lire you so generously sent us. Given the conditions of Oreste's job, we did not expect your generosity at this time.

On the 10th of the month when we wrote you we did not know whether Corinna had come out there to join you, Oreste, since we had suggested—as in previous letters—that she come home here if it didn't suit her to join you out there. Now that we know she is with you, we are very, very happy that you love each other so much.

We are very pleased to see the picture of Corinna in the bloom of life and prosperity. We will send you ours as soon as it is ready.

We are exceedingly pleased to hear that your project is going well. We hope that it continues that way always.

We are amazed to hear that Abele still has not written. We will spur him on.

We wish you continued mutual affection; it gives us the greatest joy. The greatest joy will be when we embrace you both here with us.

Your loving parents

Letter 58

Valdengo, 7 March 1911

Dearest children, Oreste and Corinna,

As you will have learned from my registered letter sent from Cagliari, I went to see Abele last week. This was to make sure for myself that Abele really had written you. He said that he had written you many times but that you gave him no answer on the subject.

It was a great pleasure to learn that he is well liked and highly esteemed by his employers. The duties entrusted to him bear witness to his ability and honesty. It's just that his salary is not at the level he deserves. He hopes that it will be improved.

He wants to come home sometime this summer, and then he would like to go join you if you could get him a job that is better and has a future. In previous letters I had already indicated to you such a plan. I hope you won't leave him without an answer.

I saw Corinna's brother Giovanni, who told me you two had sent 100 lire to her father, but he had already died when it got there. So they are waiting for other instructions on what Corinna would like done with the sum. I told them that the heirs on the spot could collect the money on presentation of the father's death certificate. In any case they are waiting for Corinna's decision. They are also [waiting to hear from her] in order to divide the inheritance left by her father. Corinna can do this with the power of attorney.

I also regret that the poor man, Matteo, did not experience the pleasure of being comforted by his far-distant daughter.

We are fine and hope the same for you off in that desert. We beg you to neglect nothing in taking care of your health because it is too precious.

Your loving parents

Letter 59

Santa Fe, 24 April 1911

Dearest parents,

I was very pleased to learn of the visit you made to Abele.

Our life here is always the same. We travel at least four days a week. Corinna gets a bit bored, but she is always content and cheerful. We are spending our days together in happiness.

I am enclosing in this letter a check for 500 lire. I can't be more punctual because of the great distance which separates me from Santa Fe.

Corinna felt the loss of her father deeply; by now she has gotten over it completely.

I have written Abele this very day in response to your letter from Cagliari.

Your children,
Oreste (and Corinna)

Letter 60

Laguna Paiva, 5 July 1911

Dearest parents,

I am sending back to you, dear father, the enclosure here because I can't find the address of Sig. Pella. A check for 203 pesos is enclosed, the amount of the interest in advance for the 2,900 loaned to me. I would like to return it all, but because of the administration's constant delay in paying its vouchers, I plan to hold on to it still. But in case Sig. Pella should have need of it or wish to collect it, let me know, and by return mail I'll carry out his wish.

The project here is going splendidly. I am enclosing two photographs taken by our section engineer in our railway car, our mobile home. Later I'll send you one of his of Corinna at her work.

Photograph 3.   Oreste and Corinna, 1911, in front of the kitchen of the camp at Laguna Paiva, where Oreste was building a railroad line.

Because of the spread-out nature of the project I have had to purchase an automobile. It is not, however, a luxury; it can carry ten persons and is extremely convenient for me. Every day I cover 100 to 150 kilometers. Since it is still cold, Corinna always prefers to stay at home, and I always travel alone or with the chauffeur. He's Swiss, not yet thirty years old, and he speaks seven languages to perfection. He is a fine companion and extremely useful, considering the different nationalities of the workmen.

I am enclosing two photographs: one with the engineer's automobile and the other at a party celebrating the completion of a bridge—it's in front of the camp kitchen.

Thank Sig. Pella warmly and say hello to him for me. As soon as I have finished the bridge that I have begun, I shall send back the entire sum, unless he needs it sooner.

Your loving children,
Oreste (and Corinna)

Letter 61

Laguna Paiva, 18 November 1911

Dearest parents,

For some time now I haven't written you; it is simply for lack of time. Yesterday I sent you some postcards, and to Abele as well, from whom I have received news from home.

We have been having raging hurricanes for days: wind, rain, it looked like the end of the world. There was also some damage; yesterday the wind in its fury overturned two trains. There were no deaths. I saw one of them near Rosario with its wheels in the air, locomotive and sixteen cars. But these are things that no one takes seriously. Last week on the line where I am, another train with cars loaded with men for digging crews overturned in the same way down from an embankment of six meters. No one was even injured; they all jumped free like cats, they are so used to it. Corinna was astonished and couldn't understand why they all laughed after the event since the locomotive and its cars were almost under water. By tomorrow the same train will be out of the water completely fixed.

I am glad [to hear about] the good times together that Abele has had with Pella of Cerretto. If he comes back for Christmas, I'll go see him in Buenos Aires.

Corinna is very pleased to hear about the purchases made for her by Mom; she is waiting eagerly.

I wanted to send you sooner the check for 500 lire I am enclosing now, but it was not possible because I don't ever get to Santa Fe. Please excuse [the delay] since I have caused you some inconvenience.

In a few days I shall respond to Abele.

I was glad to hear about the family celebration on the occasion of your name day.[1] The day after tomorrow I too shall have a celebration, for my twenty-eighth birthday, out in the country. This evening my associate Cravello came to get me with our automobile so we can get to the camp tomorrow before nightfall and celebrate my birthday together. I went to Santa Fe for necessary provisions. Three cheers! We are in good spirits and we stay that way.

Your loving children,
Oreste (and Corinna)

Thanks for life. I'm twenty-eight on the 20th.

Bye

1.   *It is the custom in Italy and many other Catholic countries to celebrate the day of the saint after whom an individual is named. October 17th is the day of Saint Margherita so presumably this reference is to his mother.*

Letter 62

Laguna Paiva, 23 February 1912

My dearest Dad,

The day before yesterday I got your letter that upset me terribly as you informed me about the awful illness that afflicts dear Mom.[1] I am astonished that you never said anything to me before except to inform me of some slight indisposition, to which I really didn't pay much attention since it is a common occurrence that one is not cheerful and lively every day. Write me often about dear Mom's condition since it [her illness] makes me very unhappy.

Some days ago while I was at Rosario di Santa Fe to negotiate a new project, I made a quick trip to Buenos Aires to see Corinna. She is fine; she asked me insistently for news of you. Yesterday I sent her your letter. It won't make her happy; she loves you so much.

I think before the end of the month I shall go to Santa Fe. Then I will be able to send you something so that you can meet the expenses that will be heavy in this emergency. I don't have to tell you not to skimp on them.

If I don't settle things the way I like concerning a new project, I'll make a journey to Italy to embrace you both as soon as I've finished up the work here; it will be about four months at the most.

Give Mom a big kiss for me; comfort her. In short, do the very best you can for her so that she recovers soon.

Corinna is sure to write you from Buenos Aires because this news will make a great impression on her.

Send letters once more to Rio Bamba 253, Buenos Aires, since in a short time I shall be at home once more.[2]

I beg you to encourage dear Mama and not to afflict yourself [with too much worry]. For both I and Corinna as well want to see you healthy and happy soon. Give her a kiss for Corinna too, who loves you both just as she loves me.

Your always more loving son,
Oreste

1.   *This letter is not in the collection. Margherita was beginning to show some of the symptoms of the disease that she died from in 1919. Probably she had a bone tumor.*
2.   *He is referring to the house that he and Corinna had lived in before.*

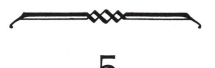

5

Abele Joins His Brother (1912–1913)

The year and a half from February 1912 to August 1913 was the period of most frequent and probably most intense communication among the family members in Valdengo and Buenos Aires. During this time, fifty-four letters, an average of three a month, plus dozens of postcards, crossed the Atlantic, far more than at any other time during the twenty-one-year correspondence. (See Table 3 in the Introduction.) Two topics in particular prompted this activity: Abele's arrival and adjustment in Buenos Aires, and Margherita's illness.

Abele's decision to join his brother created some tension within the family. Oreste was annoyed that his brother had not come several years earlier—when opportunities were better—and at first refused to help finance the trip. Luigi defended his younger son and clarified several misunderstandings. As a result, Oreste warmed up to the idea, told his brother what to bring with him (#67), and assured him that "you will be coming to your own home here" (#70). The voyage from Genoa to Buenos Aires—with stops at Barcelona, Las Palmas, and Santos—took eighteen days. Two letters written on board ship (#71 and #72) recorded Abele's feelings of closeness to his family and his observations during this trip.

Abele's adjustment was rapid and successful in large part because his brother facilitated the process. Less than a month after Abele's arrival, Oreste reported to their parents: "Abele now knows the entire city; a bit with me, a bit with Cravello, or [with both of us] together, we have made him well informed about everything. Next week perhaps we will devote ourselves to getting him a job. We are all living together as a family" (#75). Abele got a job almost immediately as an engineer with one of the major metallurgical companies in Argentina. In fact, he did well enough to start sending money home five months after he arrived in Buenos Aires. It had taken Oreste five years before he had been able to do so.

Abele's presence rejuvenated the ties with family and village. We once more hear news of Pierino Pizzoglio and the son of Sasso, friends who had been in Buenos Aires for a decade. We also learn about Cousin Riccardo in Mexico and the illustrative story of Cousin Abele's family. In one letter, for example, Abele noted: "I went, along with the son of Sasso, to visit Cousin Abele on Sunday. He and his wife are fine and send you greetings." He then explained the strain of the divided family: "He [Cousin Abele] told me quite disconsolately, that it seemed his father [Giacomo] had gone to North America, but he doesn't know any of the details. If this should be true, then Andrea [Cousin Abele's brother and Giacomo's son] would come here too" (#94).

The second major theme of the chapter is Margherita's illness. Luigi explained to his son: "It is with sorrow that I must tell you that I brought dear Mother back home last Sunday, the 11th of this month, in considerably worse condition. . . . The specialists there [Turin] treated her with electric massages and strychnine injections. The local doctor here is using the same treatment and still without any good results. . . . In the meantime she is suffering. Her arms and legs are completely paralyzed so that she cannot stand up" (#63). Luigi did everything he could to cure his wife: He took her to Turin and to the sanitarium in Andorno, where improvement came slowly. He unsuccessfully sought out a healer, which Oreste opposed.

Margherita's illness intensified her desire to see Oreste and Corinna. As Luigi wrote in April 1912: "Poor Mother, in the condition in which she is now, is afraid that she will not see you again and that she will not ever see Corinna. At the end of this month Abele will arrive to get ready to go over there. If it could just be arranged that everyone might be together once at home, it would be the greatest pleasure for us parents" (#66).

The chapter closes with Abele successfully completing his first year in Buenos Aires, but with Margherita suffering a severe reversal. In July 1913, Abele wrote home: "On the 25th of last month I completed my first year of life in Buenos Aires. . . . Summing it up, even though we don't have here our mountains and the green color, I have had a pretty good year in the dear company of Oreste and Corinna" (#97). A few weeks later Luigi told his sons that Margherita was doing much better and was walking with two canes (#99). Then on August 28, Luigi had to tell them: "Our dear Mother has suffered a new misfortune. One day as she was walking in the hallway of the sanitarium her cane slid out from under her, and she fell, hitting her knee on the floor. It caused her no small injury, so bad that she was compelled to stay in bed" (#101).

Letter 63

Valdengo, 20 February 1912

Dearest children, Oreste and Corinna,

It is with sorrow that I must tell you that I brought dear Mother back home last Sunday, the 11th of this month, in considerably worse condition. She had been at Turin for twenty days. The specialists there treated her with electric massages and strychnine injections. The local doctor here is using the same treatment and still without any good results. Everyone says that with the arrival of summer she will get well.

In the meantime she is suffering. Her arms and legs are completely paralyzed so that she cannot stand up. She must be dressed and undressed, put to bed, and gotten out of bed. We are comforted by the hope that with the arrival of the hot summer she will be able to make at least something of a comeback.

Last Sunday Corinna's brother Giovanni and his wife were here to visit us. It gave us very great pleasure. It always consoles us to hear about the excellent health of you two and your mutual affection. That is a comfort for us with these misfortunes.

We got a letter from Abele yesterday in which he says he has given up his job and that he will come home in May in order to go to Buenos Aires to join you. He has received a letter from his friend Pella, who will have told him a lot [about Argentina]. He says that he will write you at once. We hope that you can help him get a better job.

If two brothers, Giovanni and Riccardo Ramella Bagneri from Biella, should come to you with a letter of recommendation from me, see if you could hire them or get them a job as masons or masons' assistants. They have been recommended by Signora Galoppo, who thanks us both.

Here winter is not so very cold, but it's raining for long stretches [so much] that it's impeding the work in the fields.

Your loving parents

Letter 64

Valdengo, 3 March 1912

Dearest children, Oreste and Corinna,

Once again we are writing you in regard to Abele, who will also have written to you, Oreste, that he has given up his job in Cagliari in order to go over there with the hope that, between you and his friend Armando Pella, you will find employment for him.

On this point Abele says that he has not received mail from you for a long time. Nonetheless he has made up his mind to go just the same. We hope that he will be welcome.

In order to save something in the cost, I think it would be better if you were to send him the ticket. I'm not sure however.

Mom's illness is still getting worse. We are very distressed by this terrible collapse. We hope that she will get better this summer, as the doctors are saying.

It gave us great pleasure to get Corinna's postcard from Buenos Aires. You must have left her there when you went there for Christmas?

We hope that you will have received from our friend Armando Pella all the things we sent. We would like some acknowledgment.

Entrusting to you our dear Abele,
Your loving parents

Letter 65

Laguna Paiva, 29 March 1912

Dearest parents,

I got your letter today in which I am informed that Abele is coming and about the continuing indisposition of Mother, which saddens me.

I don't know whether this letter of mine will get there while Abele is still at home; I had written him some time ago. I didn't think that after several years he would need [money for] the fare. Had he come when I summoned him, he could have counted on good employment and all the best. Now Argentina is thinking about paying the debts it ran up with the centennial celebrations, and it's not the same as when they were getting ready to celebrate it. I am not sending anything for his expenses since I am unable to do so where I am and it would certainly arrive too late. But at any rate let him come; he will always be welcome, and I shall do the very best I can for him. But it will be necessary that I be informed some days in advance so that I can go meet him.

I imagine that Mother will get somewhat better and that before summer she will be well again. Try to cheer her up and keep her in good spirits.

I am writing to Corinna this very day, sending her your letter. She always waits for them with great anticipation. She is fine; she has become plump; she looks like a Mongonflier [sic].[1]

Your always more loving
children,
Oreste (and Corinna)

1.   *He is referring to the hot-air balloon that was invented by two French brothers by the name of Montgolfier.*

Letter 66

Valdengo, 7 April 1912

Dearest children, Oreste and Corinna,

Yesterday along with a letter from Abele with his photograph we received your very dear letter with the check for 500 lire, for which we thank you so very, very much.

Dear Mother is still the same and gives no sign of getting better. We are so grief-stricken that we can't put it into words. And yet we must endure it.

If it is possible, before beginning other enterprises, if you could leave someone [in charge]—perhaps Abele when he arrives—we have a great desire to see you along with Corinna at least once more before we die. Poor Mother, in the condition in which she is now, is afraid that she will not see you again and that she will not ever see Corinna.

At the end of this month Abele will arrive to get ready to go over there. If it could just be arranged that everyone might be together once at home, it would be the greatest pleasure for us parents.

In the expectation of embracing
you all,
Your loving parents

Dearest daughter-in-law Corinna,

It was a very great pleasure yesterday to get your sweet postcard along with Oreste's letter and another one from Abele. Will the beautiful baby [pictured on the postcard] now or soon be our little grandson? We hope for him and long for him.

Take our special kisses with our greatest affection.

Your parents-in-law

Letter 67

Santa Fe, 19 April 1912

My beloved parents and dear brother,

I was unable before now to arrange to send you the 1,500 lire I am enclosing for you; it was impossible because I was too far from the banks and adequate post offices.

I hope Abele has a very good voyage; I shall be there to great him in Buenos Aires if I know what ship he will be on. I would be happy if he would bring me a good camera of the standard size—he can pick it out himself.

It would be a good idea if he brought along as much as he could by way of ready-made clothing, well tailored, with the material of top quality. He should also bring some good samples of drawings he has made along with the relevant certificates. If in some way he could get a recommendation from the minister back home for his counterpart over here, an immediate opening for the future would be a sure thing.

I had back home three volumes dealing with railroads; would he bring them to me?

I've got to stop now since I must leave for Rosario in a little while, and I'm going to miss the train.

I imagine that Mom will be getting better. Give her a kiss both of you for me and encourage her. Corinna tells me she has sent you postcards. I'm going to see her at the end of the month.

Your always more affectionate
son and brother,
Oreste

Letter 68

Valdengo, 27 April 1912

Dearest children, Oreste and Corinna,

I want to respond at once to your letter that came today and put to rights a mix-up that I noted in your letter.

I refer to my suggestion—and only mine—that you might send Abele the ticket for the journey [in order] to save something if it was possible. Abele does not know anything of this. I am the one who saw fit to say it but only on the condition that the money you laid out would be repaid to you. I hope then that you won't be offended with us and certainly not with Abele for such a suggestion on my part.

As for [his] having come when you summoned him, there were misunderstandings all around. And I also was the one whose fond hope it was that he wait until he had passed the draft age. Even now I would be happy if at least one [of you] were not too far away because our lives will not last very much longer with these misfortunes. But to allow the opportunity for a better life for Abele, I'll give up this wish too.

And from Abele we got a letter this very day in which he says he will be home on the 5th of May.

Dear Mother is still the same. She suffers a bit less from the pain, but she needs sedatives (Pantapon) to get some sleep at night. I have made a kind of wheelchair, adapted also for her bodily needs. When the weather is nice, I dress her, not without difficulty, and I take her out in the sun for a few hours.

We are still putting our hopes on the heat of summer; it's taking a damn long time in getting here. If it were not for your kind help, I don't know how we would manage.

We'll see each other—when?

Your loving parents

Letter 69

Valdengo, 15 May 1912

Dearest children Oreste and Corinna,

Abele and I are fine; dear Mom is still in bad shape.

A thousand thanks for the 1,500 lire you sent us, very useful in meeting Abele's expenses. As you will have learned from me and from him, he will be leaving the beginning of June. He will also bring you the camera you wanted.

As for the recommendation of the ministry here for the one over there, it will be very hard since the Italian government doesn't even issue passports for Argentina. Nonetheless I am writing at once to Rondani, begging him to do everything he can to get it for me.[1]

As to his departure Abele will write you on this sheet of paper.

Your loving parents

We received the beautiful postcards from Corinna; we are always delighted with them.

1.   *Dino Rondani, a good friend of Luigi's, was the Socialist deputy from Biella to the Italian Parliament.*

Letter 70

Buenos Aires, 6 June 1912

Dearest brother,

I received your letter from home yesterday; I don't know whether this letter will arrive while you are still there.

I have now all at once understood the motive of your letters and those of Dad. I never answered to the point because it was not possible for me. Upon arrival of this letter I think Dad will be able to hand over to you the amount you will need to come here. Rest assured that you will be coming to your own home here, everything and everybody will be at your disposal. So then welcome and may fortune smile upon you.

So then I am waiting for you anxiously; have no fears about your well-being, and I don't think you will have anything to complain about. Corinna also is waiting to embrace you.

I have finished the project I took on and am now on the point of negotiating another one. If I don't get what I want, I shall work for someone else for a while. In any case a livelihood is assured.

Before leaving, kiss dear Mom and Dad for me and Corinna. We would love to be able to be together with them one day.

If you find any books dealing with harbor construction which might have details and exact explanations of pilings and of engineering projects, buy them and bring them to me. I am enclosing 200 lire for this purpose.

Best wishes for a good journey and a speedy reunion.

Your brother Oreste, and
sister-in-law, Corinna

Don't forget to bring a good camera, a portable Kodak with all the accessories for trips into the country.

If you find them, also bring along some monographs on underwater construction using compressed air. I think, in connection with the new bridge built over the Po near Pavia, engineering periodicals must have published some details. So long.

Letter 71

On board ship, 11 June 1912[1]

Dearest parents,

I am fine. We will arrive this evening at Las Palmas about seven or eight o'clock. The day before yesterday, at night, we passed through the Straits of Gibraltar. But since it was at night, in the morning we found ourselves out in the Atlantic. Because of the current between the Mediterranean and the Atlantic the sea is a bit rough so that many, especially the women, have been somewhat seasick.

I am writing you this from the deck aft. The ship is full, especially here in second class, where there are more than 100 people from the operetta company Caramba Scaramiglio, which is going to Buenos Aires. That's the reason we are pretty badly off for sleeping arrangements since we are of necessity compelled to sleep in full cabins.

I, and like me so many others, have been taken for a ride since, for the money we paid, we had the right to a better cabin. Never mind, the next time we will get better conditions, now that I understand the way to make the request for berths.

As to the food it's pretty good. There are five or six of us; we enjoy each other's company, and we are in good spirits.

We will be on the direct course for Santos in the middle of the ocean. Let's hope that the sea stays calm. And dear Mother? Is she going there now or is she already at Andorno?² Is she better? Write at once. And you dear Dad? Be patient a bit longer.

I have paid a 50-lire supplement for a separate table, better than that which is normal for emigrants.

From midocean I send you most affectionate kisses.

Abele

1.   *Letters 71 and 72 were added to as the journey progressed over the eighteen or so days between Genoa and Buenos Aires. As a result some of the references to time and place are inconsistent.*
2.   *Andorno, a town near Biella, was at that time famous for its thermal baths and cures.*

Letter 72

On board ship, 21 June 1912

Dearest parents,

I am still doing pretty well, just bored by the long journey and the desire to see at least a bit of land.

We left Las Palmas early on the morning of the 11th, Tuesday, at dawn, and the rising sun enabled us to enjoy a wonderful view of that beautiful city stretched out like an amphitheater for several kilometers in length.

And it really is a beautiful city. Beautiful electric trams and beautiful hotels. The city is a port for refueling since it is the last city of any importance before setting out into midocean. The stop was a real pleasure for us, even though we had just left Barcelona on Saturday the 8th. To put your feet on the ground and to leave, even for a moment, the bustle and the constant irritating motion of the ship is always a big relief. So, as of the 12th the crossing has really begun; we are in midocean, just sky and sea. On board ship here you shouldn't do anything but eat and sleep. You absolutely cannot think; thoughts crowd around and then scatter away in an astonishing manner.

By good luck we have had decent weather except for a few days, like yesterday, when there was a rolling sea and strong wind. Many, especially the women, were seasick, and the dinner tables were almost empty. I have managed to keep a pretty good appetite, and I was not seasick, except for a bit of nausea and a lot of boredom. The meals are very abundant, except that the cooking is really bad, and the reason for this is just that plague of an operetta company. If it weren't for them, we would be much better off.

Six or seven of us Piedmontesi have gotten together and make up a club, called the "Gang," united as brothers and always in good health. I am its secretary; the president is a fine gentleman who has been living in Cordova for more than twenty years.

Today, if all goes well, we will arrive in Santos. As of this morning we can see land; that is a great comfort. We will arrive perhaps around ten in the evening and naturally we will not be able to get off until tomorrow morning, the 22nd.

We have seen some other ships pass by, some quite close and others at a distance. The day before yesterday the *Savoia* also passed by with that radio-operator friend of mine on board. He telegraphed greetings to me, and I returned the favor with great pleasure. To receive a telegram on the high seas was for me a new enjoyment, and it left me with a very pleasant feeling.

We will leave Santos, I think, by tomorrow, and so I hope that I can finally get to Buenos Aires Monday evening the 24th, and perhaps I won't be able to disembark until Monday morning [he means Tuesday].

The passage over the Equator, the so-called Line, was celebrated with a party on board ship according to the usual custom. A few nasty storms also cheered us up.

In view of the heat, especially below in the rooms and cabins, I think a complete change of clothing once a day would not be too much.

All things considered, on board ship you can only live a material life. For the life of the spirit there is nothing but a kind of drowsiness, a journey like that which our body is now making.

So do not be surprised if I have to say that I have almost been unable to think of you two the way I should, of dear Mom, who I hope has begun her new treatment with expectation of a good outcome.

Nor have I had the strength and opportunity to reflect on what it will be like for me finally to embrace dear Oreste and Corinna and to bestow all those kisses and greetings of which I am the bearer.

I think only that the hour is near, and I feel a real sense of joy. One thing though I have been able to establish in confirmation of my feeling before departure; i.e., that the earth is tiny and that America is not so very far away! In the middle of the ocean as I observed the beautiful austral celestial hemisphere, the earth seemed no larger to me than Valdengo! It seems an anomaly, but it is true.

I am stopping now because the shaking of the ship is tiring and it makes me nervous, in addition to the nuisance of the passengers who are chattering all around me.

I earnestly hope that you will have great courage and confidence, which by reflection will encourage me too.

Write at once giving me all the news.

Abele

Letter 73

Valdengo, 17 June 1912[1]

Dearest children Oreste, Corinna, and Abele,

[We hope that] Abele will have arrived now after a good journey.

Today we began Mom's electrical therapy at the Andorno sanitarium, and we hope it will be successful. We left home by carriage at 1 P.M. and got there at 3 P.M. After about a half hour we left again and got home at 5.

We will have to go every other day until they see a clear improvement. Dear Mom suffers terribly from such powerful electric shocks, but she endures it stoically in her firm hope of getting well. . . .

We hope that Abele is well employed and does himself proud the way he did in Sardinia, and that you will enjoy the best fraternal harmony. Even if for reasons of employment you cannot live together, [we hope that] you will visit each other often.

Your loving parents

1. *From 17 June 1912 through 28 August 1913 there are nineteen letters from Luigi that deal with one overriding concern, Margherita's illness and her slow and partial recovery. There are, however, many details, some of casual or topical interest, and others that reflect interesting features of emigration and dislocation. As examples of each we mention: the search for a cure from any quarter; the conclusion of the Pella affair; Margherita's upper-class companions at the sanitarium; books for Oreste and Abele's Touring Club pamphlets; the death of cousin Teresa; and the construction of the Novara-Biella railway. In order to preserve the flow of the letters and to avoid wearying the reader with too much repetition, we have omitted some letters and included only excerpts from others.*

Letter 74

Valdengo, 15 July 1912

Dearest children Oreste, Abele, and Corinna,

It is a great pleasure to inform you that Mom's therapy at Andorno is continuing to make her improve. The improvement is very slow, but considering her condition at the time of Abele's departure, it is noticeably improved. Professor Vinai promises that within a month she will be walking by herself. . . .

I am sending along with this letter a roll containing a monograph in French on port construction and some plates illustrating the construction of the port of Marseilles. Sig. Secondino Rey of Vigliano, the councilman of Biella, was so kind as to give them to me. The series of plates is incomplete because these are the only ones he has. He doesn't have the rest anymore. It would be a good idea if you send him a letter of thanks for his kindness. Abele knows him.

Monographs of this type are not to be found at Biella. I have written to Turin, and if I shall find others, I'll buy them and send them to you at once. . . .

Your loving parents

Letter 75

Buenos Aires, 19 July 1912

Dearest parents,

We hope that with the new therapy dear Mother is making a rapid recovery and will be as strong as she was before, always in good spirits.

The reports Abele gave us about you and everybody were an immense pleasure. We recalled dear Biella, Valdengo, and the valleys. We talked and laughed about everything, happy in our recollections.

Abele now knows the entire city; a bit with me, a bit with Cravello, or [with both of us] together, we have made him well informed about everything. Next week perhaps we will devote ourselves to getting him a job.

We are all living together as a family. Corinna is very happy with Abele, and we like to joke [together].

I hope by the end of the month to send Pella the entire amount since I shall settle everything by this date more or less.

In the meantime I am enclosing a thousand lire. Should something more in any way be necessary for you because of Mom's illness, let me know at once.

Corinna is always waiting for news about Mom's recovery, and she is anxious to know the result of her new treatment.

In a little while we shall send you some photographs taken with the camera that Abele brought me, which came out splendidly.

Your children,
Oreste, (Abele, and
Corinna)

Give Mom a kiss and a hug to comfort her.

Bye.

Letter 76

Valdengo, 30 July 1912

Dearest children, Oreste, Abele, and Corinna,

We understand that Oreste has finished the project at Laguna Paiva. If he does not have other obligations, we long to see him, along with dear Corinna, just once again at least. Such an event would be a great consolation for us, and you can be sure Mom's health would profit from it.

We hope that Abele is suitably employed and that by undertaking new projects you will be able to be together.

Your distressed parents

We are still writing to you all at Oreste's address until we find out that Abele—in case he is—is far away [from you].

Letter 77

Valdengo, 18 August 1912

Dearest children Oreste, Abele, and Corinna,

. . . . Words are not enough to thank you for your continuous and generous assistance. We are infinitely grateful to you, dear Oreste, for the money order of 1,000 lire which you sent us and for the purpose you intended it for.

Dear Mother is getting better very slowly. She is beginning to walk, holding on to me and at a very slow pace. We hope that before the end of September she can at least walk by herself. . . .

Dearest Oreste, concerning the business with Carlo Pella, your idea is excellent since a few days before I got your letter he had indicated to me that he would like to collect the principal [on the loan].

Your loving parents and parents-
in-law

Letter 78

Buenos Aires, 12 September 1912

Dearest parents,

Since we are now all far away, and especially with dear Mother's illness, we do nothing but ask every day if something has come, meaning of course "something from home" since that is what most interests us. We always know exactly the steamers that are leaving and especially those that are arriving, hopeful that in each there may be "something."

So keep writing often, all the more now that there are three of us waiting— and we need at least one extra portion!

The news that dear Mom is beginning to get better, even though slowly, has greatly consoled us; we are happy that our most ardent wishes are beginning to be satisfied. Keep up your courage, and you too dear Dad, courage! Don't be worried, keep up your strength. We are always with you.

Since Monday the 2nd, Oreste has been back at Laguna Paiva on business, but we expect him from day to day. He got—I don't think you have been told yet—the roll with the book and the plates on port construction; it came two ships after your letter of that time.

Corinna is very pleased at the special attention you have shown her and returns it always from the bottom of her heart. For several days she has not been feeling well, perhaps [because] the weather here, too, keeps changing; but soon she will again be recovered and in good spirits.

I am here!

For a month now I have had a job with a good Argentine company, and I hope it will go well.[1]

The day before yesterday our friend Pierino Pizzoglio left with the *Principe di Udine* for over there. I went to say goodbye just before he left, and he will bring so very many of our greetings to you. Greet him for us.

Sometimes we meet up with Armando Pella, Sasso from Valdengo, and Cousin Abele, etc. They are all fine.

Your loving children,
Abele, (Oreste, and
Corinna)

1.   *Abele got a job as an engineer with Cantabrica, one of the leading metallurgical companies in Buenos Aires.*

Letter 79

Buenos Aires, 30 September 1912.

Dearest parents,

Mom's improvement has consoled us immensely, and by the time this arrives we are hoping for a complete recovery.

Abele answered your previous letter since I was traveling, as you will have been able to understand from the postcard I sent you from Córdoba.

We here are always together, and we are excellent company for each other. In the evening we always think of you with pleasure.

I am including in this letter a check for 2,950 pesos (its equivalent in Italian lire) with an accompanying letter and a receipt that you will deliver to Sig. Carlo Pella of Cossato, to be returned to me when signed. The above-mentioned amount corresponds to the principal of 2,900 pesos plus 50 pesos for three months deferred interest. I think that everything will be in conformity with Sig. Pella's expectations, and for my part I should like to thank him. I have not sent it to him directly because I don't have his Cossato address.

I am also including 1,000 lire for you; you will surely need it for Mom's therapy.

Your children,
Oreste, (Abele, and
Corinna)

Letter 80

Valdengo, 20 October 1912

Dearest Corinna, Oreste, and Abele

We are addressing this letter to you, Corinna, with the desire that you will be completely cured of the indisposition which we heard about in Abele's letter.

Our thoughts turn to you all. And when we hear of some indisposition, it grieves us a lot. If your indisposition should require the air of home, it would be our fondest desire for you to come home a while with us. We think that Oreste would also be quite pleased with this.

The excellent health that always stays with Oreste and Abele makes us extremely happy.

Dear Mom is beginning to walk very, very slowly, holding on to me or the table or the walls of the house. It's not much, but we content ourselves with the hope that she continue to improve. So that she can manage walking better I have ordered a pair of crutches from the "king." We are waiting for him to bring them.

No one of those mentioned by Oreste has been to visit us. We know from others that they have arrived.

We have received postcards with the kind thoughts of Oreste from Córdoba dated 19 September. That makes us feel better, that always and everywhere you think of us.

We have finished the corn and grape harvest, not abundant but satisfactory. Tell Abele that I have used last year's stakes.

On the vigil of All Saints' Day we will take a carriage to visit the graves of dear Narcisa and of Grandmother.

Your loving parents

Letter 81

Valdengo, 2 November 1912

Dearest son Oreste,

We address this letter to you especially because of the business with my friend Carlo Pella and to show you our infinite gratitude for your extraordinary generosity to us.

My friend Pella has been very happy with your behavior in his concerns, and he thanks you from the bottom of his heart. I am enclosing with this letter the receipt for settling the deal and the promissory note from you guaranteed by me.

Dear Mom is getting better very slowly. She walks a bit holding on to me or to the walls of the house but only when there are some chairs or something else on the other side. I still have to get her up and down the stairs, to dress her and undress her, and every night give her an injection of Pantopon so she can rest at night. Her morale is not always very high, but my encouragement makes her feel better. In spite of the season, which is inclined to be cold, we hope that she will continue to do well.

On Thursday 31 October we took a carriage to the Biella cemetery. Dear Mom was able to walk arm-in-arm with me and another friend from the entrance gate to the grave of our dear Narcisa (about thirty meters along the portico on the left as you go in). She could not go as far as Grandmother's grave, which is on the right.

This pious pilgrimage was a pleasure; it seemed to be a relief for our undying grief.

On our way home we had the pleasure of seeing your friend Pierino Pizzoglio at Vigliano. He quickly gave us excellent news about you all. He promised to come visit us here, and we are eagerly expecting him. We are always expecting you and dear Corinna.

We are very happy that Abele has a good job, so that he can demonstrate his quick intelligence.

And Corinna. Is she recovered? Should she need the air of home to recover fully, why doesn't she come to stay with us at least for a while? It would be no trouble; let us know what you think.

Your loving parents

Letter 82

Buenos Aires, 14 November 1912

Dearest parents,

Even though dear Mom has not recovered as we all were hoping and all the pains that she has been suffering for so long are still with her, nonetheless even her slow improvement has inspired us with greater optimism, and we recommend urgently that you do everything so that it will continue. And you too, dearest Father, keep all your patience and together give yourselves courage without any anxiety. Just try to be as cheerful as possible since even though we here are far away, we feel so close, so attached to you that we cannot help but feel with you all of your moods.

We are all fine except that we are beginning to feel the heat here. If only we could, we would be so happy to send it to Mom. We are certain it would be a great benefit for everybody!

We are also deeply grateful that, in spite of everything, on that day consecrated to the dear ones who are no longer with us you were determined not to fail to scatter over them those flowers which express all our grief and at the same time our affection and undying memories. We over here also remembered them.

I am employed and hope to continue to do well; at the end of the month I shall write again, and I too plan on being able to help a bit.

In regard to helping, if Mom needs crutches in order to manage better and to begin to stand up, I think it would be much better to turn to an orthopedist for a suitable device that would be much lighter and less tiring than anything the "king" will be able to supply.

Many greetings from your friends over here and say hello for us to those over there.

> Your loving children,
> Abele, (Oreste, and
> Corinna)

Letter 83

> Buenos Aires, 28 November 1912

Beloved parents,

On the 20th of this month as my birthday came around again we had a small informal party. Corinna gave me a beautiful branch of flowers in bloom and Abele a magnificent silver flower vase of exquisite taste, filled with natural flowers wonderfully arranged in a bouquet.

At midday we ate in town; then Corinna and I went to the Tigre islands, where we took a ride in a boat, on the train, in a car, and in a carriage, in short by every possible manner of travel except by air. In the evening we dined together, and at a rather late hour we came back home happily.

Abele is employed and is happy. Corinna is always cheerful and happy, and we spend the time together contentedly.

On my name day I sent you a postcard.

We are always hoping for an improvement for Mother.

I hope Sig. Carlo Pella of Cossato will have been satisfied, also with the interest for the time elapsed.

> Your dear children,
> Oreste, (Abele, and
> Corinna)

Letter 84

> Valdengo, 2 December 1912

Dearest children, Oreste, Abele, and Corinna,

Last week I was at Rivolbella, a township of Losano in the province of Pavia, to get in touch with a healer who is said to be famous, but I was not so lucky as to find him at home. I wrote asking him to come, but up to now I have not had the good fortune to see him. Since it is impossible for Mother to make such a tiring journey in this rigorous season, we have for now given up the hope of seeing him come. . . .

Your loving parents

P.S. Cousin Carmelina has come to stay with us, so when I have to leave the house, she will keep dear Mom company. This is a great relief for me.

Letter 85

Buenos Aires, 2 December 1912

Dearest Mother and Father,

   We are adding for you two photographs taken here with the camera that Abele brought along, to good purpose, since I think they make better mementos and good wishes. I am also including a check for 500 lire so that you can celebrate properly the end of this year and the beginning of the next. In this next year we confidently hope for the complete recovery of dear Mother.

   I have received your letter dated 2 November, in which Father tells me that Sig. Pella is satisfied with the remittance of his credit which I sent him. When you meet him, say hello to him for me.

   We here are enjoying the best health. I especially; I have had *seven* teeth fixed—they had wanted to give up on me—before I gave up eating forever. Now I give free reign to my appetite that never was lacking, and it's going beautifully.

   Corinna is always cheerful, and in the evening after dinner we all three enjoy very much our jokes together.

   You too stay cheerful and healthy.

Your always more loving
children,
Oreste, (Abele, and
Corinna)

Merry Christmas, a good end [of the year], and a better beginning of the year.

Letter 86

Buenos Aires, 2 December 1912

Dearest parents,

   We always remember you fondly, waiting to hear dear news of you, always hoping to get news concerning Mother that is much better. We constantly talk about you, and it is a pleasure, it consoles us, to recall anecdotes, phrases, mannerisms, your advice; and when we remember all your toil and your sacrifices, we feel proud that we were intelligently brought up. Your kindness makes us happy as if we could still feel your caresses; and we see the enormous distance that separates us reduced to nothing, and it almost seems possible for us to stretch out our arms and embrace you. And the tenderness of these sentiments is entirely your inspiration. And when a family is in such harmonious agreement, it has a right to feel proud and satisfied.

Now that the day [Christmas] specially chosen for sweet family intimacy is drawing near, we send you our infinite good wishes; do not be upset if you are alone on that day; as always we are affectionately united with all our hearts.

And so that this feeling may be more vivid, we are sending you separately two photographs taken for this purpose yesterday, on Sunday, at the beach of Sant'Isidoro [San Isidro], near Buenos Aires. From these very pictures you will be able to observe our continuous progress in the art of photography. Corinna is part of it too since she took the picture of the two of us. Another time we will send you others since it wasn't possible for us to develop them because the boat is leaving tomorrow.

It is an infinite pleasure that I too can begin to help you, and I enclose in this letter a check for 500 lire.

We hope that dear Mother will be able to endure the severity of the season better and that her improvement continues.

Say hello to everyone.

Your children Abele, (Oreste,
and Corinna)

Have a good holiday! Bye

Letter 87

Buenos Aires, 3 January 1913

Dearest parents,

It would be better to take dear Mother to some well-known specialist and not to a healer. In any case we are always hoping for some improvement.

We have spent the Christmas holidays and New Year's all three of us happily together, contented and thinking fondly of you. We hope that if this year goes well, we can go for a ride all the way home.

In case Mother's therapy should require greater expenses, do not be afraid to let us know. We will be able to send more, all the more so since Abele is happy with the job he now holds and he too will be able to contribute and he does so with all his heart.

I am enclosing for you in this letter 500 lire, which you will surely need.

Have you heard nothing from Pierino Pizzoglio? Has he visited you since the day you met him? I saw his travel companion yesterday. We had a good laugh together.

I saw in the newspapers here that work was beginning on the rail line from Biella to Novara. I remember you told me, Father, that it was going through the field near the garden. What I can't figure out is where it will go to enter Biella.

When I come back home, I'll find so many changes that I'll think I'm in America, and I'll have to run away at once, for thinking that I'm in a foreign country.

Corinna is always cheerful, and she is working at making the *pappa buona*.[1] Abele is always joking, and so we are spending the time cheerfully in the best companionship, thinking of you often and with the most tender affection.

Your children,
Oreste, (Abele, and
Corinna)

1.   *Oreste is indicating that Corinna is becoming a better cook.*

Letter 88

Valdengo, 2 February 1913

Dearest children Oreste, Abele, and Corinna,

. . . . We are waiting anxiously for the day when we can embrace you with your dear Corinna this year, as you promised.

We are very glad that Abele too is doing excellently and that he is happy that he came over.

You will have learned [by now] from our letter of the 22nd that your friend Pierino Pizzoglio has visited us, and we hope to see him again before he leaves.

About the rail line from Biella to Novara, the work has begun after a Lucullan banquet and the placement of a few stakes.

Do come without fear of losing your way or of surprises. You will find very little or nothing at all changed in this solitary region of ours.

Your loving parents

Letter 89

Buenos Aires, 5 March 1913

Dearest parents,

I am still employed making pretty good money; Oreste is busy with his affairs and is putting on weight; Corinna is the one who keeps us all in good spirits, giving us the occasion for some hearty laughs.

Sometimes we go out on excursions—in a manner of speaking because when we have gone an hour and a half on the tram, we are always still within the city.

Last Sunday we were at the house of Sig. Alfredo Garrone, who lives some-what outside the center of town; we had a jolly time with his wife and two daughters, now completely grown up young ladies, and with Sig. Bellia and his wife, the brother of the cashier of the Biellese Bank and of the ex-proprietor of the Golden Lion (Leon d'Oro).

But now we shall be alone for a while, Corinna and I, since Oreste has to go out of town for a project. He will be away for some time.

I confess that, having spent so many months together, I already feel again [with regret] his impending absence, even more so because we more or less kept each other company; [when we talked,] . . . it was enough to touch more or less seriously on any topic whatsoever to find ourselves "terribly" in agreement and to initiate discussions without end and perhaps often even—without beginning.

Our friend Pierino Pizzoglio arrived the Saturday before last with your greetings.

I am enclosing in this letter a check for 500 lire in the hope that you will by now have had a good Easter.

My friend Armando Pella, whom I see a lot of, says hello to you. He says he sends his warmest greetings to his family.

Your loving children,
Abele, (Oreste, and
Corinna)

Letter 90

Valdengo, 31 March 1913

Dearest children Abele, Oreste, and Corinna,

Today while we were watching the rain come down, your very welcome letter came, Abele, bringing very good news about you all and a bank check from you, dear Abele, for 500 lire.

The pleasure that we get from hearing that you are all getting along perfectly is just as much a consolation to us as getting your constant and generous help. It all makes us really happy. And if it weren't for the fact that Mother's illness has come to turn our life upside down, we would be extremely happy.

We hope that Mother's health will return and that I can keep mine, so that we can still spend a bit of time in peace and happiness.

We have given all the geographical maps and periodicals of 1912 to your friend Pierino Pizzoglio along with two small pictures of our house taken by our dearest Secondino. We imagine that he [Pierino] will have brought them to you. In case Pizzoglio has not delivered them to you, you can ask if by chance he has left them at Vigliano, and I'll go get them and send them to you.

If you would like to get the *Corriere Biellese* too, write me and I'll have it sent to you.

Your loving parents

Photograph 4. Oreste and Abele in a park in Buenos Aires, 1913.

P.S. We hear that Oreste is out of Buenos Aires on business; for some new projects perhaps? We wish him all the best. But first he must come to see us.

Dearest daughter-in-law Corinna,

In the hope of seeing you soon, we rejoice at the excellent harmony that you know how to maintain with your dear husband, Oreste, and with your brother-in-law, Abele. Accept a special kiss from your dearest parents.

Letter 91

Buenos Aires, 18 April 1913

Dearest parents,

For some time we haven't written you, but we always think of you with affection hoping for Mom's continuing improvement and for very good news about you.

Oreste, who is out of town, came home last week for business reasons. Now he is gone again and perhaps for several months. He asked me to write you with his loving greetings and kisses.

I have finished my twenty-three years in great shape, cheered by the beautiful flowers Corinna brought me; we had a bit of celebration together. My job is still going nicely, and in the evening I am always home reading or chatting with Corinna or the next-door neighbors.

Our friend Pierino Pizzoglio, whom we went to visit at his house, had brought for us the two pictures taken by poor Secondino, and now they are adorning our house. I also got the Touring Club material you sent me; everything's OK, and thanks a lot for everything. I urge you not to let anything get lost; now I am going to see about renewing my membership from here. Do I have a subscription to the *Corriere*? [I ask] because I haven't gotten it yet. Send us some of the local papers.

Here the first rain has begun to fall, and now it is cool. To make up for this, over there everything is blooming, and you will begin to enjoy the first warmth of spring. Dear Mother will be able to go out a bit and get started on the road to complete recovery. We urge you not to push too hard and to be very cautious, a little bit at a time and all will be well.

For news, my friend Armando Pella has got married. I don't know whether [his folks] at home know it; better not to ask and not to say anything. I haven't seen him yet [since his marriage].

The Sasso family, with whom we are friendly, is fine, as well as Zocco's son, Corrado. I am going to see [Cousin] Abele some Sunday; I haven't seen him for a while. I know the two of them are fine.

Lots of greetings to everybody, and give me news about Riccardo since I don't know where to write to him anymore after the revolution in Mexico.

Write soon. Corinna especially sends you many, many kisses.

Your always loving children,
Abele, (Oreste, and
Corinna)

We are also writing to Oreste, who will be waiting to hear about you.

Letter 92

Valdengo, 24 April 1913

Dearest children Oreste, Abele, and Corinna,

It's three days that it has been raining almost continuously, very good for the meadows and late harvests, but for sowing the rest of the corn we would need good weather that we hope will come back soon. It's not cold anymore.

The bad weather is uncomfortable for dear Mother since it aggravates her suffering. When it's nice, she feels much better. She walks a little more freely, always with crutches, but not yet by herself. The time is drawing near to start again the hydroelectric treatment, which we are confident [will produce] a good result. . . .

On the 13th of this month we got a nice illustrated postcard from you, dear Oreste, from Tandil, where you were looking for workers. We hope you will have found what you need for the new job you have undertaken.

A sense of joy comes over our hearts when we hear of your daring projects, and we wish you always the best. The same with you, dear Abele, since you have no lack of prompt and daring initiative.

Your parents

24 April 1913

Dearest daughter-in-law Corinna,

Always with our thoughts turning to the hope of embracing you sometime here with us in the company of dear Oreste, we send you our special wish for happiness and harmony.

Your loving parents-in-law

Letter 93

Valdengo, 12 May 1913

Dear Abele,

I'll get you a subscription to the *Corriere Biellese*. I will also send you some papers from here. With this letter I am sending three of them.

Some bad news. Our cousin, Teresa Maggia of Stropadarea, died the 6th of this month after an illness of a few days. I have written to Riccardo, Main Post Office, General Delivery, Mexico.

Letter 96

Claraz F.C.S., 1 July 1913

Dearest parents,

I haven't written you now for some time. On so many occasions I would like to fulfill this duty, but then thinking about work or some other nonsense distracts me. And so time goes by. But I always have you before me, and I console myself by thinking of you.

Abele and Corinna have sent me your last letter, which I read with greatest pleasure. I am always waiting to hear of the recovery of our dear mother, who, after the past improvement, unfortunately is making slow progress. We hope from the bottom of our hearts that this summer she will get well completely.

I am building roads and bridges here; I am close to Tandil, 100 kilometers more or less. The weather's a bitch—cold—and it's always raining. I have never been so cold as here. Some nights it's 7 below zero (Celsius), which is not normal for these regions.

I regret that I can't send you anything with this letter since you will certainly need it for dear Mother's therapy. I plan to get to Tandil this month, and then I shall carry out my obligations.

Abele and Corinna are home alone, and it seems that they are getting along excellently together. They both write me all the time, and cheerfully.

I imagine that in your next letter you will be telling me about a new improvement on Mother's part, to whom I send so many kisses and hugs, as well as to you, dear Father, with best wishes for good health, the way mine never changes.

Your always more loving son,
Oreste.

Letter 97

Buenos Aires, 4 July 1913

Dearest parents,

As always we are waiting eagerly for news from you, happy that in your case, dear Dad, the news is good and that dear Mother is now moving, even though slowly, toward a complete recovery. For this we earnestly recommend every proper treatment

We here are fire. Oreste is always out of town; he comes back every now and then only to return at once to the job. I am still working here in Buenos Aires, managing quite well, though I am working as hard as I can. Corinna is here too, and in the evening we enjoy each other's company since it is difficult for me to be home during the day. We talk about you often, longing for the moment when we can embrace each other together.

On the 25th of last month I completed my first year of life in Buenos Aires, spending the evening out in the company of Sasso's son and the two of us. Summing it up, even though we don't have here our mountains and the green color, I have had a pretty good year in the dear company of Oreste and Corinna.

I am enclosing in this letter a check . . . for 500 lire. If, however, for whatever reason you should need more right away, write immediately and everything will be fixed up.

An important warning: When you get this letter of mine, don't write any more to the usual address since we have to move at the end of the month, and I still don't know where. They are selling the house where we are now. Just imagine that near here, for a small house, three rooms with kitchen, bath, etc., they have the nerve to ask more than 650 lire a month. Life in America! We'll find something better, but the rents here are enormous; *one* decent room costs 100 lire a month.

I'll send you, as soon as I know it, the new address. If, however, you must write sooner, send it to:

> Abele Sola, Engineer
> Establecimento "La Cantabrica"
> Calle Martin Garcia 665
> Buenos Aires

And if you send it there, send it registered mail since I don't have much confidence in these Spaniards in the office. But I'll send it [our new address] to you as soon as possible.

If on Sunday I don't have to go out and work, we will go visit Cousin Abele and get the news about Andrea, who will probably be coming over here too.

Here we are in the middle of winter, but today is hot; and in the morning it's cool, almost cold. Out where Oreste is, he says that it's almost like a refrigerator. To make up for it you will be having fine warm weather that will restore dear Mother's strength. For my part I prefer the cold now to the heat of the past months; now I am really eating and doing justice to Corinna's cuisine!

> Your ever-loving children,
> Abele, (Oreste, and
> Corinna)

I am attaching a letter that Corinna wanted to write you, certain that you will welcome it with all your heart.

We are also sending four postcards.

Note: This evening we had polenta. Wow!

Stay in good spirits. Bye.

Letter 98

Buenos Aires, 4 July 1913

Dearest parents-in-law,

It is a very great pleasure to learn that dear Mother is getting better and better; I hope that, with the therapy that she will be getting in the fine warm weather and with the treatment of the doctor that she is getting, she will be still better. With all my heart I wish her a swift recovery. You, dear Father, keep well the way you are now and stay in good spirits, for the day will come when we can all together embrace each other. With what pleasure I would love to be there close to you now, now that dear Mother is not very well. I would relieve you in certain tasks, and I would give Mother a bit of companionship, and I would help keep up your spirits. But let's hope that it won't be so very long before we see each other soon.

And so we would make a fine journey, all of us together. What a joy for you two to see all your dear children after longing for them and waiting for them so much! Isn't it true that it would be the greatest joy for you? Especially Oreste, now that it has been many years since you have seen him, to be able to embrace them both. It would also be their fond desire, and also mine.

Oreste is still out of town on the job. He comes home once a month and, sometimes, every other. He has Abele get him what he needs and send it to him, but I hope that by the end of the month he will come home. He is in good health, and Abele too is fine. As for Abele—the two of us get along well; sometimes he takes me to the theater or to hear some music, and when Oreste is here we all go together. Sometimes on a weekday evening we go visit the Sasso family, who have always been our good friends. We have also been to visit Cousin Abele and his wife; they are fine.

Your daughter-in-law,
Corinna

If by chance you see any one of my family say hello for me and Oreste and Abele.

Letter 99

Valdengo, 3 August 1913

Dearest children Abele, Oreste, and Corinna,

Yesterday I went to vist dear Mother and have her read the dear letters from you dear Abele and Corinna dearest, received on 29 July along with a money order for 500 lire.

As soon as we got them I sent her a card to tell her about it since I had just been to visit her the day before, when to her great satisfaction she put aside a crutch and used a cane instead.

Yesterday I was very pleased that I was able to make her walk with two canes, and we hope she will continue until she leaves them behind altogether. Unfortunately she will never be the way she was, but let's be happy if she can walk by herself without the aid of supports.

We thank you all for your constant concern for us, especially with these large sums, since without your generous help we could not spend that kind of money for dear Mother's treatment, which costs so very much for us who no longer earn anything.

In the month and about a half remaining for the therapy at the sanitarium we hope to get a considerable improvement.

In this refuge of the rich she is loved and respected by everyone. I am very satisfied and happy about this.

We got a letter from dear Oreste from Claraz F.C.S. He says he is fine but that it's very cold. We answered him with a letter of ours.

I am enclosing a postcard of the sanitarium written with difficulty but by mother herself. You too will be very happy about it since you are always anxious to hear of her complete recovery.

Cousin Riccardo is going back to where he was in Mexico. . . .

Here it is pretty hot but not too much. We suffered some from drought, especially for the hay, but now there has been some rain. The grapes are very fine and abundant. We hope that we can harvest them and make a bit of wine to put aside for when you all come home some day, as I make out from your letters. We are anxiously waiting for the day when we can embrace you all once again.

We were very satisfied to hear that you too Abele have the title of engineer; it's an honor for you and for us. We hope that you continue to do well and stay successful. That will be a consolation for us.

It is good to hear that you are getting along very well with Cousin Abele and our friend Sasso and the others from here.

The fantastic price that they are asking for rents over there doesn't surprise us since even here, considering the difference in wages, they are very expensive along with everything else.

Your loving parents

Letter 100

Buenos Aires, 8 August 1913

Dearest parents,

With great joy we received your nine beautiful postcards with the news of dear Mother's considerable improvement; we shared this joy at once with Oreste, who responded exultantly. It is a pleasure to hear about these good signs, especially about the satisfaction you will have felt at the short walk she took through Andorno. When you get this letter, we expect to rceive a card written in her own hand, as a continuing proof of the good effects of her therapy.

Do not be alarmed about the cost. Don't leave anything undone, and we shall overcome it all.

Oreste is still out of town, but we expect him back, perhaps this month.

Take note in the meantime, as I told you in my last letter, of our new residence. We had to look very hard, and we found one not very far from where we were living, in a new house. It's a small apartment but convenient and with a private entrance. Our friend Zocco will be able to give you an explanation of its location, and say hello to him and his family.

Write then to:

> Sola
> Calle Corrientes 1975
> Depart. 1
> *Buenos Aires*

A few Sundays ago we went to visit Cousin Abele. Along with his wife he sends you his warmest greetings. More than that he informed us that he is going to be a father for the second time. We are planning a party for them here. Sasso and his family come here every so often, and we go there; we get along perfectly together.

A fellow from Cossato, Fiore Monteferrario, came by to bring us your greetings that he got at the last moment, and he says hello to you from here.

We are having terrible weather now; [we are] in the depth of winter.

I hear that Riccardo came home. Where is he going? If he is still at home, don't forget to give him our address and a mountain of good wishes.

> Your loving children,
> Abele, (Oreste, and
> Corinna)

Letter 101

Valdengo, 28 August 1913

Dearest children, Abele, Oreste, and Corinna,

Our dear mother has suffered a new misfortune. One day as she was walking in the hallway of the sanitarium her cane slid out from under her, and she fell, hitting her knee on the floor. It caused her no small injury, so bad that she was compelled to stay in bed. That was ten days ago. Today she is better, but she still can't walk. She was doing pretty well up to this point so that if this new mishap hadn't occurred we were hoping to see her walking by herself soon. We are hoping that she will soon be able to make a good recovery.

I went to get her yesterday. She is here with me now for the short time until her knee is healed. Then I'll take her back to Andorno to finish the season of therapy.

As you see, dearest children, misfortunes keep coming upon us, and were it not for your constant generous help, it would be impossible for us to do that which we are doing.

In these two and a half months of treatment at the sanitarium it has cost about 1,000 lire, but in the hope of seeing her cured no sacrifice is spared.

Now that Oreste is toiling so in the middle of the deserted countryside, we are always concerned lest he suffer some misfortune. And we hope that you will always excel, dear Abele. And you, dear Corinna, always stay in good health and be a help at home. Yesterday I went to visit your brother Giovanni. They are fine, and they all give you their warmest regards.

Cousin Riccardo has gone back to Mexico. He will write you; I gave him the address of the firm where you are employed. I also gave your address to a certain Aragnetti of Masserano, a school friend of yours, I think. He will come to see you.

At the sanitarium in Andorno we made the acquaintance of a gentleman, a certain Ambrogio Tognoni from Lombardy, who lives at Calle Bulnes 620, Buenos Aires, where he has a store. I also gave him your address. He will bring our greetings to you. . . .

Your loving parents

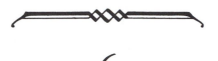

6

The Impact of Economic Crisis (1913–1915)

In 1913 Argentina entered a period of continually deteriorating economic conditions that would last for some time. Rains, the worst in years, lead to flooding and the destruction of crops (#102). Speculation drove prices up. The war in Europe curtailed shipping, created shortages, and exacerbated inflation. High prices, shortages of many goods, unemployment, unoccupied houses, and government deficits indicated that the immigrants' quest for a better life in Argentina had come to a halt, at least temporarily. Italians began to return home in unprecedented numbers, some because of the war but most because of the economic crisis (#112). By early 1915 a deep pessimism enveloped the country.

Both Abele and Oreste commented frequently on the developing crisis. "It is a frightful crisis," Oreste explained in one letter; "unemployment and poverty to an immense degree; total paralysis in every business; commerce is dead. . . . To look around you as you go through the city is something incredible. Twenty-five percent of the houses in certain districts are vacant. . . . The city of Buenos Aires cannot pay the capital of its legally contracted obligations. . . . Many plants that haven't gone bankrupt yet are closed" (#116). Abele too complained that "prices have gone up outrageously" and that "meat is now a luxury item, not to mention fresh vegetables, potatoes, fruit. . . . Add to that the terrible unemployment, the excessive rents, winter coming up, and a government that doesn't care. . . . Thus you will be able to grasp the situation here in this country, which is supposed to be rich and where no one need go without bread and meat" (#120).

Abele remained at his job in the metallurgical company and was not severely affected by the crisis. Oreste had difficulty as he moved from job to job
and had trouble collecting the money owed him by the government, but he
managed. From the point of view of the family in Italy it was a relief that the
two sons were able to continue sending money home (#102, #106, #111,
#114). Luigi lamented the crisis and the difficulty it was causing his sons.
Nevertheless, he made it clear to them how dependent he and Margherita
were on the money they sent: "If it were not for your constant generous assistance, life would be impossible for us" (#103).

As before, Luigi and Margherita longed to see their children and kept
hoping for the day when this dream might become a reality. At one point
Luigi explained: "We did not, Oreste, answer at once your very dear letter
from Claraz because we hoped to embrace you and Corinna. We are still
waiting anxiously" (#105). Later in the same letter he played directly on their
love and sympathy for their mother to induce them to visit: "Dear Mother,
still suffering, is making every effort, dragging herself along with a crutch, to
get the room fixed up for you with everything it needs." A few months later he
noted that Mother was better, although still in pain, and that "she keeps up
her courage very well, and with the hope of seeing you she is even braver"
(#110).

Corinna too expressed her longing for Biella. In one of two letters she wrote
during this period, she commented on Margherita's illness: "I would like to be
there next to her, to console her and to keep her company" (#119). She continued her thought by discussing Argentine and Italian food. In Argentina,
she noted, "there isn't any good wine. Not only that but in everything you
don't get satisfaction, like cheese, salami; none of the food we eat here is satisfactory. . . . I look forward to the moment I go back to Italy."

The network of Biellesi friends and relatives remained especially important.
Most significant for them were Cousin Abele, Carlo Boschetto, Luigi Fila,
Antonio Pella, Cousin Riccardo, and Carlo and Costanza Sasso (#107, #109,
#112, #114, #115, #117, #118, #120). A bit of special family information for
us is set forth in #108: Cousin Abele Sola and his wife gave birth to a son,
Aldo, who was to become the future custodian of the Sola family letters.

The chapter closes with a short move by the three from Calle Sarandi 1493
to Calle Sarandi 1088, the third move they made in less than two years.

Letter 102

Buenos Aires, 26 August 1913

Dearest parents,
    I am here because the tremendous rains these days have made work alto-
gether impossible. For many years they have not had such torrential rains in

these regions. The damage they have caused is tremendous. The great drainage canals in the province of Buenos Aires, which have already cost more than 200 million lire, were not sufficient. Now the weather has cleared up, and the waters are beginning to go down. For this reason I am leaving again this evening for the job, where I now expect to see the considerable damage caused [by the rains] since where I am is one of the most severely stricken regions. There is nothing to fear, however, and in all this desolation there are even some comic notes which make you forget and soften the impact.

I am enclosing a newspaper which has some pictures of a flooded city. For a week now that's all you read about in the papers.

I am sending you a check for 500 lire, which you will certainly need to finish dear Mother's treatment. . . .

We are all fine, and we laugh cheerfully together. Corinna, always lively and happy, is very pleased with Mother's improvement and is looking forward to her complete recovery.

Abele is still hard at work and is happy.

Coming from out of town I found myself now in the new place that Abele and Corinna had with difficulty discovered. We may not stay here very long since Corinna is always alone all day and she gets bored. In the evening she leaves us both numb, as she lets go with all the words she didn't say during the day. If you don't pay any attention to her, she shouts even more. It's entertaining. She's like a kid who bombards you with questions and explanations.

We are living a pretty quiet life and are always happy.

> Your loving sons and daughter-
> in-law,
> Oreste, (Abele, and Corinna)

Letter 103

Valdengo, 28 October 1913

Dearest children Abele, Oreste, and Corinna,

Dear Mother reads your letters with such great emotion that she seems completely cured because of the enthusiasm she feels while she reads them. But she isn't cured yet. She still walks with a crutch and a cane; she still suffers especially at night. Every night she has to get an injection with a phial of Pantopon. If you don't give it to her, she suffers terribly night and day. Her improvement is so slow that you can't tell the difference from one day to the next.

We hold on and hope.

I am fine. So many thanks for the money order for 500 lire. If it were not for your constant generous assistance, life would be impossible for us. Your constant help is a great consolation for us, as well as knowing that you are well in every way.

We have finished the grape harvest—it is very abundant. The local grapes were sold for between 1.30 and 1.60 lire per ten kilos; the American ones even for 20 centesimi more. Everyone is at a loss; they have no place to put the grapes. This year there's too much; perhaps next year there will be an out-and-out scarcity.

On the 26th we had the general political elections with almost everybody voting, with the Libyan war as the issue. . . . It was a real triumph for the Socialist Party. The conservatives, liberals, and clericals are upset and humiliated by this resounding defeat. Even Valdengo is beginning to open its eyes. . . .

For two days it has been raining without stop.

Winter is coming on the run. The stove and the handwarmer will soon be in fashion.

We wish dear Oreste a happy birthday. [We hope] you will celebrate it all together in the best of health and harmony. We shall remember it with joy from here.

Your loving parents

Letter 104

Claraz F. C. S., 5 November 1913

Dearest parents,

For a long time now I haven't written you, though you are always present in my mind.

I have received your very dear letter in answer to a previous one of mine written right from here. I have also seen all the other ones you have sent to us in Buenos Aires since when they get letters, they always send them on to me.

I am always waiting for good news about dear Mother's recovery, which is still too slow. I imagine that by the end of this treatment period she will be considerably improved.

I regret that I can't send you anything, as I would very much want to.

Toward the end of the month, however, I'll be in Buenos Aires since I have finished this project and am now putting the equipment into storage. So I shall be home on the 20th, and we will have a family party for my birthday (my thirtieth). Corinna is already waiting for me eagerly, and she has written me a letter alluding to the preparation for it. Just thinking about it makes me smile.

Excuse me then that I cannot always carry out this duty with the same urgency that the situation requires since I am sure that you need it—and badly. At the end of the month you can count on it for sure.

Dear Dad, try to stay always healthy, just as my health too never fails me, and so you will be able to comfort dear Mother.

Your always dearer son,
Oreste

Letter 105

Valdengo, 16 December 1913

Dearest children, Oreste, Abele, and Corinna,

We did not, Oreste, answer at once your very dear letter from Claraz because we hoped to embrace you and Corinna. We are still waiting anxiously. Since you said that you had finished the project and that you were returning to Buenos Aires to celebrate your birthday with dear Corinna and Abele, we hope that you will have spent it very well in good cheer. We are united with you in our heart and send you a loving kiss.

We are close to Christmas and New Year's; we anxiously are waiting to embrace you, dearest Oreste, and our most beloved daughter-in-law, Corinna.

If our wish does not come true and this letter finds you still in Buenos Aires, we hope that you will have enjoyed the holidays and that you won't let 1914 go by without giving us the joy of embracing you once again after so many years.

Dear Mother, still suffering, is making every effort, dragging herself along with a crutch, to get the room fixed up for you with everything it needs; she is doing as much as she can. I am waiting with pleasure to help her, hoping that it turns out well.

The weather is beautiful and comparatively cold.

I am sure that Abele will feel lost if it should fall to him to be left alone until you return, but he will put up with it.

And so, dearest Oreste, we are awaiting your telegram from Genoa to say that you have arrived, so that I at least can go to meet you at Biella.

Did we understand that our most beloved daughter-in-law, Corinna, is also with you?

Your loving parents

Letter 106

Valdengo, 2 January 1914

Dearest children Oreste, Abele, and Corinna,

We have been slow in answering your dear letter, Oreste, which came with the considerable sum of 500 lire, for which we are infinitely grateful.

The reason for the delay is that we wanted to send you our picture taken

Photograph 5.   Luigi and Margherita under the arcade of their home in Valdengo, 1913. As Luigi explains: "You see me and dear Mother going for a walk. Dear Mother with that cheerful smile of hers, a sign of contentment, even though the pain and discomfort hardly ever leave her (letter #106).

here under the arcade of our house. We are going to send with this letter the one that is postcard size; and in a little while we will send you the larger picture. I have to go to Biella to buy the envelopes suitable for sending.

Meanwhile you see me and dear Mother going for a walk. Dear Mother with that cheerful smile of hers, a sign of contentment, even though the pain and discomfort hardly ever leave her.

We have finished 1913 in happiness, and this year has begun in the same way. We hope that this will be the year to bring complete recovery to dear Mother. We hope that you too will have finished the year well and have begun the new one better and that you continue to be well.

It is a great comfort to hear that you all celebrated your birthday, dear Oreste, with good cheer and happiness. We too remembered the beautiful event with keen joy. We shared the happy day with our thoughts turned to you and your sincere brotherly harmony.

If dear Mother's serious illness had not come to trouble us, our life would be truly happy. Because of your constant and generous help, to hear that you are always well in every respect would be for us a contented old age.

We hope for you, dear Oreste, that your undertaking a new project will be advantageous for you and that you always take good care of yourself if it should fall to you to go out into the open country. We urge you always to protect yourself from the dangers of malaria since they [the places where you are going] will probably not always be free of it.

Dear Mother is working on a big letter to enclose with the picture we will send you soon.

Your loving parents

Letter 107

Buenos Aires, 6 February 1914

Dearest parents,

As I told you in the postcards, as of the first of this month, we have moved and we intend to settle down a bit. We are still in a bit of confusion, but things will soon be calmer for us since it is a small house to itself, and it has with it a nice rooftop terrace (*azotea*—our friend Zocco knows what they are like). The new address is:

Calle Sarandi no. 1493

This evening we are going to drink a glass or two in honor of Sasso, Carlo's son, who is leaving Sunday for Chile, where he is probably going to stay for quite a while, considering the general crisis we have here too, as seems to be the case, for that matter, throughout the world.

We must again thank you for the photo you sent us; it came out well; we are expecting the other larger one in a few days. And we will send you one in exchange once the heat lets up a bit.

Please notify the newspapers you've had sent to us of our new address. . . . In a few days Cousin Abele will be a father. We will go to see what it is [boy or girl]; they are fine and say hello to you.

Once again excuse the delay in writing you. The heat keeps us from doing anything we don't have to.

I am enclosing in this letter a check for 500 lire.

Your loving children,
Abele, (Oreste, and Corinna)

Letter 108

Buenos Aires, 5 March 1914

Dearest parents,

Your dearest letter of 2 January with the beautiful postcard photo gave us great pleasure to see you together looking well, and it was a great comfort to see dear Mother, if not cured, at least much improved. This gives us great hope for her recovery in the near future. . . .

On the 8th of last month we got your latest letter, of 13 January, with the larger photograph enclosed, the one you had earlier promised. We looked at it together at length, happy to see you somewhat more comfortable. Dear Mother's delightful letter also cheered us up, and we thank her for the effort it must have cost her.

And we urge that you too, dear Dad, be very careful for both of you so that we can always see you both happy and in good health.

We too, after a bit of a photograph crisis (the general crisis is still going ahead at full speed), have taken some good pictures; and we will send you some of them that you will like. One is with the Sasso family; they still recognized you in your photos. They were here the other week; their son, however, has left for Chile, and they always say hello to you. In the picture which I am in there is also a dear friend of ours, Perotti of Bioglio, who came to America after I did.

Oreste is home a bit, and then he is gone again on his project; now he has been here for several days. Corinna is working around the house and is making the *buona pappa*. I am still working at the same place.

Cousin Abele has become a father again, of a little boy, the first since the last one, a girl, died.[1] We are going to visit him.

We are getting, though not regularly, the *Corriere* and the *Tribuna*. It would be a good idea to give them our new address.

Here summer is at an end, and already we are beginning to feel the refreshing cool weather a bit more.

We wish dear Mother a good summer coming up, well suited for her recovery.

Your loving children,
Abele, (Oreste, and Corinna)

1.   *This son was Aldo Sola, the custodian of the Sola family letters.*

Letter 109

Valdengo, 26 March 1914

Dearest children Oreste, Abele, and Corinna,

Yesterday was your birthday again, dear Abele, and we remembered it with pleasure and with the hope that you enjoyed the day along with Oreste and Corinna.

Today, to add joy to our recollection of it we got the dearest letter from you, postcards, and the three fine pictures, [in which you are] different from when you left but still yourselves, in the company of your friends and the Sasso family. It's a great consolation to hear and see you always in the best of health and harmony.

We are also quite pleased that Cousin Abele is a father again. We wish the little boy good health. We have shared the news with Angiolina's mother, and she was very pleased. She too expects to hear from them. . . .

Yesterday I went to accompany Serafina Pella of Cerretto to her ultimate resting place. She died after long suffering. Give our sympathy to her son, your friend Armando. . . .

We are in spring now, but we haven't seen the swallows yet. It's still a bit cold at night, especially when it's windy.

We hope that with the coming of summer dear Mother will be able to do without the crutch and walk on her own and not feel pain.

We hear, and we read in the papers, about the continuing crisis which is troubling Argentina. We hope it doesn't affect you. Here too, because of the war in Libya, the crisis makes itself felt in just about everything.

Your loving parents

Letter 110

Valdengo, 30 April 1914

Dearest children Oreste, Abele, and Corinna,

We haven't written you since the 26th of March. Even though nothing has changed here, we feel it our pleasant duty to let you hear from us.

I, Dad, am fine, as I hope you are too. Dear Mother cannot do without the crutch and the cane when she goes out in the street. In the house she moves more freely with just the crutch, and she can take a few steps with no help at all. She is always in pain, especially at night and when the weather changes. She keeps up her courage very well, and with the hope of seeing you she is even braver. She can do the work in the kitchen and housecleaning quite easily. That is a great relief for me. Let's hope for an improvement this summer so that she can walk by herself and feel no more pain.

Tomorrow is May 1st. I'm going to Cossato for the usual gathering and conference. It's sad, but the enthusiasm I once felt is almost gone. It's true, when you get old, everything loses its zip.

The countryside—so far—looks good. If we don't have a dry spell, let's hope for the best.

Your loving parents

Letter 111

Buenos Aires, 3 June 1914

Dearest parents,

It was an even greater pleasure to know that our dear Mother keeps on improving, giving certainty to the hopes that we have continued to nourish for a complete recovery. It gives us equal pleasure to know that you, dear Father, are always in good health. Nonetheless we cannot urge you enough not to overdo—this applies to both of you, but especially to dear Mother—don't let her get careless because of her improvement. We see that the crops are also very promising, in contrast with here, where the harvest has in a large part been lost.

The bad weather has continued even through the entire month of May. Along with the extraordinary floods that came with it, it has been causing a real disaster in the countryside, where they were harvesting the corn, and this harvest is now rotting in the granaries since, to top off the misfortune, many rail lines are paralyzed because of collapsed bridges and destroyed embankments. Accordingly they can't ship the harvest to the ports of embarkation.

Even here in Buenos Aires the effects of the bad weather have been severe. Commerce and industries, those that haven't gone under, keep going just to be able to survive the crisis and hope for better times. Importing firms, which used to count in the hundreds their workmen who assembled machines, are now down to just a few or none at all. Oh well, what can you do?

I am still working at the same job, always hoping for a bit more work for the workshops, which are now reduced by half. Oreste himself has taken refuge here because of the awful weather. Where he was working has been completely flooded. We are waiting for the sun, which for a few days has seemed about to let us catch a glimpse of it, only to disappear at once so that it can rain a bit. This month we will begin winter; autumn has passed, raining and hot, but now, however, the overcoats are visible.

Your friends here are fine and give you their best.

We enclose a check for 500 lire.

Your loving children,
Abele, (Oreste, and Corinna)

Letter 112

Buenos Aires, 16 July 1914

Dearest parents,

The visit of our good friend Carlo Boschetto was exceedingly pleasant. He brought us your lovely letter and those delicious two bottles of sweet pickles, "homemade." Thanks a million; we gave them a good welcome. . . .

I tried right away that very evening to get him a job in a store of our friend Monti from Biella. I don't know if they came to an agreement. Any other type of work is hard to find, first of all because of the apprenticeship and then because of the crisis, which has kept more than half of the work force idle. A sign of this is that the ships are leaving here filled up.[1]

As always we hope that our dear Mother continues to get better, even though her treatment has had little effect, and that you, dear Father, will keep in good health.

Oreste has been gone for a while to finish up a job that the bad weather had severely damaged for him. We expect him back soon. This very evening I have written him. Corinna is fine and as always sends you many kisses; she is constantly waiting to hear from you. I am always at work.

If it has begun to get very hot over there, here it is comparatively cold, after four days of terrible weather. We hope at least that the cold clear weather continues.

We received the latest *Corriere* bringing the news of your victory in the latest elections. Congratulations!

Last week our friends Sasso and Antonio Pella came to visit us. They are fine and say hello to you. Tomorrow evening we are going to visit Sasso. His wife, Costanza, is slightly ill, but it will pass. I have also visited Monteferrario of Cossato and he gives you his best.

As always we urge you to be very careful and to stay in good spirits. . . .

Your loving children,
Abele, (Oreste, and Corinna)

1.   *Abele is referring to the Italian immigrants returning home because of the economic crisis. In 1914 nearly 61,000 Italians returned home, the largest number ever. Net Italian migration to Argentina was −24,500.*

Letter 113

Buenos Aires, 27 August 1914

Dearest parents,

We are always hoping that our dear Mother, with her continuing treatment and the favorable season, will be able to improve still more. Stay in good spirits; do not neglect anything; don't get worried, and be patient for a while yet since you will soon be happier.

Here the general crisis persists and continues, aggravated even more by the outrageous bad weather, which is ruining the little bit of the last harvest that had been saved and is hampering, by delaying or destroying it, the work of sowing for the year coming up. For a country that lives almost exclusively off agriculture this means, if not ruin or disaster, [at least] a paralysis of industrial work and of commerce. After a few days of good weather we have fallen back into this driving rain and wind, and the accompanying floods. . . .

Ever since the "European War" broke out it is the topic of the day here with the accompanying "communiqués" and "special editions" from the newspapers. . . . The news, real or invented, that the principal papers get with their excellent news services is made known at once by posters, illuminated at night, put up on the facades of the respective buildings.

Because of the war, the prices have gone up here too for foodstuffs. Coal, iron, everything in general, including the grain and corn which are for export. But now it is difficult to export anything since there is no shipping, or hardly any, to Europe. Let's hope Italy stays neutral as much as possible; otherwise even those few ships that still come and go would be stopped, and then it's goodbye to everything!

And what do they say about it over there? Things are going from bad to worse? I am concluding because it's late and also in this country they don't usually build houses with fireplaces. So with the wet weather and the water and the wind outside, I am almost frozen. Still it's winter, and you have to put up with it.

But first we want to add our most heartfelt and loving best wishes for a happy birthday which, if we are not mistaken, for you, dear Father, will be the sixty-third this 23rd September, and for you, dear Mother, will be the fifty-second on the 10th of October.

Spend those days in the best way you are able.

Your loving children,
Abele, (Oreste, and Corinna)

Letter 114

Buenos Aires, 1 October 1914

Dearest parents,

As always we hope that the proper treatment will be able to bring our dear Mother back to health in a satisfactory way, but you, however, must be calm and hopeful.

The situation here is still the same; the weather, though we are now in spring, continues to be changeable, but the cold, though it's only relative, has gone.

The unemployment is extraordinary; I honestly don't know how it can go on like this. I am afraid, however, that something really serious is bound to happen.

I see, however, that you must not be doing so well over there either, with the scourge of war in your ribs. Though it's far away, it is making itself felt here too, and who knows how long it will last still! . . .

It is a pleasure to learn that Riccardo is in good health; we have not heard anything more from him. Give us his address, and if you write him, let him have our new address. We are also pleased that our friend Eugenio Rivetti has brought you our loving greetings, even though I have seen him only once— say hello to him along with the others.

On Sunday the 20th of September we spent the entire day until late in the evening in perfect harmony and close friendship at the house of our friend Sasso, along with his wife, Costanza, and Antonio Pella. They are all fine and say hello to you. We ate polenta and the salami that goes with it. Afterward we took pictures; we will send you copies.

We have also been to visit Cousin Abele and his wife and child. They are fine and give you their best. . . .

I am enclosing with this letter a check for 500 lire. . . .

Oreste has gone back out into the country, but since he is not far away, he will come home often, and then [too] the project is a short one.

Corinna also is fine and sends you many, many kisses.

Write soon. We will too.

Your loving children,
Abele, (Oreste, and Corinna)

Letter 115

Buenos Aires, 13 November 1914

Dearest parents,

It gave us pleasure that you received our letter wishing you happy birthday on the very day of our dear Father's birthday. In this way at least we too have joined in the celebration, just as you let us share in that of our dear Mother on the 10th of October.

Oreste has been back for several days, and in accordance with your kind good wishes we hope to spend his birthday happily together. Corinna will complete her thirtieth year on the 3rd of February, though she doesn't even want to hear of having reached such an age! . . .

We hope, now that the grape harvest has been finished for some time, that the wine turns out well, though, so you say, it's not abundant. Again we urge dear Mother not to get careless and do strenuous work.

We are enclosing in this letter six photographs that ought to give you pleasure. As you will see one is of Corinna while she is doing her housework, another as she is just about to go out for a short walk, a third has Oreste and Corinna at home pretending to talk politics. In this you can see in the corner, though it is dark, one of our small family pictures of poor Secondino.

A fourth is in the house of our dear friend Sasso on the occasion of the 20th of September with his wife, Costanza, Corinna, Antonio Pella, and myself— Oreste took the picture. The last two are of a pleasant outing to a nearby village, Muñiz, with a family we know.

The weather here is still crazy; for a little it was too hot, but [now it is] mostly wind, cold, and rain.

The topic of the day is always the war.

Oreste is sending you some postcards.

> Your loving children,
> Abele, (Oreste, and Corinna)

Letter 116

> Buenos Aires, 4 December 1914

Dearest parents,

It's been way too long now that I have not written you; I only enclose every now and then a postcard in the letters that Abele sends you.

We here are living in the best possible harmony, and we think of you frequently. Our only regret is, as always, our dear Mother's illness, which has gone on for too long.

Last month we celebrated my thirty-first birthday at home with good cheer. They presented me with some beautiful vases of flowers, in addition to which Abele gave me a magnificent suitcase with all the accessories. That day I remembered you with joy: and since I could not also be with you, I am sending a picture of me with Corinna taken that very day.

There is nothing new here. . . . It is a frightful crisis: unemployment and poverty to an immense degree; total paralysis in every business; commerce is dead. Real estate, the prices for which had risen to the stars, was mortgaged at overvalued prices. Now today they can find nothing to sell to satisfy the mortgage, which averages two-thirds of the value. It is to be noted that you could say about 90 percent [of the real estate] is mortgaged, so everything is in the same condition. To look around you as you go through the city is something incredible. Twenty-five percent of the houses in certain districts are vacant; add to that that many have been that way for more than a year. And they are huge buildings.

Then too the finances of the state are at the same level. The city of Buenos Aires cannot pay the principal on its legally contracted obligations, not even the interest; that's the way it is everywhere. Many plants that haven't gone bankrupt yet are closed. Keep in mind that there is an average of thirty-two to thirty-five millions worth in bankruptcies every month; and this has been going on for more than a year. All the projects have been suspended, and the few that come up for bid are competed for at amounts and prices which serve only to point the way to ruin. That is the situation here and in all of South America.

I would have preferred that it were different, so that I too could send you some help since your expenses will be heavy. I regret, therefore, that I can't come through as I would like. I am enclosing with this letter a check for 500 lire so that you will be able to spend a cheerful Christmas, and end and beginning of the year. We here will remember you as always with greatest affection. . . .

> Your ever more loving children,
> Oreste, (Abele, and Corinna)

Letter 117

> Buenos Aires, 21 January 1915

Dearest parents,

We hope that you dear Father have gotten well again and that our dear Mother is improving. . . .

We spent the holidays at the end and beginning of the year pretty well, as always with dear thoughts of you.

We have been to visit Carlo and Costanza Sasso, and as always passing the time in the most intimate friendship. They are fine and give you their best. Their son Giuseppe in Santiago, Chile, is also doing well. . . .

I should like to know if Riccardo's address is still General Delivery, Mexico City. For a long time we have gotten nothing from him.

As you were saying, you will have made the wine by now. I hope it's good and that it will keep you in good cheer. Here we drink what we can; it's not very good, and it costs a lot. The domestic wine, *though it may be* honest and genuine, just isn't right for our "refined" palates.

In these days we are getting the full effect of summer. The heat is suffocating, even at night. And with all of this there is a region in the south that is completely flooded.

There are good hopes for the harvest, even more than is realistic since, if there isn't too much rain or a drought, there is always something [else] to spoil things. Moreover the majority of these farmers are indecently oppressed by the speculators and all who loaned them a bit of money and thereby got control of the harvest.

Here things are getting worse and worse; there is very little work.

You will certainly be seeing Antonio Pella, a good friend, a man of uncommon honesty, sincerity, and prudence, who will tell you something about things here. Greet him warmly and with best wishes. And make sure he informs us [when he is coming back] since we didn't see him off, so that we can meet him.

As for the tax on postcards, bring it to the attention of the post office that they are always stamped here at the post office and that they are quite familiar with the rates. We normally put postcards in an envelope, but since they [sic] are left open, there is no need for an increase in the rate, unless they are sealed and then they go like letters. . . .

I have not yet been able to see our friend Fila since I don't have the exact address. I'll try to see him some holiday when I have time. I do know from others that he is fine, apparently, along with his son.

The hideous earthquake in central Italy has made a big impression here, and they are collecting money to help a bit. So, even without a war, Italy has its own victims.

All the papers here have entire pages devoted to news of the war, and it looks like it is going to last a long time. . . .

Corinna sends you many, many loving kisses in response to your affectionate thoughts for her.

With this letter we are also sending you some postcards.

Your loving children,
Abele, (Oreste, and Corinna)

Letter 118

Buenos Aires, 4 February 1915

Dearest parents,

We are glad that you received our latest letters for the holidays and that you spent the day happily; that's everything we wished for. The lovely postcard from our dear Mother gave us unlimited joy; it made us remember [her] affectionately. Thanks a lot and many, many good wishes for your improvement.

We hear that it is quite cold there and that snow has come with it. Right now we over here envy you for it, considering the suffocating heat of these last few days. The change in temperature, however, is remarkable, so much so that we almost feel cold after a few drops of water and a bit of wind.

Yesterday we merrily celebrated Corinna's thirtieth birthday. Along with our best wishes she was very pleased to receive your love.

Sunday a week ago we were at the house of Signor Garrone and had a very good time. They are all fine; say hello for us to the family over there.

Last Sunday, after many inquiries I managed to visit my dear old friend Luigi Fila. He was immensely pleased with your affectionate greetings. . . . Along with his son—he's fine too—he was at work on a machine they are inventing. They are working [at it] a lot and perhaps spending their savings [on it]. They are employed as weavers in a nearby factory where many others from Biella are working. He's promised to come here and visit us, and to write you. His address is: Luigi Fila, Calle Montaneses 2941, Belgrano, Buenos Aires.

This very day I got myself up to date with my *Touring Club* subscription. I would be grateful if you could send me what you had already received after the departure of Pierino Pizzoglio, who had brought me a part of it. You can send it to me as printed matter.

I am enclosing with this letter a check for 500 lire.

> Your loving children,
> Abele, (Oreste, and Corinna)

Letter 119

Buenos Aires, 15 February 1915

Dearest parents-in-law,

It gives me greatest pleasure to see from your letter that you had a good holiday season, thinking about us, just as we too always think of you with the greatest affection.

I thank you infinitely for your kind good wishes for my birthday, which we spent happily together. Oreste and Abele brought me lots of beautiful flowers, and then in the evening we went out to dinner, and after dinner we got a carriage and went on a lovely ride. We received the postcard written by our dear mother, which gave me great pleasure. I am enormously sorry that after so much suffering of so much pain they still haven't found a cure for her recovery.

As always we have high hopes. I would like to be there next to her, to console her and to keep her company. You, dear Father, must keep her spirits up, take her on walks, tell her all kinds of nice things, something to make her laugh, so that she won't feel the pain so much. Don't let her be with anybody who is gloomy, otherwise the problem gets worse; and let her amuse herself.

You, dear Father, keep yourself in good health. When you feel a bit indisposed, drink a good bottle of Valdengo, one of the old sort, and you will see that you will feel better at once. Here you can't do that since there isn't any good wine. Not only that but in everything you don't get satisfaction, like cheese, salami; none of the food we eat here is satisfactory.

Sometimes at home we talk about not having good salami made in our way or some of the Chiaverano cheese, those small fresh ones, in short so many things that I long for, and I look forward to the moment I go back to Italy so that I can enjoy so many things that you can't get here. Take advantage of them, you who are there. Try to keep your spirits up, as we do here.

Many, many kisses to our dear mother, and for you, dear Father, a warm embrace from your ever more loving daughter-in-law, Corinna. Greetings from Oreste and Abele.

Letter 120

Buenos Aires, 4 March 1915

Dearest parents,

We are happy that our friend Antonio Pella has come to say hello and to bring you our dearest greetings and news from here. Say hello to him for us and for the Sasso family; they were here with us a few evenings ago.

As they had promised, our friend Luigi Fila and his son Ernesto came to visit us last Sunday. We spent several hours happily together digging up old times again. It goes without saying that they send you their warmest greetings. Why, he even wanted to write a note for us to include in our next letter. They are fine, though right now they are working very hard, both of them as weavers, because of an excellent contract for uniforms for the French army.

We see that the situation over there isn't of the best, with the increase in the price of bread and all. No, it doesn't surprise us at all since even here, in a country of grain and meat, prices have gone up outrageously, so much so that to a certain extent they have begun to manufacture the so-called "whole grain bread," which up to now has been unknown. Meat is now a luxury item, not to mention fresh vegetables, potatoes, fruit—the prices are sky high. It's enough to say that potatoes cost thirty-five centavos a kilo, almost eighty centesimi! And everything else in the same proportion. Add to that the terrible unemployment, the excessive rents, winter coming up, and a government that doesn't care, a budget running a deficit, so much so that it [the government] does not pay its workers and employees. Thus you will be able to grasp the situation here in this country, which is supposed to be rich and where no one need go without bread and meat.

Let's hope that the situation will take a change for the better soon, both there and here. Thank goodness that we are healthy! We wish and urge the same for you two: that our dear Mother might get well and be happy; and for you, dear Father, to take care, and that both of you stay in good spirits.

Here after a suffocating hot spell we have had a lot of rain, with the floods that go with it and a bit of cool weather, from one day to the next a difference of 12 degrees centigrade! When you get this letter, over there too the good sun will have melted the snow and warmed up the air a bit, spreading around a bit more of life. Our friend Boschetto was here the other day and says hello to you. He's fine.

Your loving children,
Abele, (Oreste, and Corinna)

Letter 121

Buenos Aires, 14 April 1915

Dearest parents,

Thanks so much for your kind good wishes on my twenty-fifth birthday, which [I] spent happily with Oreste and Corinna, thinking of you with affection. I too wanted to celebrate the occasion, and so I had my picture taken to memorialize my quarter of a century! I am sending you a copy, separately, by registered mail.

On the 16th, the day after tomorrow, we are moving to another house, close to where we are now, but a little larger. But, what really matters, it's dry and facing the sun, whereas where we are now is damp, and with winter coming on it's not smart to stay there. Our health is more important than anything else.

The new address is:

Calle Sarandi 1088

Change the address for the newspapers, especially since they have got it wrong, writing it "Carandi."

It was a pleasure to learn from your last letter, of the 21st of March, that as the good weather continues our dear Mother also feels somewhat better and that she can stretch herself a bit with some short walks. She should be cheerful and not worry, but don't let her get careless and don't let her overdo. And you too, dear Father, don't wear yourself out with your farm work, but enjoy your rest when necessary. Keep up your spirits; that's what we really desire.

Last Sunday we went to visit our friends Costanza and Carlo Sasso (Calle Rio de Janeiro 1450); we spent, as always in their company, a delightful afternoon. They were very pleased to get your greetings, and they reciprocate with pleasure. . . .

I have seen your godson, Prospero Giardino. He and his wife are fine, and he says hello to you. Say hello to his family for us.

Dear Mother, we thank you so much for your sweet letter; we wish for you a complete recovery with all our heart.

Your loving children,
Abele, (Oreste, and Corinna)

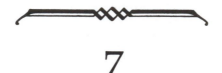

7

Italy Joins the War (1915–1917)

Although the war in Europe began in August 1914, Italy did not join the confrontation until May 24, 1915. From that date forward, the war became a major focus of the letters. Abele frequently referred to the support of the Italians in Buenos Aires for the fighting. "So then, we are at war!" he proclaimed. "The news . . . caused tremendous enthusiasm, with everyone singing the praises of Italy. . . . The enlistment of those called to service began at once, and there are already thousands signed up" (#123). Nearly two years later, on the anniversary of Argentine independence, Abele observed: "The city looks beautiful with thousands of flags, among which, after the blue and white of Argentina, our dear cheerful white, red, and green predominates" (#147). Shortly thereafter he reported: "The war continues to be the subject of enthusiasm," with many large public demonstrations to honor the Italians, the French, and the North Americans (#150).

The war, however, was more than glory and patriotism; it also meant personal hardship and suffering. It exacerbated the economic crisis in Argentina and created difficulties in Italy. Both Luigi and Oreste protested the high cost of living and noted that only the businesses profited from the situation (#132, #134, #141, #148). Abele lamented: "This blessed Republic is reduced to a state of exhaustion" (#146). The impact on Italian immigrants was severe. "Imagine," Abele wrote his parents, "that lots of families who put down their roots here a long time ago, with all their children Argentine-born, are emigrating from this promised land, in need of a larger population, for nearby

Brazil" (#145). The Solas also frequently commented with concern on relatives and friends joining the army, going to the front, and dying (#122, #131,
#139, #143).

The conflict brought many additional personal anxieties to the family. Neither Abele nor Oreste returned to Italy to fight. Abele was deferred because he
was physically unacceptable. Oreste was able to avoid being called up because
of his age and of his classification as one who was needed to support his family. Luigi, nevertheless, was continually afraid that Oreste's age group and
category might be called (#134, #135). Correspondence between Italy and
Buenos Aires was also delayed, sometimes for months, and this lack of personal communication especially upset family and friends (#143, #146, #147,
#150). The confrontation in addition further delayed the hoped-for visit of
the sons to Italy (#126, #135, #137, #146).

The war and the economic crisis affected Abele and Oreste differently. In a
confidential letter of December 1916, Abele explained to his father that "personally I don't feel the crisis since the factory is making a lot of money with
the production of sheet iron." Oreste, he continued, "has been away for more
than a year on a project of a certain importance, but for various reasons it is
not bringing in the desired return. . . . Do not worry about this, and don't get
alarmed; we are fine!" (#144). Six months later Oreste wrote his mother one
of his most solemn and moving letters. He acknowledged her complaint that
he personally did not write often and pointed out that Abele wrote for all of
them. The "real news," he explained, was so bad that it should not be mentioned; "to speak of these things would be a constant repetition of sadness. . . . About the only thing left is love for our dear ones, and even that
with meditation and in silence" (#148).

Margherita continued to improve during this period and finally was able to
walk without crutches (#138, #139, #140, #142). At that time she and Luigi
agreed to take in sick and aged Cousin Carlo. Cousin Carlo named Luigi his
sole heir in return (#140). Abele, however, was concerned about this arrange-
ment: "We would like it if you could possibly get a woman who could help
our dear mother. . . . As far as the financial arrangements go, . . . only malicious tongues . . . could spread a lot of disgusting nonsense, and it would be a
good idea to be prepared for it" (#142). Cousin Carlo died within six months
(#143).

The chapter ends on two poignant personal notes. In August 1917 Corinna
entered the Italian Hospital with uterine problems related to her 1908 miscarriage. After an operation and three months in the sanatarium of the Italian
Hospital she returned home (#151, #152). In addition, Abele reported in a
very moving passage that their closest friends, Carlo and Costanza Sasso, had
returned to Italy: "They were here that which you, dearest parents, are over

there. . . . We loved them with a constant love, without deceptive enthusiasm" (#152).

Letter 122

Valdengo, 1 June 1915

Dearest children Oreste, Abele, and Corinna,

Your dear mother is the same, as always. Some days she would be considerably better if she could walk without crutches. This year, in the period that we are going through, I don't know if we will be able to try the treatment again. Because of the war with Austria, which has unfortunately broken out even in Italy, the health establishments will not follow their normal procedure.

That of Professor Vinai in Andorno is still closed, and maybe it will open for the care of war casualties. Here the mobilization is almost general. Those born in 1876 and on have almost all been called, even those who already have done their military service. Those of the third category[1] born in 1895 left today.

Your age of the third category, dear Oreste, has not yet been called. Let's hope that everything goes well and that they don't call you. There are terrible gaps in some families: two, three brothers called up. Our friend Scaramuzzi has three sons who were recalled: Giovanni, Luigi, and Nazareno. His daughter Caterina died a few days ago leaving two very young children. Her husband has been dead for only four months. In the midst of such sorrow the good man displays considerable courage.

Our cousin Andrea wrote to us from Turin a few days after his departure (for the war). Who knows where he is now?

We are certain that there is a great deal of talk about this war over there too, and maybe you have more exact news than we do of the various developments.

According to our newspapers everyone is winning. But when the results are counted, we will all have been losers. A waste of lives and money.

If we live, we shall see things never seen before, and let's hope they are good. Here for several days we have had very changeable weather, contrary to the requirements of agriculture. On sunny days it is quite hot, but when it rains it is cool, harmful to the sensitive condition of your dear mother. . . .

Your loving parents

1. *In the third category were young men who were physically fit for service but who were normally exempt for various family reasons—sons of widows, for example.*

Letter 123

Buenos Aires, 10 June 1915

Dearest parents,

We are especially happy that you are well, dear Father, and that dear Mother is getting comfort from the warm weather. We urge you to be cheerful; that's a good remedy for everything.

Last week I gave the card to Carlo Boschetto, and he sends you his very best.

The Sasso family is also fine, and we see them often. They are very good friends of ours.

The Garrone family was also here to visit us; they are very well. Greetings.

It's started to get cold here, even though winter doesn't begin until the 21st. These days have been cold like it's not been for a long time, going down to 3 below zero (C.) How we regret the cozy warmth of the stove these days! Before I curse the winter I think back on the curses against this past summer. This cool spell (double it!) at least increases my appetite, if that is possible.

So then, we are at war! The news was received here the very evening of the declaration and caused tremendous enthusiasm, with everyone singing the praises of Italy. Though it's been expected for a long time, the declaration was favorably received. Almost all the newspapers here, besides the three Italian dailies, comment favorably on Italy's joining the war in favor of the allies, and they give it special attention, publishing it separately from the other Italian news. The enlistment of those called to service began at once, and there are already thousands signed up.

Two steamships have already left filled with more than 2,000; others are getting ready to leave. The departure was touching and grand; they talk about 100,000 people who came together to see the first ones off. The impression was extraordinary, everyone cheering, all the whistles of the ships anchored in the port blowing at great length, to send their greetings and wish them the best of luck.

Of friends, maybe our good friend Ezio, the son of the late lamented Professor Buscaglione, will be leaving soon. He has already registered though he is in the third category and he hasn't received any military training.

I, declared unfit, and without any call-up notice, don't know if they will call me. Oreste, of the third category and without military training, hasn't been called either. They are calling only those born in 1888 or since then who are in good health.

There are also many volunteers, but they give preference to the youngest and to those due for call-up.

Some time will pass before they call us for service. Then we will see. I don't know anything about our Cousin Abele, who was called back. . . .

With this letter, I am enclosing a check for 500 lire.

Your very loving children,
Abele, (Oreste, and
Corinna)

Letter 124

Buenos Aires, 10 June 1915

Confidential[1]
Dearest parents,

I am only now replying to your very dear letter of April 14, which I got at my office.[2]

Concerning the winter things, thanks so much. I too had already thought of sending you some money in addition for a few things, especially socks, which I can't have made here, but then, with the war, I saw that it would be difficult. The needs there will be too great. We will wait and see then.

I am sorry that that ignorant ass, our fine Rivetti, has come to bring you such good news and dear greetings from America. However, there is no importance at all to the things certain people can say and think. In the meantime, thanks, dearest parents, for the concern and interest that you always have for us. I saw Eugenio [Rivetti] only once. Invited repeatedly in an unassuming way to our house, he never came.

Certainly Buenos Aires made a bad impression on him, to judge from the difficulties that he had. Although I also prefer Biella, because I feel closer to it and it is natural, it is also true that Buenos Aires is a splendid city, in spite of an infinity of ugly things.

Oreste, after the railroad projects, has done other work that would have been more financially successful if the weather had not ruined half the world—just as a large number of other builders have been ruined. Then, given the enormous, ridiculous competition of ignoramuses, he has been less able to find projects. However he is always busy with everything even with good jobs, with domestic *cloacae* (interior plumbing with toilets, bathrooms, etc.), which is almost a specialty of Buenos Aires. Even now he keeps on competing constantly for projects.

As to his grand manner, it's true in part, and it's somewhat justifiable since it's been an obsession of his for many years. Since I've come here, I have cooled this obsession considerably by criticizing the crazy American grand manner. But it's always better to be a bit on the grand side than to be stingy like some people we know.

Corinna is fine, and she works hard. She does what she can, although she hasn't got that feeling for housework that only a mother can give. Sometimes I yell, but we all love each other. If that weren't the case, we wouldn't have lived together so long.

I am still at the same job, as a technical engineer. It is one of the most important firms; but [I have] never [been made] a director—an employee who works a lot, and yes, I think, is appreciated.

Do you remember when I was telling you that the hard work in Sardinia would help me a lot? I assure you that it has come true completely. I work a lot and maybe too much. I am at work between 6:30 and 7:00 in the morning, and have an hour and a half break at noon. Sometimes I even work during this break. In the evening, I leave at 7:00 or 8:00 instead of 6:00 and sometimes even later, and quite often I return after supper.

However I like to work, although I sometimes get mad, but I am always working. Many jobs have turned out magnificently for me, though at times I sweat through seven shirts. In the office everyone likes me and also in the workshop.

I speak Spanish rather well. At certain times they don't recognize me as an Italian, and I write it pretty well.

There you are, dearest parents, our current situation set before you: We live modestly, appreciated by everyone, and we hope things go better.

Be happy and don't worry about us. The day will come when we will embrace each other together.

With all my heart, your very loving son Abele kisses you.

1. *This letter from Abele is marked confidential presumably to warn Luigi that Oreste had not seen it.*
2. *This letter is missing from the collection.*

Letter 125

Valdengo, 14 June 1915

Dearest children Oreste, Abele, and Corinna,

We are addressing this letter especially to you, dearest son Oreste, because too rarely do we hear from you in your own words.

It is very true that while you are together it's good enough that one writes for everyone, but it is for us a greater pleasure to hear from everyone in their own words.

Certainly your heavy schedule will make it hard for you to send us your special regards. We keep this in mind. If you write us a letter or two and a postcard even from far away, in case you are going there often, it will be such a pleasure for us to hear your own words.

We hope this complaint of ours will not offend you. It is our great fondness [for you] that drives us to speak to you like this.

To know about your perfect harmony comforts and reassures us; but the words of all three of you will comfort us even more.

Your age of the third category has not yet been called to military service, and we hope that it won't be called.

We hope the war ends soon so that we can embrace all of you here with the greatest love.

Your loving parents

Bye.

Letter 126

Valdengo, 21 June 1915

Dearest children Oreste, Abele, and Corinna,

Your constant care for us consoles us, and it is also a great comfort in my illness.

As you see I can't write very well because my hand trembles constantly.

However I want to force myself to write too, because I am so touched by your constant great love for me and by the comfort that you always give me.

The pleasure of seeing all of you together at last would be a great comfort for me; but the current situation is not right for it, and so I am resigned to wait until things in Europe go better and there is less danger in traveling.

Meanwhile I constantly kiss you in all the letters and postcards that you send us.

I send you the dearest kisses.
Your loving mother

Letter 127

Valdengo, 8 July 1915

Dearest children, Oreste, Abele, and Corinna,

It is always a great joy to get your sweet and loving letters and post-cards. . . .

The check for 500 lire is the finest demonstration of your infinite affection for us. We can only give you our infinite gratitude for your goodheart-edness. . . .

Up to now you two have not been called up, you, dear Abele, since you are "unfit for military service."

It's better this way for all of us. Meanwhile Corinna can rest easy and de-cline to volunteer and always be with you, dearest Oreste.[1] . . .

Here all business has been reduced to supplying military needs of all types.

The industrialists who produce military equipment are reaping a golden harvest. . . . They have good reason to glorify the war.

The toughest agricultural work will soon be over. The weather, which has been consistently bad and unchanging has ruined a good part of the grapes, but we still hope to make enough wine for us and for you if you will give us the pleasure of welcoming you sometime so that we can embrace you.

We have asked Carmelina to do some knitting for all three of you. As soon as it's ready we will mail it to you, and we hope that you will be able to use it as winter comes on over there.

Your dear mother still hasn't made up her mind whether to go again for the treatment at Andorno.

Your loving parents

1. *Corinna was very enthusiastic about the war. Luigi, a Socialist, favored neutrality and took the opportunity here to tease Corinna about her enthusiasm.*

Letter 128

Valdengo, 10 July 1915

Dearest children Oreste, Abele, and Corinna,

Last Sunday we had the pleasure of a visit from Corinna's brother, Giovanni, his wife, and daughter Maria.

They are all fine and they send you their best and wish you all well. We gave them your address.

We are the same as always. Your dear mother suffers, but she has a lot of courage. As always we are hoping for improvement.

We haven't yet gone to consult Professor Vinai about the possibility of an effective new treatment. We'll be going there soon.

We are in the midst of summer, the heat isn't intense, but it will increase.

Here all the glances, thoughts, and discussions are turned on the war—that ugly bitch that stamps all the life out of our well-being. Let's hope for and expect an early end to it and the return to normal life and to profitable work for all mankind.

Your cousin Andrea, who is at the front, writes to us. He's well, and he sends you his best.

Your loving parents

Dearest daughter-in-law Corinna,

With special care and love we separately address to you our most loving wishes and many, many kisses.

Your loving parents-in-law

Letter 129

Valdengo, 15 August 1915

Dearest children Oreste, Abele, and Corinna,

We hope that you've received the things that we sent you on July 27 with a woman who had come to Cerretto and was staying with the Pellas (a package containing six pairs of short socks, twelve pairs of long ones, six flannel shirts, and four pairs of underwear, everything of wool). We also hope you've received the letter mailed to you on the same day.[1]

Your dear Mother is the same, as always. As I was telling you in another letter, we went to Professor Vinai's on July 28. He ordered some medicine that didn't help. I went back alone. He ordered another medicine, but that too was without success.

Even the professor himself gave us little hope in her recovery. We are doing everything possible to alleviate her pain, which will be difficult.

Unfortunately we must resign ourselves to this. We keep trying with sedatives to make the illness less painful. Certainly if I knew what we could still try, and where, I wouldn't omit it. Yet we always keep hoping.

There is no change in the news here. The war is the only topic of general discussion. New age groups are always being called up; even those who had been rejected are called back for another visit. Up to now you two have been exempt. You will see this from the newspapers which I believe you are still receiving.

We haven't heard anything about Cousin Andrea for some time. We hope he's all right.

Your loving parents

1.   *The letter of July 27, 1915, mentioned here and in letter #131, is missing.*

Letter 130

Buenos Aires, 19 August 1915

Dearest parents,

We too hope that you are well also and that our dear mother is cheerful in order to help her get better.

Your dear letters and beautiful postcards give us the greatest pleasure. They help us remember the old birthplaces, always so dear to us.

There is nothing new here at all now that even the war has gone out of fashion, so to speak. With the danger that it may go on for a long time still, it's becoming something normal. But it's true that we feel its effects a lot, making the crisis which has already lasted a long time disproportionately worse.

Certain materials are completely scarce, and others are becoming so, making prices sky high.

Immigration is paralyzed since they don't even come from Spain, but rather they are leaving. And, though from one point of view this is almost a good thing, reducing the number of unemployed, on the other hand it makes one worry about the next harvest, *cosecha* (pronounced *cosecia*), for which there will very probably be a shortage of labor. There is very little activity in the port, and that of construction, which was so great before, is almost nothing. . . .

Thanks infinitely for the things you had made for us, but it isn't necessary in these times, especially since everyone here is doing everything possible to ship as many garments as they can over there.

Corinna too is writing you a letter. I must not distract her, since she has begun it today in order to finish it at least by tomorrow.

Let us hear from you soon.

At this point we take the occasion to wish you, dearest Father, a happy birthday on September 23 coming up and you, dearest Mother, for yours on October 10th. We wish with all our heart that you open it [this letter] happily as we here sincerely wish for those days.

> Your loving children,
> Abele, (Oreste, and
> Corinna)

Letter 131

> Buenos Aires, 14 September 1915

Dearest parents,

We hope that all is well with you too and that our dear Mother finds comfort in the good weather. We again urge upon you extreme caution and prudence. . . .

We got your last dear letter of 27 July, telling us of the arrival of Signora Erconi, whom I think I know, or so my friend Pella tells me, with the knitwear that you kindly had made for us. However she hasn't arrived yet, . . . and perhaps she would do well not to come.

We are now waiting to hear about the two of you, about your visit to our dear Mother, and about you too, dear Father. As always we wish you the best.

Oreste, as, however, he will write you, has gone up to the northern part of the Republic to start a project, a railroad bridge. It's close to Catamarca, the capital of the province of the same name. It's a thousand kilometers from Buenos Aires. As a result Corinna and I are left alone for some time, waiting to hear from him.

Great celebrations are being prepared for September 20, and if bad weather doesn't come along to ruin it, they will be extraordinary. Every day there are parties and receptions "for those called to arms and their families," and many families are making woolen clothing for the soldiers.

On the lists of those poor men who have fallen we see the names of some of our own from Biella, and among them many whom we know.

Sunday our friend Carlo Boschetto came to visit us; he too has been rejected as "unfit for military service." He's fine and sends you his best, so give his relatives our best. Our friend Carlo Sasso is fine too, and we will probably go eat polenta and salami with them next Sunday.

> Your loving children,
> Abele, (Oreste, and
> Corinna)

Letter 132

> Valdengo, 14 September 1915

Dearest children, Oreste, Abele, and Corinna,

It's a great comfort for us always to hear from you that you are well. . . .

Your dear mother is the same as always. The consultations with Professor Vinai and the medicines have not helped at all. We must resign ourselves to this situation but without giving up hopes for improvement.

You should have received our letter of August 15, as well as the things we sent you with the woman who has gone over there. We hear that our letters are censored before they get to you. That doesn't happen to those that we get. Censorship of our letters wouldn't matter if it were not for the shameful scourge of war that is overwhelming Europe and has very serious consequences even in other parts of the world.

Riccardo too has written from Mexico, describing the almost total collapse of everything. He wrote on the 2nd of May; it got here on the 7th of this month. That's longer than Christopher Columbus took to make his first trip. He says that the scudo there is worth six of our soldi.[1] Basic products have gone up by 400 percent. Moreover there is the fear that in the end there won't be anything at all to buy.

It's a real worldwide disaster. Those who will live to see the end of this great event and those who will come along later will not believe that in this world such barbarity has ever existed among men.

Here we are so used to the war that it seems to be the normal way of life. That is, if we leave out the constant increase in the price of food of every kind. All the factories are working for the government—clothing, arms, munitions—a dream for the suppliers.

It looks like autumn is going to be good. There is a scarcity of grapes just about everywhere this year. The other harvests are pretty good. We have enough for ourselves.

We thank you so much for the dear and heartfelt good wishes for our birthdays coming up; we hope to spend them quite nicely. If it were not for the misfortune of your dear mother's illness, we could say we were spending them with great good cheer. But in the midst of misfortune good cheer is always rare and difficult. Here almost every family has someone in military service, and they are troubled about it. We, who have the good fortune that you are still out of harm's way, have the trouble of your dear mother's illness.

It was an immense pleasure for us to hear your heartfelt words, dear Corinna, in your unaffected and spirited way of speaking; that reveals the constant harmony that prevails among you. For us this is the greatest comfort.

Cousin Andrea at the front is in the greatest danger. A few days ago we received a letter in which he described the outrageous hardships those poor soldiers suffer at the front, cold, rain, snow, and scarcity of food. The sons of our friend Scaramuzzi are at the front too but in a less dangerous sector; so are Olimpia's sons.

In the hope that on a not too distant day this sad state of affairs may cease and that a bit of peace, of normal life, may come back, we send you our fondest good wishes for good health and mutual harmony, a great comfort for us.

Your loving parents

1.   *Six soldi equal 1.2 lire.*

Letter 133

Catamarca, 21 September 1915

Dearest parents,

I have been in this city for a week, where I have taken on the construction of a bridge with a span of 150 meters in partnership with another man from Buenos Aires since the necessary capital was immense.

For some time I had been competing for construction bids of every type—without success, because (of the effects) of the enormous competition on prices. Now I have snared this, and for six months I'll have work. Today I began the foundation excavations with about 50 workers, and I'll employ another 100 of them next week since it is important for me to have finished the foundations before the water rises a lot, from the end of November up to the beginning of March.

I am alone here, and I have put up a warehouse of galvanized iron for storage and for living quarters for myself and some of the workers. I have also rented a house (*rancho*) for living quarters for the remaining workers.

Catamarca, the provincial capital, is, as a city, very ugly, but its location is splendid, enclosed in the midst of very high mountains and with luxuriant vegetation. There is every type of fruit; the grapes especially are excellent for the table, not so for wine. The entire population is a mixture of Indians with Spanish (*mestiza*); most of them are very poor. The only businessmen are foreigners, Italians and Spaniards for the most part. Natives are concerned only with politics; their ambition is government employment, on the national or provincial level, and, for those who can, the National Congress.

The climate is splendid; during the day it's hot, and it will be more so in the coming months, but at night it is cool. The day before yesterday I got up with the surprise of seeing all the surrounding peaks white with snow, but by today it's already gone. It is a delightful spectacle to see the mountains and the snow since I had not seen them together for ten years.

In these regions it is completely without rain for nine months of the year, always clear and dry. Then there are powerful wind storms which raise up clouds of dirt and sand. I imagine they are comparable to those of the Sahara. I have been forced to wear glasses to protect my eyes from the dirt. I'll send you some photographs of the project and some postcards of the place.

Here we hardly talk about the war at all because of the scarcity of newspapers and, even more, of people who might read them. The only interest is local politics; everything else is of passing concern. I too have not kept up with the Great War for a week, and only today I have subscribed to one of the capital's newspapers (*La Nación*) to find out whether they are negotiating for peace yet. . . .

Corinna has stayed behind in Buenos Aires with Abele, and I expect to hear from them in a week (the train comes here only three times a week). Like me they are doing very well.

The letter and cards written by Mother gave us great pleasure. Corinna is more than happy with them and would like to embrace you both soon. I would like it too, and if this work of mine turns out well, perhaps we will come visit you.

We hope that Mother gets better and that you will continue to be well and that both of you are in good spirits. We will stay that way.

Your loving son,
Oreste

Letter 134

Valdengo, 20 October 1915

Dearest children, Oreste, Abele, and Corinna,

Just today, we received with great pleasure your dear letter, Oreste, from Catamarca.

We took special pleasure from your promise that when the work is done—and we hope with all our heart that it goes well for you—that you will come at last to embrace us after such a long time of longing for you.

You should have received the things, we hope, from Signora Erconi. We are anxious to know that they have not been lost.

We are the same as ever. I, your father, am fine. Your mother [is progressing] very, very slowly. . . .

Cousin Andrea has been promoted to corporal-major for bookkeeping. He's fine but still at the front.

In this poor Europe, with everything in flames, we are living a life of apprehension and agony. We are always hoping for and expecting the end, but we are always back at the beginning.

More age groups have left, and others will be leaving shortly.

The military services are not yet all full, but no fewer than twenty age groups have been called up, and few of them are left at home. Even some of those who had been rejected have had to go. So far those in your situation have not been called up. Of your age group, dearest Oreste, only the third category, yours, has not yet been called up. Let's hope they forget it.

War and the high cost of food are the words on everyone's lips in these sad circumstances.

Here the weather is still pretty good, considering the season. We are addressing this letter to you in Buenos Aires, dearest Oreste, since you haven't given us your address in Catamarca. Would the two of you, after reading it, send it on to dear Oreste?

Your loving parents

Letter 135

Valdengo, 2 November 1915

Dearest children Abele, Oreste, and Corinna,

For three days your dear mother has been walking around the house without the aid of crutches. This is a great triumph for her, and a great joy for me as it must also be for you. We hope this notable improvement continues until she can even walk freely through the streets.

The fond impression of your constant love and care contributes a great deal to her improvement.

Again last Thursday we had the great pleasure of receiving your very dear letter, dear Abele, with the 500 lire, and of hearing that you are always in excellent health.

It is a pleasure to hear of the sincere friendship that you have with the Sasso family. Please give them our very best.

The enthusiasm that prevails among the Italian residents there for the anniversary of September 20 is not surprising.[1] Here for obvious reasons they aren't making so much of it, especially in the present circumstance of our national life fomented by this terrible war, which has taken over and overwhelmed every single thing.

We're always hoping for and wishing for peace, and still the most ferocious human slaughter goes on.

Even those born in 1886–87 of the third category have to present themselves to the individual recruiting centers [as] of this month, and they won't be the last. Up to now you haven't been called up, but it could happen.

Saturday we went by carriage on our usual visit to the grave of our dear Narcisa and your dear grandmother. Yesterday, All Saints' Day, I went back to the cemetery.

We hope that dear Oreste's job ends soon and this barbarous war ends so that we can embrace you here with us.

Your loving parents

1.   On September 20, 1870, the Italian army entered Rome ending the temporal power of the Pope and unifying the country.

Letter 136

Buenos Aires, 26 November 1915

Dearest parents,

We send your dear letters right on to Oreste, who is also anxious to get them. We are all happy to hear good news from you, dear Father, and to know that our dear Mother's condition is better.

We gave the Sasso family your best, and they reciprocate; the same for the Pellas, who as always are fine.

Pierino Pizzoglio is sick. We visited him last Sunday and hope he gets better. You keep asking—it's understandable—if we have received the things that you so kindly and generously had prepared for us. From our letters you must now know that we hadn't received anything before, nor have we now. Are you sure that Signora Erconi has left Italy? I know nothing about her; at least she hasn't yet shown up at the Pellas. We certainly no longer expect to see her; we are sorry on your account since you made the sacrifice. Just the same, we thank you with all our heart. Nothing new here; it's very hot.

Oreste is still out of town; he writes that he's fine.

Here a special committee is doing a lot of work for the benefit of the servicemen who have been called up. They do everything; they are constantly doing charity benefits. Wednesday we went to an open-air performance of *Aida:* It was a spectacular sight, more than 15,000 people; the receipts are sure to go over 120,000 lire! They are putting it on again tomorrow and the day after.

Your loving children,
Abele, (Oreste, and
Corinna)

Letter 137

Valdengo, 31 December 1915

Dearest children Abele, Oreste, and Corinna,

Your dear mother continues to improve. She walks around the house fairly well without supports. She even sews pretty easily with the machine. We hope it continues and that she will also be able to go outside.

She is still always in pain. And to relieve it, we have to keep giving her injections of Pantopon two or three times every twenty-four hours. .

It is a nuisance, but if it weren't for these injections, she absolutely wouldn't be able to withstand the pain; we are lucky to have this treatment and so long as it's effective.

We keep hoping that she will be able to do without them and get well completely. This will be possible when we can embrace all of you here. The emotion of great joy will enable her nervous system to return to normal. As soon as the war is over, you will come home for sure, right? . . .

We hope that you spent the holidays nicely and that you will continue to be well. To our dearest Oreste we hope that nothing goes wrong for him and that he will be able to do well. We spent the holidays nicely, and we hope to finish 1915 well and begin 1916 well and to continue so.

We hear that you are in the midst of summer; here we are in the midst of winter. The weather is very changeable. Some days it is very cold, but now for several days the temperature has been mild, above zero [centigrade]. We take it as it comes.

I went to Novara yesterday for the usual session of the Provincial Council. I got back with the train that gets to Candelo at 10:30. I was home at midnight. I received a letter from our friend Carlo Sasso. Give him our best.

Your loving parents

Letter 138

Valdengo, 6 March 1916

Dearest children, Abele, Oreste, and Corinna,

Your dear mother is doing pretty well. . . . Your constant generous help is a major contribution to her improvement in view of the not insignificant expense of about 1.5 lira a day for Pantopon. It would be difficult for us to manage the cost of it along with everything else.

Again yesterday we got the letter from you dearest Abele and the check for 500 lire, for which we thank you infinitely with all our heart.[1]

We hear that Corinna has had the flu but is now completely recovered. The good news about dear Oreste, far away from both you and us, makes us very happy. In the same way it gladdens our hearts more and more to hear that you are as always in perfect harmony. That is what we hope for and recommend to you as always for your good and ours and for the honor of us all.

Here the call-up of age groups continues; even those who were rejected are being called back for a new examination. Those born in 1890 have also been called, but your type of medical exemption has not been included; so you are exempt. Those born in 1883 have not been called up—those of the third category—but they probably will since those of '84 have now been called, and it's still going on.

The European war continues, and no one knows for how long.

A few days ago we received a letter from Riccardo, he is in El Bolero, Baja California. He's fine and sends you his greetings. He complains that he doesn't get our letters, just as we don't get his. . . .

Your friend Antonio Pella and Zocco are fine and send back to you their warmest regards.

Your loving parents

1.   *He is referring to a letter of 4 February 1916, which we did not include.*

Letter 139

Buenos Aires, 17 March 1916

Thanks so much for your kind thoughts. Earlier we received your most recent letters . . . with dear Mother's postcards; we were filled with joy about her improvement, which we had so greatly hoped for. We are happy for our dear Mother and also for you, dear Father; it will be a relief for you and make you happier. Keep on doing well; that is our dearest satisfaction. . . .

We're fine; the heat is going away, and we are getting ready for winter. Here too the price of fuel is sky high. Coal is up to 180 lire a ton! And it's still going up. The same for iron; before the war it had done down to eight centavos (Argentine money), [but] is now twenty-five. The same for everything else. And it keeps going up!

Oreste is still in Catamarca. He wrote today, perhaps they will be done by the end of April. I always share your dear letters with him. He has not yet returned yours of January 22nd. He's fine. . . .

Signora Erconi has not been seen. Armando Pella, with whom we spent the other evening, says she must still be in Turin. He's probably right. . . .

We haven't seen Sasso for several Sundays since we go spend every Sunday in the country, at Moron, at the home of family friends who absolutely insist that we go there. It's about twenty kilometers from Buenos Aires, but you get there in half an hour, and there are trains at all times.

I'm still working a lot. We are producing, especially now, as much as we possibly can. We are also working on a steel mill for Brazil and one for Chile.

Tomorrow a very close friend, from Bioglio, is leaving, Gioacchino Perotti, I had already spoken to you about him on several occasions. He is coming for the war. . . . He will be sure to come visit you, and, in addition to the news about all of us, he's bringing a cane for you, dear Father. It's of a rare wood from here. Oreste had been keeping it for several years to send you. Now it has been decorated a bit, and we are sending it to you since it slipped our mind when Zocco, the younger, and Antonio Pella went back. The wood is natural, unfinished. It is long; you may have it cut since it is very hard. It might be useful to have some additional nails put in at the tip and at the ring since they are loose.

Do give this dear friend the warmest welcome; he is a serious and decent young man. He is with us right now, and we are talking about Biella and everyone.

With regard to what you wrote me about my draft status, I know about it; and I was planning to stop by the consulate for the medical examination just so that I wouldn't have problems of any sort later, and then, if I should have to leave, I would go, and so hasten the moment when I would have the pleasure of kissing you.

Therefore I would like it if it were possible for you to collect my certificate of military exemption from the town hall or from the conscription office. Then I could go in with all my papers in order. If you remember, before I left I had tried hard to get it, but they told me there was no need for it. But I see that many who are medically exempt have it with them.

> Your loving children,
> Abele, (Oreste, and
> Corinna)

Letter 140

Valdengo, 10 April 1916

Dearest children Oreste, Abele, and Corinna,

First of all, it is a great pleasure to let you know that your dear mother has improved considerably in her walking. The crutches completely abandoned, she has to use the cane only for short stretches, always walking slowly, however. Although it is necessary to continue the treatment with Pantopon to relieve the pain when it attacks her, for us it is a great triumph. I am fine.

More good news: Acting upon information which the Pellas got from Turin, we were able to flush out that Signora Erconi, to whom we had given the things to take to you.

On Saturday the 8th of this month I went to Turin, and with the cooperation of Cousin Onorino, I was able to find that person and get the things back. I brought them back home as well as those intended for Armando Pella, which I gave to his family the next day. The parcels were all intact without any alteration. She handed them over to me with the excuse that she had not left (for Argentina) and had always intended to come here and bring them back.

I won't tell you the means I used to see that woman, who has always been invisible and silent.

Let's not worry about the rest. We have the things, and at the first luckier opportunity we will get them to you since they were intended only for you, dearest children.

More important news: Cousin Carlo is living here with us; he has made a will, naming me sole heir with the obligation to keep him and care for him until he dies, and, after his death, to give his nieces Carolina and Quinta 800 lire each.

Of course it is an uncertain business, inasmuch as exact calculations can't be made with death. Since your dear mother is always at home, she is able to do the necessary housework. We have agreed in view of the fact that he preferred our house. Left alone, he is absolutely unable to take care of himself because he is suffering horribly from a violent case of asthma.

Sincerely wishing him at least five or six more years of life, it can't be a bad business. And too, we felt the obligation of humanity, in view of our relationship and the trust he put in us rather than in his nieces. . . .

With our savings and the income from his property we will go on without any harm to our interests. . . .

For two days we have had beautiful spring weather, and we hope it continues. We hope that you are well as always and that your affairs are going well, especially those of dear Oreste since they are subject to so many factors and so many ups and downs.

Carlo is always tortured in his efforts to breathe; it won't come.

The Pella family, with Antonio, whom I see often, sends you their best.

Your loving parents

Letter 141

Valdengo, 22 April 1916

Dearest children Oreste, Abele, and Corinna,

On Wednesday the 19th of this month we had the great pleasure of welcoming your friend Gioacchino Perotti, who brought us excellent news about you and the cane, an exceptional item in these parts. I thank you infinitely for the magnificent gift, which is not only a thing of great luxury but will be useful as a support in some possible and not distant circumstances.

But truly I am embarrased because it is too luxurious. I am afraid of losing it or of letting myself get robbed, and furthermore of playing the "fop" in carrying it. I shall be duty bound to render the explanation that it is a gift from my dearest children. I shall carry it on solemn occasions, especially when I shall have the pleasure of being together with you.

Your friend Perotti seemed almost discontented at having come home.

You have not been included in the most recent call-up to military service, especially you, dear Abele, you are exempt from every call-up. At any rate, if it should be the case, I'll write you at once.

This morning Cavaliere Dr. Paschetto came for a consultation with Dr. Acati from here about Cousin Carlo, who is suffering a lot and is in danger. We hope that he can get a little better and can live a bit more without suffering so much. He sends you his love.

Our friend Federico Scaramuzzi sends you his best. I'm sending you the address of a friend of his over there:

> Zuan (Juan) Amosso
> Avenida di Maio 665
> Hail Insurance Inspector

If you think you might approach him, I think he will be a good friend. Say hello to him for Scaramuzzi.

The news here isn't new. High cost of food, economic hardship, war, war, war.

A few, barely audible, words about peace, but just words. Let's hope that reality can soon ring in harmony with the words, with the desires of so many people.

Your loving parents, who are doing pretty well

Letter 142

Buenos Aires, 22 May 1916

Dearest parents,

We are happier than ever because of the good news you give us about our dear mother's improvement and your good health, dear Father. But don't overdo. Take it easy and be at leisure. . . .

I am sure that my good friend Gioacchino Perotti will have come to visit you. We heard from him from Dakar (Senegal) on the French African coast, where the ship took on coal, and I'm sure he's told you about America.

Oreste has been back for several days; he will be staying here only a short while before setting out again for Catamarca. This evening he's gone out on business. Corinna is in bed.

We are happy and surprised at the news that you got back those things you had so kindly sent to us with that piece of bad luck who had kept us in suspense for months. Thanks also on the part of Pella, who returns your greetings with pleasure. Our friend Sasso and his wife, Costanza, also say hello; we saw them the other evening. Their son Pinot may be coming back from Chile, where he is doing very well, to leave for military service, but it's not clear yet whether he will be fit for service.

A bit of news that, though it was expected, still affected us greatly: It's the end of our dear friend Pierino Pizzoglio. He died this morning; the funeral will be tomorrow. A long bout with a stomach disease, which was not treated, [eventually] developed into tuberculosis, which consumed him completely. Peace to him! He leaves a wife and three lovely children, who will be looked after by the mother's family, which is pretty well off.

It's good news that we have not been called up, but I think it would be useful to have my certificate of medical exemption in order. . . .

The news about Cousin Carlo's illness does not astonish us, and we too wish that he may still have a long and good life.

As for your taking care of him and the agreement you made with him, we consider everything you do as well done if it seems that way to you. It is right to treat him with every consideration as you have always done since he is alone and has complete trust in you. But we would not want it to be too much of a sacrifice since we want you to take it easy and be at leisure. We would like it if you could possibly get a woman who could help our dear mother with the housework and leave you too, dear Father, a bit freer. We understand that it is not such an easy matter in these times since the women will certainly have to do the men's work in the fields.

As far as the financial arrangements go, as we said, everything you do is fine with us. Only malicious tongues, and you must know of many, could spread a lot of disgusting nonsense, and it would be a good idea to be prepared for it. Dear parents, forgive this observation, it certainly will have occurred to you too, but it is occasioned by a certain awareness of that small-village environment. . . .

Here it's beginning to get cool, and right now my hands are frozen, so I am writing as best I can.

The news of the war we get right away, certainly more than you. At six in the morning we already know everything that happened the day before. On Sunday morning, the 20th, we already knew about the landslide that occurred on Saturday on the Balma rail line! Imagine then how it is with the important news!

They are now getting ready for the celebration of another centennial (the Independence Oath of 9 July 1816). . . . It is, however, a poor centennial, very poor, compared with that other one, the one for the Revolution of 1810. That was a thing of madness; no, I don't mean that; I meant to say, "in the American way." Never mind, we too will celebrate it in poverty, but sanely!

Your loving children,
Abele, (Oreste, and
Corinna)

Letter 143

Buenos Aires, 22 October 1916

Dearest parents,

Because of the lack of mail steamers, since almost all the ships are exclusively freighters, we have delayed so much in writing. . . . [1] We are sure that our friend Pinot Sasso will have brought you news about us and our greetings and that he will have told you to your satisfaction about life in America. We are waiting to hear from him. We have longed to hear from you too, dear parents, for a long time.

We were moved to hear of the death on the field of battle of our poor Cousin Quinto. I already spoke about it in our last letter since I had read it in the papers here. [2] We were also moved, but not astonished, to hear of the death of our good Cousin Carlo. We didn't think it would come so soon. We hope that the agreement you had previously concluded gives you no problems or troubles, and that everything works out well.

Your most recent dear letter, of 1 September, was received just this week. [3] I have sent it on to Oreste, who is still in Catamarca; we hope he will finish up there this month and come back very soon to be with us.

It was a very welcome pleasure to hear the ever better news about dear Mother and that with the new treatment she is undergoing she can improve ever more. Leave nothing undone and you too, dear Father, try to take it easy.

The outing you made to Oropa gave us as much satisfaction as if we had made it ourselves, especially since it seems to us and we feel as if we were close to you.

I have also received a letter from Cousin Andrea in which he tells me about his misfortunes and his imminent return (to the front). I would like to write him, but I don't know where. Would you thank him and give him my very best. . . .

Today I read in *La Prensa*, the main newspaper here, that the first snow has fallen in Biella, in the mountains perhaps. We recommend the stove and a bit of good wine.

Here on the other hand the heat is beginning; it is predicted that it will be terrible, as nasty as was the winter this year. Really it seems that the world has gone crazy.

I am enclosing in this letter a check for 500 lire.

Your loving children,
Abele, (Oreste, and
Corinna)

1.   *The last letter they sent was 29 June. It is not included in this collection.*
2.   *The Buenos Aires newspapers listed the names of those killed in the war.*
3.   *This letter is missing from the collection.*

Letter 144

Buenos Aires, 5 December 1916

Confidential

Dearest parents,

Only today am I answering your kind letter of last August 20th, which I received directly at the office two months ago.[1] I have been waiting so that I could give you more certain information.

First of all I would like to know if you received my letter of 10 June 1915, in reply to your similar one of 12 May 1915 concerning our situation.[2] I hope so.

I am still at the same place, almost four and a half years now; personally I don't feel the crisis since the factory is making a lot of money with the production of sheet iron, which has gone up in value five times from that which it had been before the war. Naturally, when the company makes money, the employees also are not losers, which certainly would have happened if the contrary were the case.

As you know, Oreste, who has come back [to visit] twice, has been away for more than a year on a project of a certain importance, but for various reasons it is not bringing in the desired return. In a few days he will be back, and we'll see.

I help as much as I can with everything, and I am not unhappy about it, nor of living honestly and with honor in the face of everybody. Oreste would have done the same if the contrary were the case.

Do not worry about this, and don't get alarmed; we are fine!

When Oreste comes back, we will write you about our military situation. As far as I am concerned, if things were going better for you as well, dear parents, I would already have left (for military service) if I had been fit. . . .

Corinna is fine and is busy about the house, only she would like things to be better so that she could embrace you as soon as possible.

I don't have anything more to say except to urge you to be of good cheer and in complete good health.

Your loving son,
Abele

1.   *This letter is missing.*
2.   *The letter of 10 June 1915 is letter #124. The letter of Luigi, dated 12 May 1915, is missing from the collection.*

Letter 145

Buenos Aires, 10 January 1917

Dearest parents,

We are happy that you too, in spite of the war, are well, and also that our dear mother feels more at ease, which means an improvement in your life, dear Father, and great satisfaction for us. . . .

Oreste came back before Christmas, in perfect health. We spent the holidays all together, though we were a bit depressed because of the bad weather during those days. Now it's turned clear again, and the heat is stifling.

We are sorry that our neighbor, Giovanni Sola, has gone back over there without saying hello to us. Never mind; you say hello to him.

Our friend Carlo Boschetto has been here for a while and is very well, Armando Pella and the family are just fine; we almost always spend the holidays together. Carlo Sasso is also fine; Costanza has gone to the country for a while with Lina Pella. She isn't very well; I think they will be going back over there soon. They send you their best.

The war is always the news of the day. . . .

Our crisis is also raging on; there are no jobs, not even in the fields. Imagine that lots of families who put down their roots here a long time ago, with all their children Argentine-born, are emigrating from this promised land, in need of a larger population, for nearby Brazil. They are all recruited by the slave-dealing agents for the notorious *fazendas*, the great coffee-growing plantations. There they are treated little better than slaves, so much so that the Italian government still enforces the Prinetti Degree of 1881, forbidding emigration to Brazil![1] It is sad to speak of the absolute *misery* for thousands of families; they even lack bread, right here in this country rich in grain. Let's hope it changes.

Oreste is sending a postcard, Corinna affectionately returns your kisses and loving thoughts.

Your loving children,
Abele, (Oreste, and
Corinna)

1.   *The Prinetti Decree was an executive order that prohibited subsidized emigration to Brazil; it was issued by the Italian Commissioner General of Emigration in March 1902 not, as Abele says, in 1881. It was named for the Italian foreign minister.*

Letter 146

Buenos Aires, 5 March 1917

Dearest parents,

As always I promise to write, and I never do. I don't know the reason; it would only be to repeat again every time the gloomy conditions which the current situation forces upon everyone.

In health we are, as always, doing excellently. Everything else goes on as best it can in these times. This blessed Republic is reduced to a state of exhaustion; and so, more or less, are all the other South American republics. All projects are literally paralyzed for lack of funds. The state cannot meet its contractual debts and is confronted with the obligation of renewing all its loans and not always on easy terms. The movement of capital has stopped. The bank deposit boxes are filled with gold and deposits that can't be removed; no one is running the risk of putting them into circulation. For quite a while now they have stopped giving any interest whatsoever for deposits in checking accounts.

The state budget for 1917 was approved with about sixty million more in expenses than in income. Now the ministers are doing everything to find new taxes and to eliminate expenses already voted. This year will be even worse than the last few.

Because of the lack of various materials, especially coal—you would think it was done as if by magic—they are discovering mines everywhere here. Some were already discovered sixty years ago. It goes without saying that none of them is getting results, nor does the government give it much attention either.

The paralysis we have here is incredible. In spite of the enormous emigration, in part because of those who have been called up for the war, severe unemployment continues, and that even in the countryside.

No one knows how this crisis will be resolved; they say after the war, but it is not clear how.

The usual discussions in every gathering place are always about the war. . . .

It is a pleasure to get letters from various soldiers; naturally, also because of the censorship, they don't say anything.

For affairs in general, that's enough.

Yesterday we went on a lovely excursion with the Pella family to a new bathing establishment, close to town. We came back happy and cheerful, as we had been all day, right from the start.

Carlo Sasso came to visit us a few evenings ago. He's fine, and Costanza is too. They give you their best.

It is an immense pleasure for us to hear of our dear mother's improvement; we hope to see her completely recovered when we return.

Often in the company of mutual acquaintances we talk about you, and we can almost see you again. Corinna too is always talking about dear Mother.

Abele is also writing to you since the *Prince of Udine* is leaving tomorrow, and steamships are very scarce now, for lack of traffic rather than because of the submarines.

Stay cheerful, and let's try to get through this difficult situation with tranquility.

> Your dear children,
> Oreste, (Abele, and
> Corinna)

Dearest parents,

I am adding a couple of lines to Oreste's letter since I too want to take advantage of one of the rare mail ships that's leaving tomorrow. I wish it an excellent crossing, like the many others, all lucky; it's hard in wartime. It is also that same *Prince of Udine* that brought me here. . . .

Our usual friends here are the Sasso and Pella families, who as always give you their best. Costanza has been away for some time in the country, at the property of our friend Lina Pella. They plan to return soon to their native haunts. In the enclosed photograph you will observe our friend Armando Pella's fine child, who is now three years old.

I am also enclosing a check for 500 lire.

At this very moment young Firmino has arrived, the son of our neighbor over there, Gaetano Sola. He has come to visit us, leaving many greetings for you and his family.

> Your loving children,
> Abele, (Oreste, and
> Corinna)

Letter 147

Buenos Aires, 25 May 1917

Dearest parents,

The long delay in letting you hear from us has been caused by the lack of mail communications. Many ships are employed exclusively for freight. One could take advantage of the few Spanish steamers, but they are such unpleasant people. Moreover their ships get torpedoed without concern and without protest. So it's better not to use them.

Rest assured, however; we are always with you. . . .

We are infinitely happy to know that you are both well and especially because of the notable improvement of our dear mother. Her letters are so dear to us, and they bring us great happiness. As always we urge you not to overdo and perform heavy tasks but to stay serene and happy the way we want you to.

It's almost natural and understandable, in view of the current abnormal situation, that the price of everything has gone up over there, but even here everything keeps on going up in price in a frightful manner, greatly aggravated by the continuing crisis, which is getting worse and worse.

I, however, am working away as always, too much even, waiting for better times. Oreste, back from Catamarca, is still at work settling his accounts, which the state, for lack of funds, is delaying in a scandalous manner.

Corinna too is at work around the house, and all together we think of you, wishing you excellent health and tranquility.

Yesterday there were great demonstrations on the anniversary of Italy's declaration of war.

Today is the great national holiday of Argentina, the anniversary of the revolution for independence from the Spanish yoke, and everything is closed. The city looks beautiful with thousands of flags, among which, after the blue and white of Argentina, our dear cheerful white, red, and green predominates. Everywhere there are great illuminations and music. Next Sunday there will be a great demonstration of sympathy for Italy, and it promises to be impressive. . . .

Dearest parents, though we are far away from you, we are doing everything possible so that one day we can be close to you and content; for now we always stay close with our dear friends. Our friend Carlo Sasso and his wife, Costanza, return your greetings with thanks; the same for Armando Pella and his family. We spend most of our free days with them. Sunday we were at their house; today we are expecting them here.

As proof of this we enclose ten photographs taken with our friends. Among them you will be able to recognize Nina Pella, our good friend. She's from Casale, but they used to live in Vercelli. Her family lives in a village close to here. . . .

I don't hear anything anymore about our friend Fila; we see various others from Biella every now and then.

Your loving children,
Abele, (Oreste, and
Corinna)

Letter 148

Buenos Aires, 11 June 1917

Dearest Mother,

Infinite thanks for your latest dear letter. I can't put into words the pleasure that a letter from you gives us. You complain that I am too negligent and in spite of my repeated promises I am always slow to let you hear from me personally. You are right too, but don't think that I have forgotten you. Quite the contrary, the main reason is that when Abele writes, he already says for both of us everything that should be said, and I do the same too. We read the letter over together, and, upon Corinna's approval, we close it up and everything is said and done. As for real news, there is none. One could only talk about crises: lack of work, the high cost of food, and the tragic war that keeps going on. . . .

As you see, dear Mother, to speak of these things would be a constant repetition of sadness, and when talking to people who are dear to you, you want to talk about things that are lovely and dear. And this too is the reason that even when I write, I am "crippled" in what I say. Yes, dear Mother, the moment we are living through is too sad. About the only thing left is love for our dear ones, and even that with meditation and in silence. So great is the passionate hatred today that to speak of love is almost a paradox.

Here nothing is being done, or rather every day less. The government can't find a way out to mitigate the prevailing crisis. They try every way, but they don't ever hit on the right one. . . . The lengthy political arguments distract them completely from the economic question and thereby the population suffers more from it than it really should. The ones who have struck gold are the commodities dealers, who corner the entire market and then make the consumer products shoot up to fabulous prices, never even dreamed of, since for the most part they are products of this country.

I am sure that it costs less to live in a Europe at war than here when we are still at peace. But all this will pass. As great as is today's suffering will be tomorrow's happiness. . . . So then we will live in real peace. It is a joy just to think that we too will see that day.

All our friends and acquaintances here are fine, and they give you their best in return.

Corinna and Abele are also very well; they send many kisses to Father too.

Your son,
Oreste, (Abele, and
Corinna)

Letter 149

Buenos Aires, 12 July 1917

Dearest parents,

We hope for both of you that our dear mother continues to do well, that she takes care of herself and does not overdo. We are happy for you, dear Father, that you are enjoying good health, as we always wish. . . .

I am writing in a hurry because I must leave tonight for Santa Fe on urgent company business. Last month I was at Resistencia (Chaco) and at Corrientes, near Paraguay. Now I am extremely busy, so please excuse me if I don't write as much as I would like. This will apply to the next letter—within fifteen days I think I'll have another steamer.

Oreste left on June 30th for Asunción, the capital of Paraguay. He is going there to do the planning for the installation of a large refrigerating plant on behalf of the firm where he works (the Swift Company), one of the largest in the world, with its home office in North America. He will be away a couple of months. Corinna is fine; she always talks about you; she is happy that you think of her so much. Tuesday she came here to Buenos Aires (I went to pick her up); she stayed with the wife of our friend Pella, and today she returned home.

Here we are in the midst of winter with an unheard of cold; it has even snowed, to our pleasant surprise and the amazement of the Argentine nationals, who are unacquainted with it. . . .

I won't go on any longer since I have to go back to the office and leave at ten tonight. I'll get there tomorrow at noon.

Your loving children,
Abele, (Oreste, and
Corinna)

Letter 150

Buenos Aires, 31 July 1917

Dearest parents,

From your last very dear letter we learn with joy of your good health, dear Father, and of the continuing improvement of our mother. The good weather of the summer season will certainly help and will make all of us content. . . .

We are always seeing our friends Sasso and Costanza; we give them your best, and they return your greetings with pleasure.

Our friend Armando Pella and his family also give you their very best—we were together Sunday and yesterday evening for dinner. They are upset that for more than six months they haven't heard from home, whereas they assure us that they have written many times.

We have also seen our friend Antonio Pella. He's fine and says hello.

Since you were saying in your letter of May 8th that Eugenio Rivetti kept asking you about the wallets that are in fashion here, I went and bought two of them as samples. I sent them in a registered parcel, which I hope will get there all right. I selected two good varieties, but they were expensive. I didn't want to send ordinary stuff since I imagined he would want something elegant. That is why I am sending only two of them, and when you give them to him, please tell him that should he want others at a good price (two pesos each more or less), I shall send them to him as soon as I get the word. I think, however, that he could have them made over there very nicely since at the current rate of exchange they turn out to be too expensive. One is sealskin and is worth 14.50 pesos, and the other is 5 pesos. Together they are 19.50 pesos, as you can see from the enclosed sales receipt. Don't ask for anything, but if he should wish to pay, tell him that you don't know how much they are worth in lire, so that you could see how he applies the rate of exchange. In any case don't take less than 61.50 lire, which was the exchange rate on the day of purchase. As one who has been here, he is sure to recognize the firm. Give him my best.

Because of the shortage of mail steamers I have been slow to carry out a duty. I'll make good now, though a bit late. I am enclosing a check for 500 lire. . . .

For about fifteen days Oreste has been in the nearby city of La Plata, the capital of the province of Buenos Aires. He comes back, however, every Sunday. (The city of Buenos Aires is the federal capital of the Republic and is completely independent administratively and politically. I can believe it. [Of the] more than eight million inhabitants in the Republic, a million and a half are in the capital! The towns are stunted; a great head with a body.)

La Plata, however, is a beautiful new city, though Oreste works in a nearby town.

Corinna is fine, though a slight indisposition will oblige her to undergo treatment for a while.

So far I am doing great (it's hardly necessary anymore to make an effort to play the "big man"!).

So dearest parents, try both of you to stay happy and content. One day, as soon as conditions permit, we shall have the satisfaction of embracing each other.

Here the winter is again making us feel its rigor; for several days the sky has been overcast, and it has been raining. It's all right if it doesn't freeze afterward; if it does there will be havoc in the countryside.

The war continues to be the subject of enthusiasm. The public demonstrations are coming one after the other, and they are bigger and bigger. After the one for Italy, in which more than 100,000 people took part, there was another one, equally huge, in honor of France. And yesterday evening there was also a very successful torchlight parade organized by the Italian societies in honor of the United States. The occasion was the arrival of a North American military detachment on a visit of the Republic. The visit has given rise to the most varied discussions. It left today after a stay of eight days. . . .

Since we will probably have to move, if you write, address it to me at the office, Calle Martin Garcia 665. We will write soon giving you our new address.

Your loving children,
Abele, (Oreste, and
Corinna)

Letter 151

La Plata, 8 September 1917

Dearest parents,

We are as always doing well in health, except Corinna, who is in the hospital.

For a long time she has been feeling poorly because of a miscarriage she had at the beginning of our marriage. Since she had recovered, however, she neglected to have the small operation that the doctors had recommended at the time. Everything went on quite well until a year ago, more or less. From then to now the pain has been getting worse, and the doctors advised that she go into a hospital because she would be better cared for there. We did just that, and for exactly a month she has been at the Italian hospital, looked after with every care; I am a personal friend of many of the leading physicians. Before she went in they were all in agreement that Corinna would have to have a small operation (a scraping of the uterus); now it seems that this won't be necessary anymore because of the effect of the treatment and the absolute rest she has had. She stays strong and cheerful, but when any woman in a nearby room dies, and she finds out about it, she too is afraid of dying. It makes me laugh, and the doctors laugh too. Today I got the news that she is much better and has gotten up now and walks through the gardens for several hours a day. That improves her appetite, she says. That's a good sign certainly.

I have been working here in a refrigerating plant of Swift, a North American company. It's a gigantic factory; about 5,000 people work there. I had never seen a factory of this type. Imagine that on an average 3,000 animals daily are put to sacrifice—some days even 2,000 cattle, and then the sheep and pigs, only these three kinds. They begin slaughtering at 4 A.M., and by 8 P.M. everything is already canned or in frozen quarters. The fat is also canned or put in barrels like oil. The bones, separated and carefully cleaned, are divided into sections. The remainder is processed, put into sacks, or packaged like *guano* (fertilizer), and the blood gets the same treatment. The skins are cleaned, salted, and prepared for tanning. It's really an example of the North American system. The management too is, in general, English or North American; I doubt that there are ten of other nationalities, myself included.

I have been charged with the planning for a new refrigerating plant to be installed at Rosario; construction will begin shortly. They are waiting for materials to arrive from the United States.

Because of the closeness (exactly one hour by express train) I go to Buenos Aires every Saturday, and I keep Corinna company at the hospital until Sunday evening, when I come back here. I would like to be there more often, but I have no free time during the day, and they don't let you enter the hospital at night, so we see each other only once a week.

Abele is still at home in Buenos Aires, and he visits Corinna more often. He wrote you some days ago also letting you know everything that's happened. He is very well and is getting fatter every day. He is already over 80 kilos [176 pounds], and I am pretty close to it. It must be the effect of the climate, which is just right for this.

When I went home on Saturday I saw your dear postcards and your last letter. Our dear mother's postcard from Oropa gave us the greatest pleasure; we all enjoyed it. I took it to Corinna, who wanted to keep it to read it over several times, as always. She's anxious to come join you so that she too can go and eat the "polenta cunscia"[1] at one of those farms, as shown in Mother's postcard. We hope for better times and also that that day will come.

You could say that life here is paralyzed so far as jobs are concerned. The only factories that are working are the refrigerating plants, because they export their entire production to Europe and the United States, and some steel mills, because iron isn't coming in from abroad, and some few textile mills, also because of a lack of imports.

Your son,
Oreste, (Abele, and
Corinna)

1.   *A special local polenta enriched with butter and cheese.*

Letter 152

Buenos Aires, 30 November 1917

Dearest parents,

Corinna, after about three months in the sanatorium of the Italian Hospital and after an operation, performed by one of the best surgeons here, which was very successful and she came through it very well, . . . has been home for a month convalescing nicely. It's going slowly, but well. A woman is doing the housework for us, and soon she will be completely recovered. Oreste and I are as always doing great.

We hope that you too are always well: that our dear mother with her improvement be patient and careful, and you, dear Father, take great care to keep yourself healthy.

We have delayed writing you because we were always waiting for mail ships. After several departures in the early part of October we haven't seen any more of them. . . .

Things are the same as always here, in spite of the splendid *cosecha* (pronounced *cosecia*)—a crop in full harvest. The railroads are functioning haphazardly after a strike . . . which lasted nearly a month. The other industries are also in great turmoil: factories, metal works, refrigeration plants, etc. In the plant where I work there has been a strike for almost two months, and it's likely to last that much longer again or more.

A bit of news! Yesterday at four our very dear friend Carlo Sasso and his wife, Costanza, left on the steamer *Garibaldi*. After hesitating for so long, they made up their minds, and we hope with all our heart that they will arrive happily. I saw them off at their departure and stayed as long as it was possible for me to see them, and even after. We felt it deeply; their house was our house. They were here what you, dearest parents, are over there—friends with all sincerity and heart. We loved them with a constant love, without deceptive enthusiasm, and you may believe it, dearest parents, that if I am now weeping, it is not out of weakness but, you may be sure, because of that honest selfishness which is more keenly felt when we miss the love of our dear ones. We hope with all our heart that the friendship left behind can continue always between you. It will be a joy for everyone, for you and for us.

I did not write yesterday because the day after tomorrow a large and fast Spanish steamer is leaving. This one of ours is sure to get there before they [the Sassos] do and before the Christmas holidays. If no one knows anything about it, you don't know about it either, but, with this letter, you know that you will be getting a part of our soul. You will have an opportunity to chat about this country and to talk about us. Greet them for us as soon as they arrive, even before *they* greet you for us.

I am enclosing a check for 500 lire with our best wishes that you may have a good Christmas season and a better New Year's, well protected from the cold, in perfect harmony, and with every happiness; that is what we want.

Another check for 200 lire is for you to distribute to our dear ones at the front and a part of it, if you think best, for any of our families in need because of the war. Above all don't forget our cousins Virgilio and Andrea and our dear friend Giuseppe Sasso. . . .

Once again our best wishes to you, please give our very best to everyone.

Our friend Armando Pella keeps asking for news of his family. When you say hello to them, speak to them about it. His family gives you their very best.

Your loving children,
Abele, (Oreste, and
Corinna)

Today, the 1st of December, it was a very great pleasure to get your letter of 15 October with one from our dear mother enclosed. Corinna thanks you very much for your good wishes. As I was saying, she is getting better.

This time the censor has used his scissors, cutting out three or four lines. I forgot to say that Eugenio Rivetti has neither written nor paid. Don't say anything to him. If you see him, you can ask him for me if he liked the wallets.

Oreste arrived this evening. He said that he too wrote you some days ago.[1] Once again our best wishes. We give you again many kisses. Your loving sons

1.   *Letter of 28 November 1917 not included.*

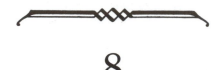

8

The Death of Margherita (1918–1919)

In September 1917, Oreste took a job with the Swift Company, the U.S. meat-processing firm, in the nearby town of La Plata (#151). As a result, in April 1918, he and Corinna moved to Berisso (#153). Oreste apparently did well because shortly thereafter he was promoted. "His employers must have a reasonably high opinion of Oreste," Abele wrote his parents, "since they are putting him in charge of a new refrigerating plant in Paraguay, and that in a company where they are all Americans and English" (#155). Corinna stayed behind in Berisso taking care of the house, the flowers, and the chickens.

Abele remained in Buenos Aires and moved to a hotel near his work and then later to an apartment. For the first time since his arrival in 1912, Abele was separated from his brother and sister-in-law. He continued to do very well; "The company has struck it rich," he explained, "and I too have gotten a small reward from it. . . . There are several thousand lire that I shall jealously keep in reserve for the future along with some other small savings, but they will always be available for any need whatsoever you or we may have" (#155).

Luigi thanked his sons for their financial generosity and indicated just how important their contributions had been. He noted with precision that Oreste had sent home a total of 14,300 lire and Abele 9,000 lire. The money, he explained, went to fix up the house, to purchase some land, "to meet the expenses of Cousin Carlo's legacies," and to pay for Margherita's medical treatment (#157). In short, the money earned by the sons in Argentina was essential for the survival of the parents in Italy.

Toward the end of 1918, Margherita's health declined (#159, #161), and as she got worse Luigi implored his sons to return home. The message was clear;

Your mother wants to see you at least once before she dies. In November 1918, after the war was over, Luigi urged them to make up their minds to come home; "Oreste," he pleaded, "after eighteen years, please don't deprive us of this joy" (#162). Luigi tried everything he could think of to encourage his children to come home: Oreste could send Corinna for a visit since she was alone in Berisso (#159); Abele could return home to find a wife (#165).

In the early months of 1919, Margherita got worse. In his letter of February 23, 1919, Luigi began: "I don't know if your dear mother will still be alive when you get this letter" (#166). He then described her pain and suffering and concluded: "Only morphine in large doses relieves the pain a bit, . . ." yet "it kills her sooner. And yet what's to be done? Either let her die in despair from the pain or make her die with pain killers" (#166). In March and April Margherita's condition deteriorated (#168, #170). Oreste and Abele nevertheless found it impossible to return at that time because of business and because of the uncertainty of their draft status (#160, #169, #175).

On May 8, 1919, Margherita died. In several emotional and touching letters the respective members of the family expressed their feelings of sorrow and loss. Luigi noted his satisfaction that he had done everything possible for Margherita and that "Valdengo has never seen such a funeral," but "this worst of all misfortunes" so upset him "that I don't know how to pick up the thread of my daily tasks anymore. Even though the poor creature gave me so much to do, that was nothing in comparison with the void she has left in our house and in my heart" (#172, #174).

After he heard the news, Oreste told his father: "I am writing with a heart full of anguish. . . . I cannot describe how I took it and Corinna too." He then reminisced about the past, the house in Biella, the day he left, and the farewell given to him by his mother (#173). Abele lamented that when he learned of Margherita's death, "I don't know what I did. . . . I could not understand a thing. The lunch hour came, and I remained alone for a while giving vent to my grief in tears" (#175). Both sons expressed concern for their father and urged him to be brave: "Our kisses, our affection, everything is for you," Abele assured Luigi, and then suggested: "Should you wish, dear father, to make a trip over here to us, our homes are yours" (#175).

The chapter ends with a letter from Oreste attempting to console his father: "The tragedy to be sure is grave; however it is necessary to come to terms with destiny" (#179).

Letter 153

Buenos Aires, 1 April 1918

Dearest parents,

A bit of news. After much delay, and as you have already been informed, today is the last day that we shall remain together as a cozy little family. It has been several weeks since Oreste found a house in La Plata (Berisso), and tomorrow he will move in. I all alone have searched for a place with a family. However, out of a population of a million and a half it looks as if I can't find a place to suit me. As a result I have settled for a hotel; I'm moving all my stuff there this very day.

Berisso is a suburb of La Plata, capital of the province of Buenos Aires (the city of Buenos Aires is the federal capital of the Republic and is autonomous). Berisso is twenty minutes by electric tram from the city of La Plata (twelve kilometers), and La Plata is an hour by train from Buenos Aires (fifty-three kilometers) with trains every half hour or less, so that almost every day off I will be able to make a quick trip out there to be together with them.

The new address of Oreste and Corinna will be:

> Calle Lisboa n. 633, La Plata (Berisso)

I am taking up residence at the hotel to sleep and eat there. It is near where I work, the address is:

> Gran Hotel del Sud
> Calle Bernardo de Irigoyen n. 1608
> Buenos Aires

I'll try it for a while, and if I don't like it, I'll move.

Thank you for the birthday greetings to Corinna and me; we spent them happily together.

Yesterday, Easter, we were with our friend Armando Pella and family. They give you their best, returning your greetings.

I won't go on any longer because I have a lot to do. We will write soon when we are all settled.

I am enclosing in this letter a check for 500 lire.

> Your loving children,
> Abele, (Oreste, and
> Corinna)

Letter 154

La Plata, Berisso, 17 April 1918

Dearest parents,

I haven't written for a while, in part because the news that Abele was giving you was for the entire family. As Abele informed you in his last letter, we have now had to separate from him, though with the greatest regret, since from where I am working now it was too much trouble to go back home, something I could do only on Saturday because of the distance. So I rented a small house in town here, which we have to ourselves. Now that Corinna is completely recovered, she can also take care of the housework, for which she has engaged a young girl from the town as helper.

Last Sunday already we had a nice visit from Abele and two families we are friends with. The trips that I used to make to Buenos Aires to visit friends they will now be making to visit us.

Abele, unable to find a place to his liking, has settled at a hotel. However, it is a first-class one which is pretty comfortable. We here are living a simple domestic life, in part because of the lack of convenient places to go; but it's peaceful and we are happy. In the evenings I read newspapers or books, and Corinna sews and chatters away.

Since you got me a subscription to the *Tribuna Biellese*, which I always read thoroughly, it will be necessary to have our address changed. I have left instructions about it here at the post office.

Everybody's attention here is fixed on the war in Europe. . . .

Here all the products that used to come from North America and Europe are lacking. The railroads have been running on wood for some time; gas also is made from wood. And everything is at exorbitant prices and always going up. So far as we can make out, even in the neutral European countries they aren't doing too well. In a Swedish paper of two months ago there were advertisements for the sale of a kilo of butter and two and a half kilos of potatoes, and so on, and this is as if one were dealing with rare items. . . .

We hope that shortages won't concern you very much, though it is necessary to limit oneself to the utmost. Living in the country the effects should not be felt so very much [sic]. And then too the war must be won; for this, every sacrifice will bring victory closer.

We wish you everything good. Try to get through this period the best way you can; that's all we wish.

Tell the Sassos that we think of them so much, and give our best to their son in case he's at home, and to all our friends.

Your loving children,
Oreste, (Abele, and
Corinna)

Bye, Mother, be happy with Father.

Letter 155

Buenos Aires, 2 August 1918

Dearest parents,

Oreste is still in Paraguay, but he hopes to return soon.[1] Corinna is alone in Berisso; fortunately there is a nice Piedmontese family in the neighborhood. Last week she was here for several days as a guest of Signora Pella. We are on the best of terms with them; I am at their house several times a week.

I keep on working the same as always, too much even. The company has struck it rich, and I too have gotten a small reward from it, though to a modest degree and less too than what I had hoped for and had deserved. There are several thousand lire that I shall jealously keep in reserve for the future along with some other small savings, but they will always be available for any need whatsoever you or we may have.

As for our situation here, I had answered your two special letters of 14 April 1915 and 20 August 1916 with my letters of 10 June 1915 and 5 December 1916, but I haven't found out whether you received them. I should like to know separately—by means of a note in a letter addressed to me.

His employers must have a reasonably high opinion of Oreste since they are putting him in charge of a new refrigerating plant in Paraguay, and that in a company where they are all Americans and English. And so we hope for a raise in salary.

Corinna is fine now; she is taking care of the house, the flowers, and the chickens.

Give us the news of our friends and relatives and say hello to them.

I am enclosing in this letter a check for 500 lire. A second one, for 100 lire, is for our soldiers. Please give twenty each to Andrea, Virgilio, and to Sasso. The rest as you think best.

Your loving children,
Abele, (Oreste, and
Corinna)

1.   *Although we have no reference to Oreste's departure for Paraguay, we assume he told his parents in a postcard that has been lost.*

Letter 156

Valdengo, 22 September 1918

Dearest children, Abele, Oreste, and Corinna,

We have delayed answering your very nice letter, Abele, until now so that we could let you know the result of a consultation Professor Vinai had here at our house with our local Dr. Acati concerning your dear mother's condition.

Today we had the consultation. Professor Vinai, who is so nice and warm-hearted, gave us much, even everything, to hope for concerning your dear mother's recovery. He ordered a prescription to take effect at once so she would get her appetite back. It was agreed that we go this week with our doctor to his sanitorium at Andorno to get a battery-powered electrical device so she could have a temporary treatment this winter, and then in next year's season we will take her back to the sanitorium to reinvigorate her more. Certainly in this winter season we must achieve an improvement in her strength so that she will be able to undergo the treatment.

In the meantime we are living more or less contentedly in the hope that your dear mother recovers in the best way possible. The professor's words went straight to my heart, especially at the thought of what a tragedy it would be to lose my beloved companion, who for all of our lives spent together has been all this time a perfect joy of sincere affection and love, both between ourselves and for you, our dearest children.

On the 20th of this month it was our pleasure to have Carlo and Costanza Sasso at our house to celebrate the fateful anniversary of the everlasting downfall of the temporal power of the popes. We took the occasion to celebrate in advance my birthday, which comes tomorrow. We thought of you with affection.

Their son has not written for some time. As soon as I know where he is, I shall send him without fail the 20 lire you entrusted to me.

I handed over the same amount to Cousin Andrea, who was here on a short leave of ten days and left yesterday. He thanked me warmly. He has your address and will write you.

His heroic behavior in all the circumstances of his military life should be rewarded for merit and bravery. But those men who are heroic, sincere, and guileless, without fanaticism, are not ambitious, nor do they lay claim to rewards. Rather they do what they do out of a selfless sense of duty. That's the way our dear Andrea is.

For Cousin Virgilio I gave his mother as much as you told me to. I am sure she will deliver it to him.

I shall make other donations, as I have always done, to other relatives or friends who are enduring the hardships of the war.

We thank you so much for the 500 lire you sent us. They will be very useful for your dear mother's recovery. . . .

If our dear Oreste has still not come back when this letter gets there, you will please be sure to share it with him and also Corinna.

Your loving parents

Letter 157

Valdengo, 22 September 1918

Special

Dearest son Abele,

You are right! We have given no answer in response to your letters of 10 June 1915 and 5 December 1916. The reason for that was that we were satisfied with your explanations.

In any case we hope that things continue to go well and that dear Oreste will have modified his excessively grand plans, and you will play the role of a good, well-heeded prompter for him.

We have never doubted your generosity considering that dear Oreste has, since he has been over there, sent us 14,300 lire, several thousand of which were spent on his and your behalf. And you, dear Abele, have sent us 9,000 from over there.[1]

It amazes us to think that we have spent a good part of it: a part to fix up the house a bit, a part to round off some of our land holdings, and a part to meet the expenses of Cousin Carlo's legacies, so that we could maintain the family estate intact. . . .[2]

Our assets in cash now . . . come to 10,000 lire in registered bonds at 3.5 percent and about the same amount in deposits.

As to your poor mother's illness, which has cost a considerable sum, I don't wish to spell it out because the poor creature gets too upset if I name it.

We are doing everything possible, confident that you will not be displeased. Consider that you have only one mother.

We think that our dear Oreste, because of his generosity, may well have suffered losses he didn't have to. We hope, now that Corinna is healthy again and with the greatest prudence, he might be able to make up as much as he may have lost.

And you dearest Abele, with so many merits, as the Sassos also have said, continue with your good management to be the master of the house until one day we can embrace you all with the greatest love. Your dear mother lives and hopes to live even while suffering until she can embrace you.

From our letters you will easily be able to understand our sentiment especially in regard to your current living alone.

Your loving parents

1.   For an estimate of the amounts these figures represent, see the Appendix.
2.   Luigi had previously borrowed 2,700 lire to take over a part of the family property that Carlo had inherited.

Letter 158

Buenos Aires, 14 October 1918

Dearest parents,

Oreste is still at Asunción; Corinna is at Berisso, but she has been here for a while for a treatment of injections which had already been prescribed after the operation. I am fine; I have had a touch of the flu epidemic and nothing more. . . .

Our dear mother's continuing troubles notwithstanding we still feel confident about a good recovery, and we can only recommend, as always, peace of mind and don't get discouraged. Our dear mother's words have moved us deeply, and we consider them to be the result of a temporary mood of discouragement. Keep your spirits up; don't worry yourselves with certain ideas that are bad for you. We will without fail embrace each other in perfect harmony. . . .

Here it has been an entire month of glory. The demonstrations began after the Italian triumphs and victories, and they are now going on all over. It's delirious!

There are huge demonstrations where the women are counted in the tens of thousands, the allied and Argentine flags by the millions. In certain areas the entire week is a holiday with pay. Today is a general holiday by government decree. At long last! Long live Italy! . . .

Your loving children,
Abele, (Oreste, and
Corinna)

Letter 159

Valdengo, 18 October 1918

Dearest children, Abele, Oreste, and Corinna,

Your dear mother suffers constantly. Sometimes she gets discouraged. My words of consolation and her steadfast hope of seeing you all again are her comfort. With extraordinary determination she keeps her hopes up, and I hope too, and I'm sure it's the same with you.

The grape harvest is over. The yield was very poor as was that of all the harvests because of the long dry spell in the summer. Life here is a disaster. Prices are ten times normal, and foodstuffs are scarce.

All this is the result of the war; we hope that its finale is now here, with the defeat of Kaiserism and its fine associates.

We hope that there isn't so much disruption over there and that life goes more smoothly.

We hear that Oreste is still in Paraguay, Corinna is at Berisso, and that you, Abele, are in Buenos Aires. There are five of us, and we make four family groups. In our opinion Corinna could have made the journey here, even if she went right back, to give us the invaluable consolation of getting to know her; it would be a great comfort to your dear mother and to me.

We make so many plans, we have so many wishes, and the longed-for day will finally come when we embrace you all here at home.

Costanza Sasso has been here to visit us today. I visited Carlo. They got a card from Abele. They thank you and greet you will all their heart, on behalf of their son also.

Your loving parents

Letter 160

Zeballo, Cué, Asunción, 7 November 1918

Dearest parents,

I came to Paraguay with a two-month contract, and now four have passed, and I still haven't finished. I have held off writing so that I could inform you of my return to Berisso, where Corinna is anxiously waiting for me. Corinna has sent on to me a lovely letter from you, one from Abele, along with another from the Sassos.

Though, as you can imagine, it gives us the greatest pleasure to get your sweet letters, you can also imagine how saddened we are by our dear mother's letter, to see her so depressed and in such great fear. You can imagine with what longing I would like to be with you, but it is impossible for me, though I am not saying I don't want to come back. All of us here believe that our dear mother's illness won't be as serious as she thinks and that it is rather a passing mood of discouragement that affects her. Indeed we think of, and when we were together the talk was of, going back, even if it were just to go for a walk all together. And, yes, that day will come, and we hope that it is not too far off.

It is a very great pleasure to observe and we duly appreciate all the concern that you have for our dear mother. Sasso also speaks of it in his lovely letter. That is certainly a comfort for her and a joy for us.

It is a pleasure to see what a close friendship you have with the Sasso family, and it makes us think of those lovely Sundays spent together here; it was a lot of fun.

I have promised and informed them that I'll be back in Buenos Aires for Christmas. I would like to have been home for the 20th of this month. The excessive amount of work prevents me. I'll do what I can to be free for Christmas.

We are extremely jubilant as we read the good news about the war and the glorious, almost incredible victories. These victories will certainly lead to peace. . . .

Dearest parents, even if I am often slow in writing, you may be sure that you are always dear to my heart and that I want all the greatest happiness for you. Give many regards to the Sassos; we think of them too always with love.

Your son,
Oreste, (Abele, and
Corinna)

Dear Mother, cheer up and don't be depressed. Your son Oreste sends you many loving kisses.

Letter 161

Valdengo, 17 November 1918

Dearest children, Abele, Oreste, and Corinna,

We have been slow in responding to Abele's lovely postcards, . . . hoping to hear from Oreste too since he had promised in his last letter that he would write soon and send photographs from Paraguay, where he happens to be now.

But now a month has passed since our last letter; we'll get moving and let you hear from us.

I, your father, am fine as always; your mother is doing rather poorly. Every two to three weeks she is seized by a fever, which has weakened her so much that the doctor is also worried because he can't give the reason for it.

Her extraordinary courage, along with the hope of seeing you all together, makes her so strong at heart; the fact of a secure peace in the immediate future keeps her cheerful in the certainty of seeing you at least once before she dies.

Together we hope that as soon as peace has been established once and for all, you will give us the joy of being able to embrace you all and also to talk about some of our interests. For at this point I too, though I am in good health—advanced age can bring changes—. . . could come to the end.

We are then confident in our hope and that you will give us this great joy, which could be our last.

And dear Corinna? We hope that she is healthy and as good as new again, and that she too will want to give us the joy of a loving embrace.

We are always hoping for improvement and that the coming of peace in Europe, which has been so greatly longed for, may also bring a little peace even to the terrible sufferings which are torturing your dear mother.

Repeating our hope of embracing you all, we send you kisses with our utmost affection.

Your parents

Letter 162

Valdengo, 25 November 1918

Dearest children Oreste, Abele, and Corinna,

Exactly on the 20th of this month, your birthday, dearest Oreste, we had the joy of getting the lovely postcard from Assunción [sic]. . . .

We hope then that you spent dear Oreste's birthday nicely, even though you are separated, since you, dear Oreste, are still in Paraguay. . . .

We are the same as ever. Your dear mother suffers constantly, except that the injections dull for the moment the cruel pains.

We hear that it is very hot there, unlike here, where it's terribly cold. Your dear mother huddles up to the stove filled with burning wood.

Now that the war is over, there is hope that normal conditions will return in everything. Otherwise it is a disaster to go on with these fantastic prices for everything that is necessary for life, even medicines.

Since the war has finished in Italy's favor, we hope for an honorable peace for everyone that will last and that you will make up your minds to come see us. Oreste, after eighteen years, please don't deprive us of this joy.

Your loving parents

Letter 163

Buenos Aires, 21 December 1918

Dearest parents,

I've held off writing because there were no steamers, and we were expecting Oreste for Christmas; but he keeps on working at Asunción. Corinna, who is still at Berisso, comes to Buenos Aires sometimes. She is very happy to get your repeated sweet sentiments, which she returns from her heart.

I have been down with the flu, "grippe," but now I am as happy as a lark, and I feel great, all the more so since from the 1st of this month I live, eat, and sleep—in my own home! Those few days of illness made me decide almost violently. The hotel was all right as far as the room went but not for the food. Once my mind was made up, I bought what was necessary; I looked up the maid we had in our previous house and who knows what we are like (Sasso and Costanza must know her, I think). She comes in the morning and leaves at eight or nine in the evening—she's married—when she has finished cleaning up the kitchen. She is Spanish but she is good and works hard.

I have rented a small apartment with three little rooms (a dining room, a bedroom, and a second bedroom for when Oreste or Corinna comes). There is also a bathroom complete with a toilet. It's a little place, the rooms are 3.8 meters by 3.8, but it's nice. It's on the second floor, and so I have all the light and air I need. I am eating our kind of food, and I have the pleasure that those families of friends are returning all those visits I always make to them. Pella and his family have already been here, Cravello (Oreste's former partner) and his family, Fassolo, etc. They all congratulate me on how well I have been able to manage things (the hell with the expense, health comes first). Corinna came during the first days to help me and went back yesterday. She too is happy that she can come to Buenos Aires without having to bother friends or adapt to the hotel. I too am happy because their room is always ready for them, and the bed is made.

Sasso knows quite well what these small apartments are like here, but this one is nice . . . in its own small way, and it's absolutely private. When I get home from work in the evening, I am completely free in my slippers and shirtsleeves. If I want I can take a bath without having to go out. I eat, and I take it easy arranging my stuff and putting it in order. The maid prepares everything: She does the laundry, cleans up, and fixes the meals. It will cost a bit more perhaps, but I am living the way I like to if it goes on like this. I'm also close to work.

The new address is:

> Avenida Montes de Oca 250
> Depto. 34

This evening Corinna and I are going to Pella's house. We will make plans to spend Christmas together. Last Sunday Pella, his family, and I were all at Corinna's in Berisso, spending a cheerful day off together.

We are happy about your growing friendship with our friends the Sassos. . . .

Though this letter will be late in getting there, our good wishes for a good holiday season and a better New Year are as always the best and dearest ones we offer.

I am enclosing a check for 500 lire.

For our soldiers I am also enclosing a check for 100 lire. Please distribute it as always, a modest gift but straight from the heart.

> Your loving children,
> Abele, (Oreste, and
> Corinna)

Letter 164

Valdengo, 14 January 1919

Dearest children Oreste, Abele, and Corinna,

You have received our last letter . . . written to you both and in which the hope of seeing you soon is repeated.

Our dear mother, who always speaks of you, is afraid (and sometimes I am too) that she won't see you again if you delay so much. On the third of this month she got one of her usual fevers, which kept her bed-ridden for several days in grave danger. It's been two days [since] she can get up a bit; the weakness is overpowering. Every fever she gets leaves her weaker and weaker. As long as I am in good health, we can just drag out our existence.

Now that the danger of German submarines is gone as well as the war on land, we hope that you won't raise difficulties about coming to see us one more time, especially you, dear Oreste; it's been eighteen years since we have seen you. We believe and are confident that we will see you soon or at least find out when that day will come.

If this letter gets there in time to say happy birthday, dear Corinna, we do so with all our heart. And if it will have passed (nicely, we hope), may she continue, and always be well.

[Broken off without a closing]

Letter 165

Valdengo, 2 February 1919

Dearest children Abele, Oreste, and Corinna,

Your letter, dear Abele, made us feel better to know that you are all well and that you have set up housekeeping; we hope that's a sign that you are looking for someone to be your faithful companion in life.

It is our wish that it turn out well for you. And if it is your intention to come home to find her, it will be an occasion of greater happiness for us, especially to see you and embrace you. Your dear mother always speaks of you with the fear of never seeing you again since the various phases of her illness make both of us very anxious and troubled.

And dear Oreste is still at Asunción? If he had to stay there so long, wouldn't it have been better, and an immense pleasure for us, that she [Corinna] should have come to spend some time with us? That would be a reason for Oreste to come here too, when he came to pick her up. These are all our ideas and, in our opinion, quite practical. Don't you think so, dearest Abele?

We thank you so much for your check for 500 lire, which you so generously sent us. The same for the 100-lire check for our relatives and our friends in the army.

Your dear mother suffers, and suffers always. She gets the most encouragement from the hope of seeing you one more time before she dies. . . .

In New Yorck [sic] Maria and Margherita, the sisters of Carmelina, have died, along with their husbands within a few days of each other. They leave behind children of a tender age. The notorious and famous Spanish kiss is leaving a trail of death behind it just about everywhere.[1] Let's hope we are among the survivors.

Your loving parents

1.   *The flu epidemic was thought to have come from Spain.*

Letter 166

Valdengo, 23 February 1919

Dearest children, Abele, Oreste, and Corinna,

I don't know if your dear mother will still be alive when you get this letter. For several weeks she has gotten painfully worse. She hasn't gotten out of bed for the past fifteen days. She suffers terribly; only morphine in large doses relieves the pain a bit. Consider that this doesn't cure her; it kills her sooner. And yet what's to be done? Either let her die in despair from the pain or make her die with pain killers. It is tragic.

The doctor doesn't know what to say anymore, except to be a support to her in her disastrous decline. I am so upset that I don't know what I am doing anymore.

The poor creature will take heart for a few moments and then often loses hope. Her greatest concern is the hope of seeing you before she dies.

I don't know if it's possible to hope for your coming home. That would be so important for me too and also to draw up an agreement for our family interests. In every letter we have always expressed our desire to see you, especially dear Oreste, whom we haven't seen for almost eighteen years. You will all be our dear, dear welcome children, just to be able to embrace you at least one more time before dying since, if fate takes your dear mother, I won't be around much longer, If it were possible to make a trip home, it will be a joy for us, perhaps our last.

Since this letter will be there in time, we wish you, dearest Abele, a happy birthday.

Many, many kisses from your loving parents.

Letter 167

Valdengo, 13 March 1919

Dearest children Abele, Oreste, and Corinna,

After a few days of crisis a bit of hope has returned which alas will be just a hope. In her weakened condition she is worn down and the pain never leaves her; it's only relieved a little by the injections of the terrible morphine. What can we do? This tragedy has overtaken us. Her single thought is the hope of seeing you again before she dies. When she mentions your dear names, she weeps; and I weep too when I consider the vast distance that separates us, but without giving up the idea that you will come see us.

I don't know about your situation with the government. Perhaps [there are problems] for you Oreste, but I am sure that you, Abele, are in the clear. In any case it will be a great joy for us to see you at least one more time. . . .

Here life is still the same as if we were at war. Everything is at fantastic prices and with no sign of coming down. We have little confidence in the outcome of the famous Paris conference. Meanwhile the crisis in industry is coming into the open. The workers' agitation for an eight-hour day and a half day on Saturday has been received by the industrialists with clenched teeth.

Your loving parents

Letter 168

Valdengo, 25 March 1919

Dearest children Abele, Oreste, and Corinna,

Today, dear Abele, is your birthday. We remember it with great affection, hoping that you spent it nicely in good health in the companionship of dear Oreste and Corinna. We imagine that Oreste has come back from Asunción and is at Berisso with Corinna.

I, Father, am fine. Your dear mother keeps getting worse and worse. Some days she is very ill, and then she gets a little better. Only morphine in heavy doses brings her a bit of relief from the terrible pains. . . .

We got your last letter on the 29th of January. We hope it won't be long before we get others. For, as we keep saying, since we are unable to see you, it is our joy at least to get your letters frequently. Your dear mother has almost given up hope of seeing you, but at least [hopes] to get good news from you.

And Oreste is still at Asunción? And Corinna alone in Berisso? And you, dear Abele, are alone too?

That is the way life goes. Small families reduced still more for various reasons. We hope at least that you are all well.

Your loving parents

Letter 169

Buenos Aires, 12 April 1919

Dearest parents,

We are expecting Oreste in a few days, Corinna as always at Berisso, and I as always am here. . . .

The alarming news about our dear mother made a deep impression on me. We want, however, to hope for a turn for the better and that by now she has improved as we sincerely and ardently wish. You too, dear Father, be brave, for yourself and for all of us.

I am expecting Oreste soon to see about planning a trip to embrace you with all that love that you have instilled in us. For if your longing is great, ours is just as great or greater. Don't lose hope! We hope, now that the war is over, there will be no serious restrictions for residents abroad [who wish to return], encouraging that day when we can embrace each other all together.

Many thanks for the kind thoughts and good wishes on my birthday, the best good wishes [I received].

I spent it alone since Corinna didn't come. Only in the evening my friend Armando Pella, his wife, and their child came. I thought of you that day as I always do every day.

I enclose in this letter a check for 500 lire.

It is as always a modest tribute; please remember in case of greater need we can do more, always with the same pleasure in being helpful in the best way. Leave nothing that might be necessary undone; your health and contentment are our happiness.

Dear Mother, take courage, be patient in undergoing every treatment. Think of nothing else but to get well and to go on living, as before, for us.

> Your loving children,
> Abele, (Oreste, and
> Corinna)

Letter 170

> Valdengo, 13 April 1919

Dearest children, Oreste, Abele, and Corinna,

Your dear mother keeps to her bed tormented by the most piercing pain. As usual morphine in extraordinary doses tranquilizes her a bit. The hope of getting well has almost disappeared. But with the arrival of good weather there is still hope for some improvement. It is a joy to hear that you are in excellent health and that Corinna has recovered completely.

Is Oreste still in Paraguay? Those are a long two months. Here's hoping his health remains excellent and that he gets a good profit.

It would have been very nice if Corinna, instead of staying alone in Berisso, had come home to be with us, at least until Oreste came back.

And you, dear Abele, are always alone too? It's nice that you visit each other frequently and exchange those marks of affection that you always feel within.

By the way, I met your friend Fiorentino Strobino, who had come back from military service, and he asked me a question I could not answer but I would like to be able to answer affirmatively—[whether] you will be coming to Biella soon to get married. If it is true, we are waiting for you with open arms to come and get for us a loving daughter-in-law like Corinna and for yourself a faithful companion in life. Will we be able to have this pleasure? We hope so.

> Your loving parents

Letter 171

> Valdengo, 24 April 1919

[Postcard with a view of the mountains around Biella]

Dearest children, Oreste, Abele, and Corinna,

Things are continuing badly for us. Your dear mother suffering without hope of recovery. Sure that she will die soon. This is the worst trouble that afflicts me. The thought of being left alone is for me, your Father, grief that will be worse when it happens, which alas won't be long.

Your loving parents

The view on this postcard will, I hope, reinvigorate your desire to see [it] again.

Your loving father

Letter 172

Valdengo, 8 May 1919

Dearest children, Oreste, Abele, and Corinna,

I am writing you as a follow-up to the telegram sent to you by our friend Giuseppe Sasso.

Your dear mother, after long and cruel suffering, died today at 4 P.M.

For several days I had noticed a sinister change, but I would not have believed that it would be so soon, this worst of all misfortunes for me, the loss of my beloved companion in life, your dearest mother.

A few days ago I got dear Oreste's postcard from Asunción with expressions of encouragement for us. Yesterday I got the nice letter from Abele [#167] with the same encouragement and 500 lire. It gave me reason to hope that in the not so distant future you would come back home at last.

Your dear mother, contrary to her usual enthusiasm, seemed indifferent since she saw her strength was going, and she was certain she would not see you. She seemed so disheartened that it was pitiful.

And yet it *has* happened. I don't know what comfort there will be for me now that I am old and deprived of my sweet companion. Your constant loving help will give me courage.

I am satisfied, as you can be too, that nothing has been left undone. Just yesterday I got a letter from Professor Vinai . . . asking me for information. Now I am letting him know about the terrible catastrophe.

The burial will be Saturday at 3 P.M. with a strictly civil ceremony. There will be music according to the explicit request of your dear mother. I shall scrupulously carry out her last wish.

I won't go on any longer.

Your desolate father

Letter 173

Berisso, La Plata, 15 May 1919

Dearest Father,

I am writing with a heart full of anguish. I came home the night of the 4th; Corinna and Abele met me at the door. I am very glad to be back with them after ten long months. I had sent you a postcard from Asunción, dated the 29th of April, the day before I left, informing you that I was going back to La Plata. In these days I was tidying up the work that I had finished in Paraguay, when at midday Monday of this week Abele called and told me of the terribly sad misfortune, that loss of our dear mother.

I cannot describe how I took it and Corinna too when I gave her the news. Many, many things came to my mind all at once; I remembered well the house in Biella and the day I left, when you saw me off at the station, and the "remember" said to me by our dear mother. Oh, if even for a moment I have forgotten you and even less our dear mother! Even though too many times I have proved negligent in writing, you are always present in my mind.

We had learned sadly of the continued worsening of our dear mother's illness from your last letters. I had consulted a doctor friend about this type of disease, and he sadly told me that there were no real cures. Though it was sad, this information was at least very useful since it prepared me for the ugly outcome.

With what pleasure we would have liked to be there close, to see us all together with our dear mother! It was not only her desire; we wanted it too. Current conditions hinder everything I should have wanted most.

We can imagine the depression you feel. You who sacrificed yourself so much to relieve and comfort her during the torments of her illness and to see her lose ground in such a way bit by bit. There are things that are too hard. . . .

We don't know what to write to give you comfort; it's the same with us. Try something else for a change as seems best to you. Give up the worries of farming; take some trips. In short look for some pleasures that might get your mind off it.

If one day conditions change, we will be able to embrace each other all together at home.

Your sons,
Oreste, (Corinna, and
Abele)

Letter 174

Valdengo, 18 May 1919

Dearest children, Oreste, Abele, and Corinna,

It has been ten days now that your dear mother is no more. I am so upset that I don't know what to do anymore. I don't know how to pick up the thread of my daily tasks anymore. Even though the poor creature gave me so much to do, that was nothing in comparison with the void she has left in our house and in my heart. And yet I must get used to it in any case. This week your aunt and Pierino have been here to put the house back in shape. They went home yesterday. They will come back as soon as I need them.

You should have received the telegram and my letter sent right afterward.

My life is only for you now, so I beg you to write me frequently and give me your comfort and encouragement.

Following your dear mother's wishes that I make some contributions in her memory I have paid 50 lire each to: 1) the Valdengo Institute for Charity, 2) Institute for Needy School Children; and 25 lire each for the 1) *Corriere Biellese*, 2) the Biella "Casa del Popolo," 3) the Trade Union, 4) the Union of Textile Workers—in all a total of 200 lire. I am sure you won't mind, especially considering the honors paid her by an immense number of comrades, male and female, and by friends and acquaintances who reverently accompanied your dear mother to her last resting place. Valdengo has never seen such a funeral. You will see the detailed account in the *Corriere Biellese*.

In view of this terrible tragedy that has happened to us I hope you will make up your minds to come some time and visit your desolate parent.

Your loving father

Letter 175

Buenos Aires, 26 May 1919

Dearest Father,

Your very kind letter of February 23rd, with the first alarming news about our dear mother, had saddened us, but we ardently hoped for a turn for the better. Later, your letter of March 25th had relieved us somewhat. Oreste had returned in those days, and we all hoped for the best.

On the contrary! On the morning of Monday the 12th of this month, at about twelve o'clock they brought me a telegram from abroad at the office. I waited a moment, almost suspiciously; I opened it; it was the tragic news from my friend Sasso: "Your mother died today. A letter follows. Sasso."

I don't know what I did; a little later when the manager, the assistant manager, and various other employees expressed their sympathy to me, I could not understand a thing. The lunch hour came, and I remained alone for a while giving vent to my grief in tears. Afterward I telephoned Oreste and Corinna, and they too were stunned by the sad and unexpected news. . . .

We are waiting for reassuring news that at least she died peacefully. Remember us also at the beloved tomb. Here we shall make her sons' kisses fall upon it.

And you, dear Father, be brave. Seek that diversion that is necessary among your friends and save yourself for us. Our kisses, our affection, everything is for you.

We hope, if our military status doesn't create a new obstacle, to see you again soon.

I am now rereading the wishes expressed by our dear mother a year ago, and, should you wish, dear Father, to make a trip over here to us, our homes are yours. We ourselves are separated, but we visit each other constantly. You might find it difficult getting used to life here, shut up within four walls and with no acquaintances. However, if you wish to try it, let us know so that we shall take care of everything. Meanwhile it is our wish that you stay completely calm and serene. Try to get others to cultivate the land and to have at home someone you can trust for everything else. It will be our pleasure to provide for anything you may need. . . .

Sunday a week ago Oreste and Corinna were here. This Saturday I went there in the evening and came [home] yesterday evening, Sunday. All our talk was about our dear mother and you, dear Father.

How painful it is for us not to be able to write these dear words "parents" any longer. Now, dearest Father, you have our kisses and our great love all to yourself. . . .

> Your loving children,
> Abele, (Oreste, and
> Corinna)

Letter 176

Buenos Aires, 16 June 1919

Dearest Father,

After the painful and irreparable misfortune we have been somewhat relieved that you have expressed sentiments of legitimate satisfaction at having left nothing undone. Having done everything one could is the only solace for such great grief. It has also been a great source of satisfaction to learn about the unanimous outpouring of sentiments of condolence for our dear mother. We too gratefully thank everyone.

From my dear friend Federico I have received the issues of the *Corriere*

Biellese with the expressions of deep sympathy given in tribute to our dear mother and of affection for you and for us. I shall write thanking him.

You, dear Father, try always to enjoy yourself, taking short pleasure trips. Perhaps you could take advantage of the inspection trips that your friend Scaramuzzi makes for business reasons. As always it will be a great satisfaction for us to know that you are in good spirits and happy. You would do us a great wrong if, needing anything whatsoever, you did not let us know.

Within a couple of months I shall be more explicit concerning our coming to embrace you; I am waiting for the balance sheet of my firm. In the meantime it would be useful to get acquainted with the law's provisions about draft evaders.

As to my coming home to get married, as I was telling you, I take it as an omen since I honestly know absolutely nothing about it.

Oreste and Corinna were here last Saturday. Yesterday, Sunday, I was supposed to go there, but it was raining, and I worked.

It has begun to get cold here. My hand is half frozen and keeps me from writing more clearly. . . .

We hope you will have found a way to manage things around the house and that you are at leisure and rested.

Your loving children,
Abele, (Oreste, and
Corinna)

Letter 177

Valdengo, 17 June 1919

Dearest children, Abele, Oreste, and Corinna,

I am glad that Oreste has finally come back to Berisso from Paraguay to be with his dear Corinna and that you will see each other frequently and among other things talk about our dear one and your desolate father, alone and old here.

To make what little money I have more secure, I have done the following: I have deposited in the Bank of Biella ten bonds of 1,000 lire each, payable to the bearer and renewable at our request. The letter of deposit also includes the two of you. So should it by chance happen that I die you two will remain as the legal possessors. At the same bank I have an account book no. 2888, payable to the bearer and also in your names. At the savings bank too I have an account book, no. 2848, which I also put in Oreste's name. There are other deposits at the Banca Italiana di Sconto. They are also in Abele's name as you will see from the letter here enclosed, which Abele should sign and send back to me so that I can deliver it to the bank at once. I already have the contract receipt.

I still have sufficient money at home for the necessary expenses. I have had the tombstone made for your dear mother and the portrait to attach to it. I have also had small ones made for a pendant which I'll send to you as soon as I get them. I have to think some more about the tomb inscription. I'll send you a copy. Don't worry about sending me money. I have what's necessary and am in no need. But I do ask you to write me frequently since that is my only joy.

It made my spirits soar to hear from Abele's letter that there is reason to hope that we might embrace each other on the occasion of the thirtieth anniversary of your birth. Will that apply also to dear Oreste and Corinna? I hope so.

In these areas the drought has caused immense damage to the crops in the countryside. We keep hoping and waiting for the rain that doesn't come.

I received condolences from your friend Armando Pella; since I don't know the address, would you please thank him for me.

Your loving father

Letter 178

Buenos Aires, 15 July 1919

Dearest Father,

As I was saying in my last letter, I am waiting to see how things develop so that we may all be able to embrace each other. In the meantime let's hope that things improve and that travel is more reasonable.

We have received our dear mother's obituary from your friend Scaramuzzi and also your letter, dear Father, edged in black.[1] It is a very respectable way to show respect, but I, and Oreste shares my view, am opposed to all external display. I carry my grief always in my heart, in such a way that you will certainly excuse me if on the outside there will be no sign of our sorrow within. And yet I understand how difficult it would be over there to rebel against customs that are absolutely general; one must submit to them.

With the return home of our brave veterans we hope the cultivation of the fields will be easier and that you will have more leisure, giving you time for the relaxation that is really necessary.

The demonstrations against the high cost of living are understandable and are the subject here of a lot of talk. . . .

Winter this year has been mild, but in exchange we now have awful weather and worse humidity. There is serious flooding in various parts of the country resulting in the interruption of rail service and enormous losses of livestock. That will be the reason for a new increase in food prices.

Next Sunday, if I am not working, I'll go to Berisso to be with Oreste and Corinna. The other evening I was at my friend Pella's, who is changing his residence, coming back to the center of the city, close to his office. He, along with his family, gives you his best.

In this letter I am enclosing a check for 500 lire.

> Your loving children,
> Abele, (Oreste, and
> Corinna)

1.   *One of the rituals of mourning in Italy was to put a black border around any letters one wrote.*

Letter 179

Berisso, La Plata, 3 August 1919

Dearest Father,

It saddens us to hear that you are inconsolable over the sad loss of our dear mother; we would all like to be near you. Corinna too always talks about it. The tragedy to be sure is grave; however, it is necessary to come to terms with destiny.

We have received your last letter, which was in truth too sad, and just today the postcard from Oropa. Surely these trips will divert you and restore your peace of mind. Try to take advantage of them while the weather is favorable.

We were pleased by the kindness shown to you by your old friend Signor Scaramuzzi. I too remember him well: from the time he went to Sala and on another occasion to Valle Mosso and then on the frequent occasions when you visited each other since I always accompanied you.

We have also heard from our dear friends the Sassos. As always they have shown affection for us, and it's equally true for you. We are pleased about that.

In your last letter you speak about an offer made for the house in Valdengo.[1] As far as I am concerned you should do what suits you most, and I think it will be the same for Abele. We saw each other last Sunday, but because other people were with us, we didn't discuss it; he has kept your letter. Today we haven't seen each other because of the bad weather; everyone has stayed put in his own house. It's rare for a week to go by without our seeing each other. And then, when he isn't coming on Sunday, Corinna serves notice on me and leaves me flat to go visit him, and she comes back in the evening. Believe me, dear Father, the most perfect harmony prevails between the two of us, that of true brothers.

> Your children,
> Oreste, (Abele, and
> Corinna)

1.   *The letter he refers to is missing from the collection.*

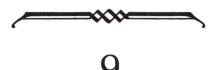

9

The Impossible Return (1919–1922)

When Oreste originally went to Argentina in 1901, he expected to return to Italy for at least a visit and perhaps even to remain there permanently. Similarly, when Abele joined his brother in 1912, he too assumed that he would return. Margherita and Luigi most certainly believed that their sons would come back. Yet in fact the sons returned for only a visit and that was after the death of both their parents. The letters in this final chapter provide special insight into the reasons why the return proved to be impossible: Oreste always seemed to have a project he had to finish; Abele was too deeply involved in and successful at his job; previously the war had made travel impossible; the uncertainty of their draft status presented problems; and the cost of the trip was high. At the end of 1919, the Italian government issued an amnesty decree that removed one potential obstacle to the return (#180, #181, #182). Oreste, however, went off to a new job in distant Misiones, and it was more than a year before there was further serious talk of return.

In November 1920, Abele told his father that he was waiting for Oreste to return from Misiones "in order to be able to fix approximately the time when we will be able to embrace each other again" (#185). He then asked his father about jobs, wages, and the cost of living "so that I could see how much it would take to live modestly but in a certain comfort." However, he refrained from making any definite commitment to return, referring to these potential plans as "castles in the air" and "dreams." Luigi, nevertheless, interpreted the letter differently: "I had the great pleasure, Abele, of getting your sweet letter with excellent news, that special letter that assures me that you are coming home" (#186). Luigi at the same time provided the information on the economic situation in Italy that Abele had requested; prices for everything were high, and wages not so good. But, he quickly added, "please don't let this unbalanced situation frighten you."

In an especially revealing letter to his father, Abele debated the pros and cons of returning. "It's true that it is very expensive [in Italy], but at the current rate of exchange almost everything costs more here. . . . On the other hand it's true that I make quite a lot" (#188). Oreste, he noted, was still away and would not return until the end of March, but Abele hoped that "if it all goes well, he will be able to save something, and it will be easier for us to come." The cost of the trip, he explained, would be "about 50,000 lire if it should have to be round trip. Do not, however, let this frighten you because the money is there and enough left over" (#188). Luigi, in a touching response, said that he did not want them to spend a fortune on the trip. "It is my greatest wish to see you," he wrote. "If, however, I were certain to keep my health the way it is now, if your interests hold you back, and if the cost of the trip will go down, you could postpone your arrival for another year" (#189).

The postponements continued, and finally Luigi sharply reminded his children: "Dear Oreste, it's twenty years that I haven't see you; Corinna, I haven't met you; and you, dear Abele, it's ten years" (#192). The next letter Abele wrote he promised that "we shall without fail come to embrace you" next spring (#193). Oreste, however, went off to Catamarca on yet another project to build a railroad bridge. Luigi seemed to resign himself to the fact that the return would not be permanent; the best he could hope for was a visit. "I am far from expecting you to come here to visit me and then to stay here" (#196). In the last letter of Luigi included in the collection, he summed up his thoughts: "I am waiting with open arms for the day of your so greatly longed-for arrival" (#201).

Abele's letter of April 19, 1922, is especially interesting because of the information it contained on the situation of immigrants in Argentina at the time. He told his father that he would try to meet Emanuele Scaramuzzi and help him get established as requested. However, he explained, he was very busy and was not certain he could do as much for Emanuele as he had done for others in the past. "Counting new arrivals recommended to me and veterans of America coming back," Abele said in an effort to explain his reluctance to help, "I shall have about fifty!" He warned Luigi that it was not a good time to immigrate to Argentina because there was not much work in the factories: "Others who came over from Italy have already gone back. Many don't know that America has already been made, almost finished, and the salami doesn't hang from the hedges" (#202).

Letters from Abele, Oreste, and Corinna in June and August of 1922, only a few months before Luigi's death, mentioned an imminent return and urged Luigi to be patient. Corinna stressed her strong desire to return (#203). Oreste, writing from Catamarca, assured his father that they all wanted to visit but that it would not be possible for a little while longer (#204). Abele talked of his success and also assured his father that they wanted to come (#205). On October 12, 1922, Abele wrote that they would finally return. "I repeat with total certainty," he told his father, "that it will be next spring" (#207). Next spring, however, was too late. Luigi died on November 13, 1922, his wish for the return unfulfilled. The book ends with a moving letter from Abele to Cousin Abele in Valdengo mourning Luigi's death (#208).

Letter 180

Buenos Aires, 10 September 1919

Dearest Father,

The Saturday before last I was at Berisso, coming back on the evening of Sunday, the 31st. All three of us—Oreste, Corinna, and I—had a good time together, talking happily about your hike almost right up to Mont Blanc!

That's good, and we imagine that, with the necessary precautions, you will keep on taking those lovely walks. Scaramuzzi must be a good companion. Give him, along with his family, our very best.

I shall always remember those brief "ascents" of ours. Those dear memories are unforgettable. Here they are impossible. I worked last Sunday as I almost always do (I got home from work this evening at nine), and I couldn't make the outing to Berisso. I hope to go there this Sunday.

Here spring is beginning, but the weather is changeable.

I got letters from our friends the Sassos. Give them my very best. My friend Armando Pella, along with his family, also gives you his best. Say hello to his sisters for us; they complain that they don't hear from him.

As to the house in Iaccheto, which you ask me about again, we have already said that it's our wish that you should do what suits you most. From what I could make out, you don't seem very keen on it, especially with your exclamation: "If we sell it, we won't have it any more!" Here you show that you are as always a great conserver, but, believe me, in that area I am one no less than you.

By the way I am aware that our friend Sasso has sold his property at Salpasco, and naturally he will have made a good profit. Still, unless he has purchased some other one that is more suitable I think that money is consumed more rapidly than land. Do they perhaps intend to come back here among us? Their age doesn't seem favorable for it, especially now.

I got a postcard from Corinna announcing the blessed event of fifteen chicks. She says they are so beautiful that she doesn't do anything at all anymore but look at them. I will be going there Sunday, and I shall take an interest in them so that they may quickly reach the age of the frying pan! That's what I have done for the others.

Dear Father, though they get there late we hope you will be pleased to receive our loving best wishes, as always, for your birthday. We do not doubt that you have spent it happily. The 23rd of September will be a holiday for us, and even from afar we embrace you with the greatest love.

The text of the amnesty decree has arrived here, and if the telegraph office has not made a mistake, we think a potential obstacle has been eliminated. We will talk about it again shortly.

Your loving children,
Abele, (Oreste, and
Corinna)

Special—Confidential

Dear Father!

You know how much I have always been attached to my native region. Accordingly the gist of my desire won't astonish you.

As I had already told you, last year there came my way as a bonus several thousands of lire, and this year there was also a little more. It has all been saved for possible unforeseen needs.

Now I was thinking, if it were possible, and of course with your complete approval and advice, of buying over there the small property of our neighbor (formerly, I believe, belonging to the Rosazzas). I am more or less certain that the current owners paid 10,000 lire for it, and though it must of necessity have increased a good deal in value, I am confident that I can reach the figure and still have enough left over for a trip over there and for unforeseen contingencies. All this, believe me, is in a modest spirit, without the slightest illusion of being a small capitalist.

I would be satisfied with this, dear Father, because you could then give the entire property to a family to cultivate the land and keep for yourself the small house without other problems. However, I should always like to be sure that someone was taking care of it [the house], so that you would not sacrifice yourself and be left alone.

So, then, if you think the thing is feasible and if you approve of it, you could, confidentially except for me, sound out their willingness to sell and the price. I would be extremely grateful to you if you would undertake this task and let me know the results. In case it is possible and the answer is yes, I would immediately send what is necessary.

Pardon me if you think this is an idiotic plan, and I beg you to believe in my good intentions.

Your loving son,
Abele

Letter 181

Buenos Aires, 30 December 1919

Dearest Father,

I have been to the consulate with Oreste getting our civil and military status as Italian citizens formally straightened out, on the basis of the well-known amnesty decree.

One thing is already smoothed away. We hope to settle some other things, and I am certain that we shall embrace each other in this year that is about to begin. Let's wait and be patient!

On Christmas day, the traditional day for the family, I was at Berisso with Armando Pella, his wife, Lina, and their child, Nino (six years old), and with Oreste and Corinna. We had a fine reunion. In the afternoon, taking advantage of the beautiful weather we went on a motorboat ride along the Santiago River and the port of La Plata. Afterward we ate dinner at home in Berisso; we got back to Buenos Aires at midnight.

As always we thought of everyone back there and especially of you, dear Father, wishing that you too might enjoy congenial companionship like us. We gave them one of the small pictures of our dearest mother. I still have one like it, with you, that I shall always keep with the greatest affection. I am going to have an enlargement made of it to make it the most precious ornament of my small room.

After the parties for the end-of-the-year holidays I am expecting Oreste and Corinna here, and we will have dinner here in my small house with Armando and family. The first day of 1920 we will all go to the Pellas, and so we shall conclude and initiate the year all together.

I am the one who manages all this; I am completely in command of them all, yet always in a spirit of complete harmony.

But we do still feel the absence of our dear friends the Sassos, our unforgettable friends, but we hope that you will always be in touch with each other. Give them the fondest greetings from all of us.

Here the heat is dying down. Notwithstanding the fact that it made us spend five or six rainy Sundays, we have already gotten to the point where we are enduring 37 degrees (centigrade) in the shade, and we are at the beginning! Yesterday evening I had begun to write, but I had to quit because I was sweating so much. It was unbearable. Today we have had a downpour to cool us off a bit, bringing it down to 30–32 degrees. Today because of an urgent piece of work I worked from 6:30 A.M. to 7:30 P.M., all in one shot without a break for the midday meal, and after supper I kept on until midnight, so that now I am writing you hurriedly—it's almost 1 A.M.—so as not to miss the steamer that's leaving.

Your loving children,
Abele, (Oreste, and
Corinna)

Letter 182

Buenos Aires, 24 February 1920

Dearest Father,

Too much time has passed since my last latter, but you may be sure that it is not our forgetfulness; . . . the *Tommaso di Savoia* has arrived happily after a crossing of forty-four days, caused for the most part by long and absurd quarantines. . . .

Last Saturday, the 21st, after dinner I had the delightful pleasure of receiving your very dear kisses [, which] I had been waiting for, and giving ours in return, in the person of our good friend Corrado Zocco, who had arrived with the *Tommaso di Savoia*. We naturally talked a bit about everything. Yesterday evening I invited him to dinner with me, and we continued the conversation about Italy. I was very happy to learn that you are in good health; that is the most important thing for us. He also brought the package with the woolens you had told us about: four pairs of shorts, three flannel shirts, ten pairs of long socks, and three pairs of short ones.

Though it was a long time ago, prepared for us then by our poor, dear mother, we thank you infinitely, all the more since you might have great need of them over there. They are very fine, and we shall use them with great care in loving remembrance. But excuse me, dear Father, if I make an observation; the only purpose is to find out where the things went. . . .

I am rereading the dear letter of 15 August 1915, where you told us about the things that you were sending us by means of that woman who then never left, and you listed the contents of the package as: four pairs of shorts, six flannel shirts, twelve pairs of long socks, and six pairs of short ones. If you used them, we would be very happy, sorry only that you had not done the same with the rest. It could, however, be the case that by bad luck they had fallen into the hands of someone who abused your trust.

Excuse me again, but it is good to know and to keep it all in mind.

I had already thought about finding a job for our friend Zocco, and since they didn't have anything for him at the company where I am, I gave him a note of introduction to a small laboratory where we send work and which is exactly in his line. Since I had previously spoken to the owner, I think he will have found a job for himself this very morning.

Sunday I was at Berisso to share with Oreste and Corinna the news from you that is so dear to us. This week I am expecting them here. One of these Sundays I'll take Zocco along.

From our dear friends the Sassos I have gotten letters and postcards; I also got a long letter from their son Giuseppe, who had finally arrived in Mexico in good health after three months of traveling. He had to cross the United States from Philadelphia to New Orleans!

We also appreciate the greetings from our cousin Riccardo Maggia, as well as all the others from relatives and friends. It shows that they remember us fondly, and we return them to everyone with the same fondness. . . .

Here it's the same as always; the price of everything keeps going up, but, thank heavens, we lack nothing. . . .

As I wrote in my last letter of December 30th, our status as Italian citizens has been completely straightened out, and in that sense we don't think there is any obstacle to our coming to embrace you. I thought I would come this year, and naturally with Oreste and Corinna, but I am not yet able to make a definite decision. The firm where I work has increased its capital from one and a half million pesos to three million, and it is expanding. They have already purchased the land and houses [that are] to be torn down for a new building in the center of the city [and used] for office space and for a head office of our firm. Then there are other acquisitions: large warehouses at the port—with a railway and a mole for unloading. And so it is in the organization stage, and I too am playing a role in it. So I really would not like to lose my seniority in rank right now, having earned a certain trust and respect after eight years of hard work, especially since I am the one most in touch with all the projects. I should have to ask for leave, and if they should raise objections, I would have to leave everything flat, just to start over again afterward and who knows on what conditions?

In any case, if it should not be this year, next year will be a certainty at whatever cost. In the meantime let's hope that things improve over there as well as the conditions for travel

> Your loving children,
> Abele, (Oreste, and
> Corinna)

Letter 183

Buenos Aires, 6 April 1920

Dearest Father,

It was a very great pleasure for us to learn that you had recovered from the bad cold which had been afflicting you; we hoped with all our hearts that it would go away soon.

Thanks so much for your kind birthday greetings on my thirtieth. I spent the evening with my friend Pella, his wife, and child, after working all day, . . . since Oreste and Corinna were at La Plata.

We also got the picture of our dear mother. I had already ordered the enlargement.

Within a month it will be the first anniversary of the death of our dearest mother. We ask you again, dear Father, to remember us on that day with a bouquet of flowers. Nor will we forget.

The greetings brought to us by our good cousins Andrea and Pierina, our delightful new cousin, were especially appreciated, and the good news and the respect and the gratitude with which they spoke of you, dear Father, fill us with joy.

They had a rather long crossing, and it wasn't too good; they got here the 27th of last month. Andrea, in the company of his brother Abele, whom I hadn't seen for several years, came to visit me at the factory on the morning of the 31st of last month. I went out with them, and we went to my house to have a vermouth. Afterward we each had to go our separate way since we all had business to attend to. Then in the evening, as agreed, Andrea and his wife came to my place for dinner, and we spent a very cheerful and pleasant evening together. After dinner I went with them on a carriage ride through the city, getting them back to Abele's house at about midnight.

From our cousin Abele's house to mine is almost an hour by tram. He has a nice little dairy business; he works very hard and is making a profit. They hope to get along well together and to give Abele some relief in his work.

I am also glad that we are close together again, hoping that the good relationship will continue.

His wife, Angiolina, is fine, though very delicate in health; the child,[1] who is now six years old, is doing great. Last Sunday, on Easter, with Oreste and Corinna who had come on Saturday night, we went in the morning to say hello, spending a pleasant moment together—well, like cousins—they give you their best.

Andrea informed me that it is not going well with his father.[2]

For dinner we went to the Pellas as had been previously arranged. In the evening Oreste and Corinna went home. I may go there on Sunday.

I am enclosing in this letter a check for 1,000 lire.

Your loving children,
Abele, (Oreste, and
Corinna)

1.   *The child he is referring to is Aldo Sola, the custodian of the Sola family letters.*
2.   *His father, Giacomo Sola, was in New York. (See letters #93 and #94.)*

Letter 184

Buenos Aires, 17 September 1920

Dearest Father,

I am here at Abele's place getting ready for a new trip. I am leaving tomorrow for the Province of Missiones [sic], and I am going near the Iquazu Falls to organize a new settlement on a rich man's property. He has several of them; the one I am going to is 67,500 hectares (167,000 acres), and it's one of the smaller ones.

Corinna will stay behind in Berisso for now, and if things go well she will be coming too. Missiones [sic] is regarded as the paradise of Argentina, and it must be true, considering its fertility, its gentle hills, and its clear waters.

We here are as always in the best possible health and wish the same for you too.

The topic of the day is the discussion of the situation in Italy. . . .

Your son,
Oreste, (Abele, and
Corinna)

Letter 185

Buenos Aires, 25 November 1920

Dearest Father,

I am taking advantage of the last steamer going this year to wish you with our greatest affection good Christmas holidays, a good end and better beginning of the year. We hope that in those days of joyful family gatherings you too will be in the company of some good friends, and we too, dear Father, will be present with all our heart.

I have received a letter from Oreste; he's fine and so is Corinna, whom I went to visit last Sunday.

I am waiting until Oreste is able to find out how long his stay in Misiones might last in order to be able to fix approximately the time when we will be able to embrace each other again and so to realize our fondest wish, a dream we have cherished for so many years. Keep on waiting, dear Father, and stay contented and happy; your anxious hope is ours too.

And so, as on a whim, I should like to know, more or less, the current prices over there, compared with the earlier, prewar prices, for the most common items: rail travel, hotels, restaurants, etc., so that I can get an approximate idea of what is needed. I should also like to know, again compared with the prewar ones, the salaries of employees who are at a fairly high rank, in Biella of course, so that I could see how much it would take to live modestly but in a certain comfort.

I keep devising plans, or rather castles in the air, which, without a factual basis, turn out splendidly until they fall apart all by themselves! Dreams are also a good part of life; they are as legitimate as hope, even if, like these, they are much too abstract. And yet there are moments of reflection that succeed in moving us. . . .

Let's come back to earth. What do the latest Americans to arrive, Pella and Motta, have to say? They will boast a lot, but do they plan to come back here or are they happy there? . . .

All right, dear Father, try to stay content and don't let yourself get annoyed too much.

I am enclosing in this letter a check for 1,000 lire.

Your loving children,
Abele, (Oreste, and
Corinna)

Letter 186

Valdengo, 5 January 1921

Dearest children Abele, Oreste, and Corinna,

On the 1st of this month I not only began the new year in excellent health, but I had the great pleasure, Abele, of getting your sweet letter with excellent news, that special news that assures me that you are coming home. In addition there was the check for 1,000 lire, which I shall save scrupulously since I don't have any need to spend it now.

As to what you ask me about prices, I can tell you the following: Everyday life is out of whack in comparison with before the war; rail travel costs more than four times as much; from Biella to Valdengo you sued to pay 40, later 55, centisimi; now you pay 2.05 lire one way, second class, and that with wretched service.

In the hotels and restaurants to have a main course, soup, cheese, and a half liter of wine costs from nine to twelve lire; a room costs from five to 10 lire.

It costs four lire a liter for wine of the poorest quality, and a cup of coffee no less than fifty centisimi. Butter is at twenty-five to thirty lire a kilo; it used to be 2 or 2.20 lire. Eggs are from eight to twelve lire a dozen depending on the season; before they were from sixty to eighty centisimi.

In the *Corriere Biellese* for 31 December you can get the maximum prices in Biella for all the most commonly consumed products.

Woolen cloth, for which we used to pay six or seven lire a meter, now starts at forty or fifty. Shoes were from fifteen to twenty lire; now they are seventy or eighty.

Wages have gone up a lot but proportionately below the price of the rest. An employee who used to receive 200 or 250 lire can have a salary of 800–1,000 or more. Everything is comparative.

Please don't let this unbalanced situation frighten you. We have polenta, potatoes, and wine, and some eggs here at home.

In these regions there has been a tremendous amount of work since the war on damming the mountain reservoirs for the production of electricity as well as so many other projects. I think and I hope that, if you will be planning to stay here or not far away, it will not be difficult for you to find employment. All the more so since you have special technical knowledge that many do not have and they get along quite well.

If you all are of this opinion, I shall go about talking to some of my acquaintances to find out whether a fairly good job would be possible.

When you are here, it will be easier to find it at your convenience.

In the hope of embracing you soon.

Your loving father

Letter 187

Valdengo, 25 January 1921

Dearest children, Oreste, Abele, and Corinna,

It gave me the greatest pleasure to get your postcards, with views of the wilderness between Brazil and Argentina, from which I learn of your continued state of excellent health even in those virgin territories.

I note, however, that there are vipers there in large numbers, surely poisonous ones, and flies. I hope these creatures will have no occasion to get you, dear Oreste, because I hope with all my heart to embrace you along with the others this coming summer with all of us in the best of health.

I had written to Abele that if Corinna does not come to be with you, she could come here rather than stay by herself in Berisso. . . . And so then when you two come she will be here with me to welcome you, for I want so much to have some one of you be here and better all together. These are my wishes, not demands.

I hope and wish that you will always be well, and Corinna and Abele too, and no misfortunes should befall you.

I have heard from cousin Riccardo Maggia, who is at Coluca,[1] San Francisco. He's fine and says hello to everyone. I also hear from our friend Giuseppe Sasso from Mexico. He's fine and says hello.

I have not seen the Sassos for several weeks, but I think they are all fine. On Saint Martin's Day they moved to Borghetto, where they have modernized a pretty nice house.

Your loving father

1.   *We can find no town near San Francisco of that name. Perhaps Luigi made a mistake in the spelling.*

Letter 188

Buenos Aires, 13 February 1921

Dearest Father,

Thanks for the information you give about the economic situation over there. I too had taken note of that article in the *Corriere* about the maximum prices in Biella. It's true that it is very expensive, but at the current rate of exchange almost everything costs more here, especially certain items manufactured here with the exorbitant raw materials of this country. Rents are more and more expensive; for this hole-in-the-wall apartment of mine starting this month I'll be paying 1,000 lire a month! On the other hand, it's true that I make quite a lot since I am able to have at my disposal for average monthly expenses more than 5,000 lire.[1] It's true that I am leading a relatively simple life but reasonably in keeping with my status and employment. I could perhaps make it more austere, but I think that it wouldn't save that much and would conflict with the reasonable needs of my life, which is of necessity influenced by the hard work of my job. Nevertheless I always save enough, and my health is especially important.

Oreste is still away; he writes that he is pleased at the progress of the new settlement. We were expecting him this month, perhaps to come get Corinna, but he writes now that he won't come before the end of March, and we will see then. If it all goes well, he will be able to save something, and it will be easier for us to come. Corinna is fine; I was there at Berisso last Tuesday, Carnival. We talked a lot, looking forward to the happiness of the longed-for embrace, all together with our dear father.

Of late the travel situation has been very burdensome: our sea voyage alone, in modest second-class accommodations, would cost us about 50,000 lire if it should have to be round trip. Do not, however, let this frighten you because the money is there and enough left over.

Just yesterday, along with two other friends, I had to dinner an officer of the steamer *Principe di Udine*, the one that brought me here. He foresees a transportation crisis in the near future with a reduction in rates as a result. In any case do not give up hope since we will come just the same, no matter what the travel situation may be. As far as staying there, we will see; don't say a thing.

I already have at my disposal several tens of thousands of lire, and though that's not much in the present situation, they might just be useful for some small enterprise, at least to get it started.

We'll see about this when the time comes. Everybody keep quiet!

Your loving children,
Abele, (Oreste, and
Corinna)

1.   *For an estimate of the amounts represented by figures in this letter, see the* Appendix.

Letter 189

Valdengo, 12 March 1921

Dearest children Abele, Oreste, and Corinna,

I must make up for an oversight. I did not in any of my most recent letters send you my best wishes on your birthday, dear Abele. I hope you will forgive me, and since you will get this afterward, my wish is that you spent it pleasantly. . . .

I got a postcard from dear Oreste from Misiones; I am not answering him since I imagine he has already come back there.

Yesterday I got your sweet letter and postcard, dear Abele. It is a great pleasure to learn that you are all well and are working on coming to see me. It pains me a lot to think that you will have to spend a fortune on the trip. It is my greatest wish to see you. If, however, I were certain to keep my health the way it is now, if your interests hold you back, and if the cost of the trip will go down, you could postpone your arrival for another year. . . .

These words of mine are motivated by the desire not to obligate you to a huge expense for the trip. This does not mean that I am giving up my wish to see you. I shall be satisfied to postpone it to another time. Do as you wish. No one will know anything.

Yesterday I was at Novara for the Provincial Council. I came back in the evening.

Your loving father

Letter 190

Valdengo, 21 May 1921

Dearest children, Abele, Oreste, and Corinna,

On the eighth, the second anniversary of your dear mother's death, I went on the sad pilgrimage to take flowers to where my dearest one lies forever. I still cannot forget the pain.

You must have learned from the newspapers the outcome of the elections in Italy, not much changed from those of 1919.

The situation here is serious, exacerbated by fascist mobs, which are corrupting the bourgeois party, which wants to govern at all cost. There is the labor crisis that is raging through the entire economic sector. An atmosphere everywhere pregnant with troubles puts all of humanity in a state of agitation. Not without danger of a new war. . . .

In your last letter, dear Abele, you don't talk about coming home any-more.[1] The season is beautiful, just right for it.

If I knew for sure that you were coming, I would like to have the house cleaned up nicely, to prepare a worthy reception for my dearest children, so greatly longed for.

In the meantime, in expectation I send you many affectionate kisses.

Your loving father

1.   *He is referring to the letter of 4 April 1921, which is not included here.*

Letter 191

Buenos Aires, 15 June 1921

Dearest Father,

As I had already told you,[1] Oreste came back from Misiones with the fever, but now he has recovered perfectly and has gained back the weight he lost. It was an extraordinary situation since the region is beautiful with many streams of clear water; however the tremendous flooding of the Paraná River and the persistent rains led to the formation of many small lagoons, and, because of the great numbers of insects, caused malarial fever. Oreste held out for a long time, but in the end he too fell victim; he is now in perfect health. They are still at Berisso.

We are waiting to get settled and perhaps to be together once again and to spend several months waiting for the time when we will all be together satisfy-ing our and your great desire for that long-awaited moment. I am fine, the same as always, constantly working.

The woman who did the work for me in my small apartment has just re-cently left for Spain with her husband. I regret it because she was absolutely trustworthy, hard working, and clean, but I am content that she went away with a great feeling of regret on her part and so did her husband. They wept for several days before leaving, and they will always think fondly of me and Oreste and Corinna, whom they liked very much. If you treat people well, the effort is never lost. It is a great pleasure to be remembered. I have another maid now, a Tuscan, and I hope for the best because much is gained by treat-ing people kindly. Right now I am instructing her in my ways, and she is prof-iting from the instruction.

After having been invited repeatedly, on Sunday I went to say hello to my friend Armando Pella. . . . On the 18th of this month he will be going back to Italy for good, with his wife, Carolina (the sister of the late Pierino Pizzoglio), and a nine-year-old boy. He will bring you our dearest greetings. He's a good fellow. . . .

Last week our cousin Andrea came to visit me in the office. Afterward I had him over to dinner with me. His brother Abele, Cousin Angiolina, and their boy will probably also be leaving soon. Angiolina has definitely made up her mind because of her continuing delicate health; he is not so sure since he wants to keep on making money. Cousin Pierina, Andrea's wife, is not very well either, but it's something that will soon pass. Andrea told me he would remain here and that he would like to stay with the dairy business, which is quite profitable, in spite of the fact that his life has been sacrificed to it. The hard part will be in arranging things with his brother. . . .

Pietro Pella-Carlai has arrived and has already purchased a "panatteria," and it seems he's had good luck. He has spoken to me several times on the telephone; I'll go visit him.

We too will be coming, easily by next spring, or perhaps sooner, depending on the economic situation. But expect us for sure by the spring. It is cold here now, and in addition today was a windy day, but it was clear.

We hope, dear Father, that you will take advantage of the good season over there to take some nice walks, and we will be happy to hear good news from you. But don't tire yourself, and if you go into the mountains, don't trust yourself either to some of the smallest difficult passes.

Today, with my friends Armando Pella and Alfredo Garrone, I was at the unveiling of the monument to Christopher Columbus, a majestic work by the sculptor Arnaldo Zocchi. It is a gift of the Collettivitá Italiana to Argentina for its centennial. An enormous crowd participated in spite of the cold, windy day. Tonight there will be extraordinary lighting effects and a characteristic torchlight procession.

I shall let you know what kind of arrangements we will have made. Keep in good spirits since we are fine.

Your loving children,
Abele, (Oreste, and
Corinna)

1.   *He is referring to the letter of 4 April 1921, which is not included here.*

Letter 192

Valdengo, 10 July 1921

Dearest children, Oreste, Abele, and Corinna,

On June 15th I received a postcard from you, Abele, where you said that you would write when the next steamer left. Now it's the 10th of July, and I haven't gotten anything. I'm getting anxious. Perhaps it's gone astray or been lost?

It would be better if the delay were the result of your coming here without writing anymore. If that were the case, I should be very happy.

You should have received postcards from the Valsesia, where we had a lovely excursion. I was with my friends Scaramuzzi and Rondani. This week I have been to Turin to visit our relatives, the Beccutis. They are fine, and they give you their best.

Here things keep going by fits and jerks, but so far they never go well. Perhaps it will go better over there. Fine.

Your loving father

P.S. This letter, already written, closed, and stamped, was ready for mailing, but I opened it up again to tell you that I had received your letter of June 15th just a moment before. I am happy about all the contents, except for the reservation that I hope to embrace you. Dear Oreste, it's twenty years that I haven't seen you; Corinna, I haven't met you; and you, Abele, it's ten years. For me it would be a joy beyond words.

Your loving father

Letter 193

Buenos Aires, 25 July 1921

Dearest Father,

As I already mentioned in my last letter, after a lengthy search, we have found a place to stay and, after almost three and a half years, we are together once again.

In Buenos Aires, as everywhere, the crisis is intense. However, though difficult, it is possible to find housing, especially small apartments in pretty good condition. Then the rents are exorbitant, never equaled in any period of madness.

Like me, Oreste and Corinna are very well; they moved last Friday, 22 July, loading everything on vans of a moving firm, which are specially designed for that purpose. I moved on Saturday the 23rd; our vans arrived almost together around six in the evening (from Berisso it takes sixteen hours for the trip).

So we have been in our new home since Saturday. Sunday it was a big job to start getting everything distributed, a job we hope to finish, with everything organized, this week.

It's an apartment on the second floor with four rooms facing the street (that's hard to find in Buenos Aires), an inner room for the maid, a kitchen, a bathroom, a servant's lavatory, a washtub, an entrance vestibule, and a roof terrace free for hanging the laundry, etc. As to location it's not bad; it's quite central and convenient for the trams.

When we are nicely settled in, I think we will be able to spend several months together nicely, until next spring, when we shall without fail come to embrace you.

To give you an idea of the price of rents, it's enough to know that, at today's rate of exchange, we are paying 1,400 lire a month, and imagine that that is still reasonable.

The new apartment is:

Calle Brasil 1508

Would you please have the address changed for the newspapers?

Your loving children,
Abele, (Oreste, and
Corinna)

Letter 194

Valdengo, 23 August 1921

Dearest children Oreste, Abele, and Corinna,

I am glad that you are all together again and that you are well. . . .

From Abele's previous letter and the delay in receiving a letter, I had convinced myself that you were on the way to join me. I see from this last letter that you have decided on next spring. I am anxiously waiting. Perhaps next year will go better in our poor Italy. . . .

A question for you, dear Abele. You have now finished your thirty-first year; you never speak about getting married. Do you want to say single like this? Are you waiting for some fine and lucky opportunity? Without getting into the details of your thinking, it would be my wish to see you in someone's good companionship. If you are planning to marry someone here, I will be quite happy. In any case, do as you think best and as you wish. My words are not binding.

Let's go on to something else. Here the summer has almost run out. It has been very hot; now it's reasonably cool at night. The weather is changeable.

Your loving father

Letter 195

Buenos Aires, 7 September 1921

Dearest Father,

. . . We are all fine; Corinna takes care of the housework; I am working the same as always; only Oreste is getting ready to leave in a few days for Catamarca, for a few months, where he is undertaking the construction of a new railroad bridge, close to that very one he built in 1917–1918. But there is no danger there of disease, and it has good communication with Buenos Aires. He will write you. . . .

Your loving children,
Abele, (Oreste, and
Corinna)

Letter 196

Valdengo, 23 September 1921

Dearest children Oreste, Abele, and Corinna,

It's now the 23rd of September, my seventieth birthday. . . .

The past few days our dear Pierina has been here visiting me. She returned home yesterday evening. . . .

I am far from expecting you to come here to visit me and then to stay here since it would be absurd. Your best interests and your plans can very well be different. Therefore I don't want to be an obstacle to your affairs.

The only pleasure for me will be to see you, if I may, once before I die, and to settle our family interests. Your last promise, to come next spring, has me counting the months and days that separate us.

Your loving father

Letter 197

Buenos Aires, 29 September 1921

Dearest Father,

We are happy to have good news from you, and your lovely walks are a pleasure for us. We hope, dear Father, that you will have had a good seventieth birthday, the 23rd of this month, a day we too remembered with good wishes.

You didn't say anything to us about our friend Lino Pella; didn't he come to bring you our greetings?

Oreste writes from Catamarca that he is fine.

Cousin Andrea has been to visit me. . . . His wife, Pierina, also came. She had to undergo an operation, and now she's fine (don't say anything if they don't speak to you about it). They give you their best.

This evening [Cousin] Abele also came for the first time [to the new apartment] since if he doesn't change his mind again, he will be leaving with his wife, Angiolina, and their boy, Aldo, on the 13th of October coming up. They will all three come to say hello to you and will bring you our dearest greetings. He will tell you stories of America. . . . He sold the dairy business, which was making a good profit, they say, and Andrea couldn't buy it because he was unwilling and unable to pay as much as he [Abele] was asking. They are also somewhat at odds because of a family matter.

Here the cold is gone; and after a drought so bad that it is a danger to the crops, we are having terrible weather. And then we will be right in the middle of summer.

On the other hand, you must be very careful about the cold and take every precaution.

Your loving children,
Abele, (Oreste, and
Corinna)

Letter 198

Buenos Aires, 14 December 1921

Dearest Father,

We are as always happy to hear you too are well and as always we cherish that moment when we will embrace you. . . .

And for our part thanks for the sacred remembrance of our dear ones who are no more; we too remember them with devotion.

The news of your good health is always a source of great satisfaction to us; we repeat our constant urgings for relaxation and complete serenity, especially in this cold season.

Here we are in the midst of summer; its already getting up to 39 degrees centigrade!

In my last postcard of the 1st of this month we hastily sent you our new address:

Calle Carlos Calvo N. 1627
Depto 2
Buenos Aires

Unforeseen reasons made us decide to change residence; this new one is just as nice. It has four rooms, a kitchen, a bath complete with hot and cold water (we need the hot water in the winter), and a courtyard that is quite large, completely paved with mosaics, which we are adorning with flowers.

Because of the torrential rains Oreste has had to suspend his project for now, but he will start up again soon. In the meantime we are getting ready for the longed-for journey. Have patience; a few months go by quickly.

We have received a letter from our dear friends the Sassos. Our best to them.

We are happy that Cousin Abele and family have been to visit you,[1] bringing you our best greetings. I haven't seen Andrea anymore, and I don't even know his address.

Our friends here are fine and give you their best.
Oreste and Corinna are sending postcards.
Enclosed I am sending a bank check for 1,000 lire.

Your loving children,
Abele, (Oreste, and
Corinna)

1.   *This information was conveyed in a letter not included in our collection.*

Letter 199

Valdengo, 1 January 1922

Dearest children, Oreste, Abele, and Corinna,

It's the 1st of the year, and there's a nasty New Year's gift.

Thursday, the 29th of last month, I went to Biella to collect the interest at the Banca Biellese and the Banca di Sconto.

Since I didn't have any need for the money, I deposited the sum in my account: 205 lire at the Banca Biellese and 86.25 lire at the Sconto. After an hour of business the Banca di Sconto closed its windows to everyone. It had obtained a one-year moratorium from the High Court in Rome. We are going to see if the principal creditors will adjust to such a situation.

I hope that it won't go further than the loss of interest.

Since I don't feel safe keeping the bonds at home because I could die and some light-fingered person could get hold of them, I found it convenient to keep them on deposit: at the Banca Biellese certificates for 10,000 lire at 3.5 percent; at the Banca Sconto for 3,000 at 5 percent; in addition to the small savings accounts all in your name too.

At the time I had told you about this; I don't think you will be cross with me over this disaster, which isn't my fault.

I still have at home eight treasury bonds that come due on 15 February, with a total face value of 4,000 lire, and a certificate for 1,000 lire at 4.5 percent plus two of 100 each. . . .

I haven't seen any more of Cousin Abele. All the others are fine and give you their best.

Your loving father

Letter 200

Valdengo, 12 January 1922

Dearest children, Oreste, Abele, and Corinna,

Last night I had a dream so beautiful that I must tell you about it since it indicated the truth. I dreamed that I was with your dear mother in a room full of lilies and flowers of all sorts. It was the signal from dear Abele's letter [#198] . . . where he says you are busy adorning your new apartment with flowers—a beautiful dream, an indication of a joyful truth, a sign of enduring sweet harmony between all of you and me.

I am infinitely grateful for the 1,000-lire money order; I will scrupulously keep that sum in reserve.

I am overjoyed that you will soon come to embrace me. I should like to know a little in advance in order to get the house into good shape, worthy of receiving my dearest children, whom I have not seen for so long. . . .

You know about the bankruptcy of the Banca Italiana di Sconto. I hope that you are not affected by it; here one hopes to save whatever is possible from it. The Banca Commerciale Italiana also looks as if it's not in good shape. That's what they say.

I hear that it's very hot there. Here it is very cold. The continuing dry weather is making trouble for industry because of the lack of water.

The rest of life is going forward helter-skelter.

My health is excellent as always, as I gather and hope for the three of you. If Oreste is going back to Catamarca, I hope that he does well and stays in excellent health.

Your loving father

Letter 201

Valdengo, 8 March 1922

Dearest children, Oreste, Abele, and Corinna,

Winter has passed, and the cold weather has gone away after such a long time. I have kept in good health thanks to the stove and its warmth, fed by unstinting use of firewood.

I hope that you too are all well, getting yourselves ready for the journey to come visit me. I am waiting with open arms for the day of your so greatly longed-for arrival. Our friend Sasso is also waiting to see you.

Yesterday I saw Corinna's brother, Giovanni. I gave him your address since he wants to write you.

Here things are as always going to pieces. You must be well informed about Italian politics and finances, where no one is finding the way to a good solution.

Your loving father

Letter 202

Buenos Aires, 19 April 1922

Dearest Father,

We are happy to know that you are well, having gotten through the winter, and that the stove has kept you good company. We are entering upon the nasty season; it's raining and cold.

Oreste is still gone. He was expected for Easter, but he didn't come; he is very well. Corinna and I spent the day with the Pellas; they are fine and give you their best.

The presidential elections are over too. Although they are still counting votes, a great triumph for the governing Radical Party is assured. What can you do! . . .

I got a postcard from Cousin Abele; I'll send him an answer. I also got your letter of 13 February (it came today), in which you tell me of his arrival and recommend to me Emanuele Scaramuzzi, who embarked on the 7th of this month and will probably get here on the 26th.[1] I think I remember him. . . . I'll do what I can to go meet him since at work I am getting busier and busier every day until I can't do it anymore; and I shall try to look after him like a good friend. However, I think it's a poor time for it. Counting new arrivals recommended to me and veterans of America coming back, I shall have about fifty! There is not much work in the factories. Well, we'll see. Others who came over from Italy have already gone back. Many don't know that America has already been made and almost finished, and the salami doesn't hang from the hedges. . . .

I enclose with this letter a bank check for 1,000 lire.

Your loving children,
Abele, (Oreste, and
Corinna)

1.   *This is the son of Luigi's dear friend Federico Scaramuzzi.*

Letter 203

Buenos Aires, 13 June 1922

Dearest father-in-law,

It is a great pleasure to hear that you are doing fine in health. I am infinitely grateful to you for the beautiful and charming postcard. Your kind thoughts for me are my delight, and I too shall always keep them in mind. I have a great desire to see you and embrace you, and I hope the day will not be far off when you will have the pleasure of embracing your children; they look forward to it so much. Be content then, for we shall see you soon.

Oreste and Abele have a special affection for their dearest father, whom they adore so much. Oreste is away; he's working in haste so that he can finish up soon. He's fine. Abele is waiting for Oreste to finish so we can leave. In my opinion Abele needs a rest; in the ten years that he has been working at Cantabrica he has never been on vacation, and I've never seen him home for a week. He's fine, however, and he's fat, only that now he's beginning to go bald, but that doesn't matter to him. He says "it runs in the family" and laughs. Oreste has been bald for some time, but he's always well.

Take then, dearest father-in-law, the most loving embraces from your loving daughter-in-law,

Corinna

Letter 204

Estación Mota Botello, 27 June 1922

Dearest Father,

Corinna has sent on to me your beautiful postcard addressed to her; she is very pleased with it. She has written me, sharing it with all her heart. Abele has also written me, sending on to me your last letter of May 10th, as he always does when I'm away from home.

I too have sent you several postcards from here, only I don't think you have gotten them because you don't mention them in your letters. This isn't uncommon because of the terrible mail service from here and especially because it's so far away from the great centers.

My project, which has suffered various interruptions for different reasons, now looks as if it's about to go forward swiftly. In this interval I have been working on other construction projects.

Abele has a great desire to make an excursion . . . all the way home. It's my wish too, and even more Corinna's. The circumstances don't ever let me do it because I'm tied down by the projects when the season is favorable. I think that when the project I have taken on is finished, we will all come to embrace you.

Your son,
Oreste, (Abele, and
Corinna)

Letter 205

Buenos Aires, 4 August 1922

Dearest Father,

We send immediately all your very dear letters to Oreste, whom we now expect soon. He has successfully completed two of the projects he had begun. The last one remains; it too should be almost finished by now if there have been no unforeseen hitches. When he gets here, we will see how to arrange things.

Dearest Father, we, as much as you, long for that dear embrace we have been waiting for so very, very much. For our part, believe me, we are doing what we can to hurry it up. In the meantime don't you worry about anything, don't get upset, don't wear yourself out, try to find diversions, and stay completely calm and serene. The worst wrong you could do us would be that of failing to take sufficient precautions for your good health since your health is our health and happiness. Do not neglect anything at all you might have need of, and let us know at once.

I too have an overriding need for rest. This very day they have begun the move of the management and administration offices (about sixty employees) from the factory to a large new building right in the center of the city, with very large salesrooms and showrooms. As a result I shall be left alone as director in chief, and, believe me, you have to keep moving day and night to attend to the technical office and more than 550 to 600 workers for an establishment about 20,000 square meters in area, almost all of it covered!

I get tired, I get mad, but I take care of everything and everybody.

Oreste too is tired of his life in encampments, but he doesn't mind it if things are going well.

And so, dearest Father, you must think of our situation too, as we think only of yours.

In the meantime we hope with all our heart that you will be able to enjoy pleasantly your seventy-first birthday coming up on the 23rd of September because if we won't be there yet, we will be there with all our heart. . . .

Telegrams from there, which we saw in the papers, tell of a serious hailstorm. We hope the damage is not too great.

I am enclosing in this letter a check for 1,000 lire. . . .

I am closing now to get there on time to catch the mail.

> Your loving children,
> Abele, (Oreste, and
> Corinna)

Letter 206

Buenos Aires, 31 August 1922

Dearest Father,

We were pleased by your excursion with your friend Scaramuzzi, especially after the not so very good news of your indisposition, and now we are glad to know that you have recovered.

Oreste has been back for a week; he is sending you a postcard separately. He's fine, happy that he's finally finished two of the projects he had begun.

The third had to be stopped because of unfortunate unforeseen events; he expects a solution to the problem soon. If it weren't for this, I think we would already be on our way.

And so we shall have to wait on events for several months, to our great regret, but we absolutely promise that the beginning of next spring will not pass [without our return]. For this we ask once again for the last time to be patient; we urge that you take every precaution and that you be absolutely serene and cheerful. A few months go by quickly, and they will increase, if that is possible, the happiness of the longed-for embrace.

As to the sharecropping, dearest Father, everything will be fine as you do it; we are just happy to know that you are free of worries and well taken care of.

I refer you to my letter of 10 September 1919, where I alluded to my desire to purchase our neighbor's small piece of property so that we could give it all to a nice family and you would have someone for company. You answered that it wasn't possible. Still if it were feasible today, I insist.

If not, I've been thinking of another solution, though not as good: to buy the small house adjoining ours . . . or to make do with the other house, the one in Iacchetto, and to have it fixed up appropriately, putting in a balcony in the front, to make room for a family which would take charge of the land and look out for you. And so you would be able to stay independent in the small house. They are solutions thought up thousands of kilometers away. Consequently please forgive me if I should be in error. However, every last thing you may do to be sure that you are well taken care of will in our eyes be quite well done. Let us know at once of whatever you might have need of.

This evening our friend Armando Pella has been to dinner with us. He will have to remain alone for some time since his wife had to take their boy to Zarate, a city about 100 kilometers from Buenos Aires, for treatment of his leg, which will take rather a long time. He sends you his best.

Once again we offer you our dearest best wishes for a happy birthday, this 23rd of September.

> Your loving children,
> Abele, (Oreste, and
> Corinna)

Letter 207

> Buenos Aires, 12 October 1922

Dearest Father,

From our last letters you will have learned about our decisions concerning our longed-for arrival. Oreste still has some work that is incomplete, and he hopes to wind it up as soon as possible. In any case I repeat with total certainty that it will be next spring. Have patience still for a few more months, dear

Father, and try to stay cheerful and amuse yourself as we would like, and be extremely cautious and careful.

As far as the house is concerned, we repeat what we wrote: Whatever you do will be fine.

We hope that you will have had a cheerful seventy-first birthday; we too have remembered it with affection. . . .

Here the nice days are beginning with the arrival of spring, after a terrible winter.

Thanks for the greetings from relatives and friends, which we return in kind. Our friend Armando Pella also returns your kind greetings. We expect to see a lot of him at our house because his wife is away with the boy, who has to stay for some time under treatment for the dislocation of his thigh. They are at Zarate with her family.

From the papers we learn that the fascist movements are also in the Biella area. . . .

If our friends at the *Corriere Biellese* are always so organized, why have they still not managed to get the address right?!

Oreste is also writing you. Corinna is always delighted by your affectionate greetings and along with us embraces you.

Corinna has also heard from her nieces, Giovanni's daughters, one of whom seems to be on her way here with her husband. Give our best to her family.

> Your loving children,
> Abele, (Oreste, and
> Corinna)

Letter 208

> [Addressed to Cousin Abele in Valdengo,
> after the death of Luigi on November 13, 1922]

> Buenos Aires, 31 December 1922

Dearest Cousin,

What can we say? Our grief is so great, so intimate, that we are unable to communicate it.

Every comfort is impossible. Our greatest wishes have been shattered. We have desired that longed-for moment of the purest and most sublime embrace too much to be able to believe that it will no longer be possible for us to embrace and kiss our dear father.

Just at the very moment when we were on the point of pressing him to our heart.

We can only thank you sincerely for all that you have done for him and for us.

We hope to see you soon.

A hug and kisses for dear Aldo, Angiolina, and yourself.

Your loving, grief-stricken
cousins,
Abele, (Oreste, and
Corinna)

Appendix: Pesos, Lire, and Earnings

It is not an easy task to determine the monthly earnings of the Sola brothers, how well they did compared to an average Argentine worker, and how much— in terms of days or months worked—they sent home to Italy. Published data on hourly and monthly wages in Buenos Aires at the time are fragmentary, frequently inaccurate, and often contradictory. In addition, there are the problems of wages and salaries given in gold pesos, paper pesos, and lire; of fluctuations in wages and the cost of living; and of dramatic inflation during World War I. Nevertheless, it is possible to combine existing data with information in the letters and come up with a rough approximation of the financial situation of the Solas.

In the 1900–1912 period the Argentine peso was the equivalent of 2.2 Italian lire (#37, #43). During the next decade there is a decline in the value of the lire, and although it fluctuated it was worth about three Argentine pesos (#150). The cost of living is approximated by the index in Table 4. It rose gradually until 1914 and increased dramatically during the war, reaching a peak in 1918 (#98, #139). Although the cost of living rose rapidly in both Argentina and Italy, it rose more rapidly in Italy (#132, #186).

Oreste began sending money home after five years in Argentina. By 1909 he was earning 400 pesos a month (#37), or more than three times the average monthly salary of a skilled male worker in Buenos Aires (see Table 4 and #25). In 1912 he sent 1,500 lire home to cover Abele's migration costs (#67). Obviously he was successful financially during this period. From then on, however, he had some problems and did not continue to do as well. Neverthe-

TABLE 4: *Estimates of Wages and Cost of Living in Buenos Aires, 1910–1921*

| | Average male wages, pesos | | | | Index | |
| | Unskilled workers | | Semiskilled and skilled workers | | | |
Year	Daily	Monthly	Daily	Monthly	Real wages[a]	Cost of living[a]
1910	3.06	77	5.45	136		100
1911						101
1912						105
1913						108
1914	2.90	73	4.39	87	68	108
1915					61	116
1916					57	124
1917	2.62	73	4.00	104	49	146
1918					42	183
1919					57	173
1920					59	201
1921	3.91	140	6.75	174	73	189

SOURCES: James R. Scobie, *Buenos Aires: Plaza to Suburbs, 1870–1910* (New York: Oxford University Press, 1974), p. 266; Robert E. Shipley, "On The Outside Looking In: A Social History of the *Porteño* Worker during the 'Golden Age' of Argentine Development, 1914–1930," Ph.D. diss., Rutgers University, 1977, pp. 133, 354–376, 390–398.

[a] Data in the following sources confirm the general trends of the real wages and cost of living indexes for Argentina: Roberto Cortés Conde, *El progreso Argentino, 1880–1914* (Buenos Aires: Editorial Sudamericana, 1979), pp. 226, 263; and Carlos F. Diaz Alejandro, *Essays on the Economic History of the Argentine Republic* (New Haven: Yale University Press, 1970), pp. 43, 460. The following documents the cost of living in Italy: Istituto Centrale di Statistica, *Sommario di statistiche storiche Italiane, 1861–1955* (Rome, 1958), p. 172.

less, by September 1918 he had sent home a total of 14,300 lire, or an average of 1,200 lire per year (#157). The total sum was the equivalent of approximately four or five years of remuneration for a skilled male worker in Buenos Aires.

Abele did considerably better in Argentina than his brother. In 1910 he was making 150 lire (68 pesos) per month in Sardinia (#51), a little less than an unskilled male worker in Buenos Aires. In Buenos Aires, he soon found a good job and did increasingly well thereafter. Whereas it took Oreste five years before he could send money home, Abele began to do so after just five months. By September 1918, he had sent home 9,000 lire, or 1,500 per year

(#157). In 1921 he noted that he had about 5,000 lire per month to spend, out of which 1,000 went for rent (#188). He estimated that the round trip from Buenos Aires to Biella for the three of them would cost about 50,000 lire, and he did not see any problem in raising this sum. That was for him nearly a year's salary and perhaps as much as seven or eight years' salary for a skilled male worker in Buenos Aires at the time.

If we compare these sums to what money Luigi had (the family estate) at the end of his life, we get a sense of how successful the two brothers, and especially Abele, were. In 1922 Luigi explained that he had approximately 20,000 lire in liquid assets and some land that more than doubled his worth (#199). Yet the total worth of Luigi was the equivalent of approximately eight months' pay for Abele (#188).

Index of Names

(By letter number)